CHANGE IN SOUTH AFRICA
Blind Alleys or New Directions?

CHANGE IN SOUTH AFRICA
Blind Alleys or New Directions?

CHRISTOPHER R. HILL

REX COLLINGS LONDON 1983

First published in the United Kingdom by
Rex Collings Ltd,
6 Paddington Street, London W1

© Christopher R Hill 1983

ISBN 086036 200 0

Typeset and printed in Great Britain by Photobooks (Bristol) Ltd

Contents

Acknowledgements

I have too many debts to be able to acknowledge them all individually. I must, however, mention the friends and colleagues at the University of Stellenbosch who received me so kindly and contributed so much to my understanding of South Africa during a term's leave from the University of York at the beginning of 1980. I am particularly grateful to Antony Melck, Professor S. J. Terreblanche and Professor Ben Vosloo.

A number of people have read parts of the text and generously given me the benefit of their advice. They include Peter Collins, Nico Du Bois, Steven Georgala, Sir John Leahy, Tom Lodge, Martin Reid, and Major-General Henry Woods.

I have a special debt of gratitude to Steven Georgala, who was an invaluable research assistant at Stellenbosch.

The Tablet, The Times and *The Times Literary Supplement* have been so good as to allow me to use material first published by them.

The Chairman of the Southern African Studies Trust, the late Sir Richard Graham, and his fellow trustees have given me unfailing support, for which I am most grateful.

I am also much indebted to the Southern African Studies Trust and the Joseph Rowntree Charitable Trust for grants towards the cost of visits to South Africa.

Mrs Sue Osborne and Mrs Hardy have patiently typed the manuscript, without complaining about my handwriting. Hugo Watson Brown devoted great care and skill to the tasks of preparing the bibliography and index; Dr Anne Akeroyd cast her eagle eye over the bibliography and read the proofs. I am most grateful to them all.

CRH

Abbreviations

ACP	African, Caribbean and Pacific
AFCWU	African Food and Canning Workers' Union
AFL-CIO	American Federation of Labour—Congress of Industrial Organizations
AHI	Afrikaanse Handelsinstituut
ANC	African National Congress
ASB	Afrikaanse Studente Bond
ASSOCOM	Association of Chambers of Commerce of South Africa
AZAPO	Azanian People's Organization
BAAB	Bantu Affairs Administration Board
BAWU	Black and Allied Workers' Union
BMWU	Black Municipal Workers' Union
BOSS	Bureau of State Security
CCBU	Consultative Committee of Black Unions
CFL	Confederation of Labour
CPSA	Communist Party of South Africa
CUSA	Council of Unions of South Africa
DONS	Department of National Security
EDP	Economic Development Programme
EEC	European (Economic) Community
FCI	Federated Chamber of Industries (*see also* SAFCI)
FCWU	Food and Canning Workers' Union
FOFATUSA	Federations of Free African Trade Unions of South Africa
FOSATU	Federation of South African Trade Unions
HNP	Herstigte Nasionale Party
ICFTU	International Confederation of Free Trade Unions
IIR	Institute for Industrial Relations
ILO	International Labour Office
IRC	Industrial Relations Committee
ISCOR	Iron and Steel Corporation
JCC	Johannesburg Chamber of Commerce
KP	Konserwatiewe Party
MAWU	Metal and Allied Workers' Union
MIWU	Motor Industries Workers' Union
MNR	Mozambique National Resistance
NAFCOC	National African Chamber of Commerce

NP	National Party
NRP	New Republic Party
NUSAS	National Union of South African Students
OAU	Organization for African Unity
PAC	Pan-Africanist Congress
PEBCO	Port Elizabeth Black Civic Organization
PFP	Progressive Federal Party
PRP	Progressive Reform Party
RAU	Rand Afrikaans University
RSA	Republic of South Africa
SAAK	Stellenbosche Aktuele Aangeleendheidskring
SABC	South African Broadcasting Corporation
SABRA	South African Bureau of Racial Affairs
SACCOLA	South African Employers' Consultative Committee on Labour Affairs
SACP	South African Communist Party
SACTU	South African Congress of Trade Unions
SADCC	Southern African Development Co-ordination Conference
SAFCI	South African Federated Chamber of Industries (*see also* FCI)
SAIRR	South African Institute of Race Relations
SALB	South African Labour Bulletin
SALDRU	South African Labour and Development Research Unit
SEIFSA	Steel and Engineering Industries Federation of South Africa
SRC	Students' Representative Council
SWAPO	South West Africa People's Organization
TCI	Transvaal Chamber of Industries
TNC	Transnational (Multinational) Corporation
TNIP	Transkei National Independence Party
TUACC	Trade Union Advisory Co-ordinating Council
TUCSA	Trade Union Council of South Africa
UAW	United Auto Workers' Union
UF	Urban Foundation
UG	Union Government
UNIP	United National Independence Party
UNISA	University of South Africa
UPE	University of Port Elizabeth
UTP	Urban Training Project
WFTU	World Federation of Trade Unions
WPGWU	Western Province General Workers' Union
WRAB	West Rand Administration Board
ZANU	Zimbabwe African National Union

FOR MY MOTHER
GWEN HILL
WITH LOVE

CHAPTER 1

Interpretations of Apartheid

South Africa, now that the American involvement in Vietnam is over, is the single issue on which all kinds of people can agree, ranging from revolutionary socialists to conservative-minded liberal humanitarians. For some it is all a question of class; for liberals the present sad state of affairs stems from undue emphasis on race; for many white South Africans its origin lies in the failure to keep the races apart: indeed, one objective of this book is to draw attention to the variety of ideology, interest and intention that lies behind the general concern and to the superficiality of such agreement in interpretation as exists. Nevertheless, however variously South Africa is analysed, its internal policies move an extraordinary range of people to indignation and some to passionate involvement.

There is so much about which to be indignant that it is difficult to know where to start. The system of regulation and control known as apartheid, which labels people by race as European, African (formerly Native, then 'Bantu', now 'Black' in the official terminology) and Indian, or by mixture of race as 'coloured', is a grotesque absurdity. Under a massive conglomeration of laws, most of them passed since the National Party came to power in 1948 (which means that, even if children become politically aware as early as at the age of six, no South African under the age of forty remembers any other ruling party) the racial groups are kept apart, from birth to death, from the labour ward to the cemetery. Some whites see the absurdity, for others separation is habitual and natural, but for almost all Africans, Indians and coloureds it is a searing and continuous insult. By extension, it is seen to insult all the black, brown and yellow peoples of the world, or at least their international representatives, and implicates all white people in the perpetration.

It is not part of my purpose here to list the disabilities suffered by 'blacks'—a term which I use here to cover all the 'non-white' groups. There are many existing accounts—perhaps for the newcomer the quickest introduction to the subject is to turn to the meticulously researched publications of the South African Institute of Race Relations, especially its annual *Survey of Race Relations in South Africa*. The facts of apartheid are well known and unite a wide variety of groups in denunciation of South Africa, or at least of some major aspects of its system. Not all the groups are equally well informed, nor equally passionate, but all call for significant changes and some for root and branch demolition and reconstruction of

1

South African society. The groups include the following (the list is not exhaustive): liberals and humanitarians, in South Africa and abroad; many academics, who tend to be divided, sometimes bitterly, into Marxist and non-Marxist groups and, within the Marxists, into a number of factions; other intellectuals, who tend to make less detailed analyses and therefore to find more common ground; *verligte* ('enlightened' or reformist) Afrikaners, as distinct from the *verkrampte* (hard-line) majority; some firms and bodies representing business interests; black organizations, including the African National Congress (ANC) and the Pan-Africanist Congress (PAC), both banned in 1960 and operating in exile; the Black Consciousness Movement; numerous black bodies inside the Republic, ranging from the Azanian People's Organization (AZAPO) to Chief Buthelezi's Inkatha, the last nominally a cultural movement, but in fact a powerful political force, largely among Zulus; the governments of the western industrial powers ('the west' for short); third world representatives in such fora as the United Nations Conference on Trade and Development; representatives of the African Caribbean and Pacific (ACP) countries who are partners with the EEC in the Lomé Convention; the majority of delegates at the United Nations General Assembly and of members of the Security Council.

The main purposes of this book are to discuss recent trends of thought which have occurred among various white South African élites, and to assess such real changes as have flowed from them. By way of introduction to that major theme Chapters 2, 3 and 4 are devoted to an examination of three approaches to the South African predicament, the official policy of 'separate development' of the races, liberalism, and the revolutionary or violent way forward. For the remainder of this Chapter I turn briefly to some of the issues which preoccupy academics.

THE ACADEMIC DEBATE

The debate among academic commentators is in one sense unimportant, since much of it takes place in conferences, seminars and learned journals which are obscure, or unknown to the general public, or indeed (except perhaps by hearsay) to most members of the decision-making élites. On the other hand, academics do contribute to, as well as draw upon, a general intellectual atmosphere within which, consciously or unconsciously, decisions are made. Furthermore, the pupils of today may be the decision-makers of the day after tomorrow and their decisions will be influenced by the vision of the past that is created for them now. For these reasons, and because the Marxist/non-Marxist division offers a framework which can accommodate many of the groups listed above, I start with a brief account of some of the academic debates, as they are conducted between Marxists (or 'neo-Marxists') and others.

The debate between liberal and radical historians of South Africa has been summed up by Harrison M. Wright (Wright 1977) in a short book which has been attacked both because Wright's sympathies lie with the liberals rather than the radicals and because he relies heavily, when

2

criticizing the Marxists, on off-the-beaten-track publications, including privately circulated seminar papers, which may not represent their authors' mature thinking. The latter criticism is fair, since papers are often written to test out a line of thought, or give preliminary research findings, and may be extensively altered in the light of comment by the authors' peers. But in Wright's defence it must also be said that the authors he examines (e.g. Martin Legassick) have not yet committed themselves to a major text which sums up their thinking thus far, so to some extent he was obliged to rely on more ephemeral material.

The first question is, are we to regard race as *in itself* an explanation of apartheid, or should it be seen as subordinate to another factor, class interest? Is it, in other words, an independent variable which directly influences the state of affairs; is it dependent, in the sense that it plays a part only indirectly, its influence subordinate to that of some other variable, such as class; or has it perhaps changed in nature? From the answer to this question much else follows. If race is an independent variable, then race relations is a legitimate field of study; questions such as why people are racially prejudiced may be answered without necessary reference to economics, and disciplines like sociology and social psychology assume a central rather than a peripheral significance. (Of course some practitioners of these disciplines may also be Marxists.)

If race relations may be studied, there may also be theoretical 'cures' for bad ones. Such cures, if they are to be translated into social action, may also bring with them measures of an economic nature—all social measures have an economic dimension—but they would not necessarily originate in a class analysis of South African society. Thus explanations of racial prejudice like the Jungian, would not be out of court, nor Michael Banton's image of the black man in Britain as 'the archetypal stranger' (Banton 1967: 381) (an image complemented in Africa by the Swahili word for 'white man', *mzungu*, also meaning 'stranger'). A good summary of such theories is Philip Mason's *Common Sense about Race* (1962), written shortly after the setting up of the Institute of Race Relations in London in 1959.*

If, however, economic factors are assumed to be primary, a different set of questions has to be asked. Some scholars would even go so far as to say that once the problem has been 'correctly' analysed, the answer is entailed, and can be 'read off', as if from a slide rule; in other words, to 'identify the issues' is to solve them. This is at least dubious; one might as plausibly suggest that to identify the issues is to aggravate them. Even if it were true that to analyse correctly is to solve, the difficulty would only be pushed back a stage—how would we know when a correct analysis had been found?

---

* So far has the intellectual climate changed that no-one would think of setting up an Institute of Race Relations now. The Institute, at one time an influential body, declined, though it is not yet defunct, because it became a battlefield between liberals (often characterized as 'the Establishment') and radicals. The radicals won, but the liberals controlled the purse strings—and closed them.

3

Not all devotees of economic explanations are Marxists. What is sometimes called 'the O'Dowd thesis' (O'Dowd 1974; also Horwitz 1967) of which Mr Harry Oppenheimer, Chairman of the Anglo-American Corporation of South Africa, is usually taken to be the 'godfather', argues that apartheid will, so to speak, cure itself as the increasing demands of the economy impose rationality. I shall look at this view later, but meanwhile am concerned, in very bald outline, with Marxian attitudes and explanations.

For the Marxists the whole point of apartheid is that it established and maintains a variant of capitalist exploitation, which in South Africa has taken the form of racial oppression. Thus, if South Africa is to be put right, it is capitalism which must be destroyed and racial oppression will then wither away, since its only function is to maintain capitalism. This is, of course, a simplified account; some Marxist authors would allow that, although in strict logic race should be seen as subordinate to class, it has, because of the passage of time and the consolidation of racialist habits of behaviour, acquired a quasi-independence, which must, however, in the ultimate analysis be illusory. There are those, too, who try to amalgamate a Marxian approach with some aspects of pluralist theory, though enemies of pluralism would say that the classification of societies as 'plural' (i.e. as ones in which different groups co-exist) does not explain anything about them, but merely redescribes. The effort to save something from the mass of pluralist theory and combine it with Marxism may be attractive on grounds of economy, without being altogether successful (see e.g. Leftwich 1974).

Within the Marxian group a number of questions are of the first importance and have generated a considerable literature. 'Race relations' may well be an illegitimate field of study for Marxists and therefore customarily put in quotation marks by them, and black nationalism may be merely an obfuscation of the real (class) issue, yet white workers persist in distinguishing themselves on racial lines from black workers and, having by their own efforts secured privileged access to many jobs, strenuously seek to maintain it, rather than showing class solidarity with the blacks and regarding themselves as a single working class. Blacks who have been 'co-opted' into the middle class continue to see themselves as black first and middle class second, and black nationalists persist in preaching nationalism, rather than anti-capitalism, though this is more true of the PAC than of the ANC, which is divided on the issue. The question whether social progress in South Africa should be furthered by mobilization on class or on racial lines is at least as old as the South African Communist Party, as Dr Sheridan Johns showed in his seminal thesis (Johns 1965) and is still strenuously debated, as we shall see in Chapter 3.

A further debate, much of whose force is now spent, concerns the analysis of the South African economy. It is nowadays seen as a single economy by most economists, dominating those of its neighbours (and even beyond, at least as far as Malawi) rather than, as in much of the older literature, as two economies, the traditional and the modern, going on side

4

by side, where the function of the more advanced economy is to modernize its backward neighbour (this is often called 'the Lewis model' after Sir Arthur Lewis). The former view (of the economy as a single unit) would be accepted by many non-Marxists, but is essential to a Marxian position, which needs to see migrant labour as in some sense part of the exploited class (there is much debate about exactly what sense) and the process of exploitation as a continuous one going on both in the reserves and at the point of production. An elaboration sees the reserves (now incorporated as mini-states, or popularly, Bantustans) as internal colonies, within the South African economy. This again is not just a Marxian notion: no less a scholar than Professor Carter, the *doyenne* of American Africanists, subtitled her work on the Transkei 'The Politics of Domestic Colonialism' (Carter *et al.* 1967).

A related elaboration links the analysis of the southern African economic system with the 'dependency' theory of Frank (1969), who developed the theory in the Latin American context, and Baran (1970). Frank's central thesis is that the extension of European influence over the whole world created a *world* capitalist system by incorporating areas until then untouched. Metropolitan capitalism then proceeded to 'underdevelop' the peripheral areas in the interest of the 'metropole', thereby distorting the peripheral economies. The result was that, instead of becoming (or, in some cases, remaining) self-sufficient, they turned into suppliers of a limited range of products required in Europe, and so became increasingly dependent for their survival on exports to Europe of those products and on imports of everything else. The theory is refined by the introduction of 'sub-metropoles' (e.g. in Brazil and in South Africa itself) with their own peripheries.

This view of the world has obvious difficulties; for instance, it is not altogether easy to specify the degree of capitalist contact with a given area which constitutes incorporation of that area into the world capitalist economy. Nor does the theory (if it qualifies for that label) readily generate testable hypotheses, and it is not clear what type of evidence would be accepted by its supporters as tending to disprove it. Nevertheless it has stimulated books on, for example, East Africa (Brett 1972 and Leys 1975) and a number of collections of articles (e.g. Oxaal *et al.* 1975 and, specifically on southern Africa, Palmer & Parsons (eds) 1977).

Another problem which necessarily preoccupies Marxists is that of intention. If the state is ultimately run in the interest of the capitalist class, do both parties to the arrangement (if, indeed, the parties are not identical) know that it is an arrangement, or is it a state of affairs reached without conscious direction? The same question has to be asked about missionaries and humanitarian bodies like the Anti-Slavery Society, which are often seen as essential factors in the worldwide extension of capitalism. In recent times it can usefully be asked about such London-based organizations as the Institute of Race Relations, the Capricorn Africa Society, the Africa Bureau and even the much more radical Movement for Colonial Freedom (for the last three of these see Sondashi, 1980). In these areas hypotheses can be formulated and evidence found; an interesting recent example is Norman Levy's account of the co-operation between state and mineowners on the question of importing Chinese labour to the Transvaal in the early 1900s (Levy 1978). It must, however, be added that the believer in the necessity of collaboration between state and capital in capitalist society will not be deterred by lack of corroborating evidence, or even by contrary evidence; the latter can always be interpreted as an aberration, or perhaps as a prudent regard for appearances on the part of government or capital, or both.

At a more detailed level, there has been much debate on the left about recent reforms in industrial practices in South Africa, and it is worth noticing the kind of response provoked from Marxists by assertions that conditions have improved. Merle Lipton has published a great deal of evidence (e.g. Lipton 1976) to this effect and has been extensively attacked for it by Legassick and Innes. The authors argued, first, that Lipton was mistaken because she had taken the wrong base date (Legassick & Innes 1977: 440), and continued with a number of similar criticisms. They then, in a pronounced shift, altered the base of the argument to say that in any case she was asking the wrong questions. Even if black wages were improving, the underlying structural relationship between exploiters and exploited would not be altered; what needed to be asked therefore was how this relationship had come about and how it was maintained (*Ibid*: 468). This change of ground of course renders relatively unimportant the detailed argument about the extent of the improvement that had occurred.

Reactions to the recent major reports of the Riekert and Wiehahn Commissions (RSA 1979 a and b) will be discussed in a later chapter. Meanwhile, it will be seen from the last few pages that in Marx's house there are many mansions, but the central theme is clear enough. For the Marxist, South African apartheid is a unique method of administering capitalist exploitation, but it is only a method. What matters is the South African capitalist system, its origins, current contradictions and future prospects: indeed, in some versions South Africa begins to look like little more than a case study in capitalism. The participants in the debate, though few in number (many exiled, or self-exiled, from South Africa, and virtually all white) have been influential within the academic world—and perhaps elsewhere. Indeed, the importance of the debates within Marxism and between Marxists and others lies not in the cut and thrust of academic discourse but rather in the possibility that from the creation of a new orthodoxy among specialist intellectuals will flow a more widely held belief that apartheid is a specifically capitalist phenomenon, which in turn will lead to a gradual acceptance of the proposition that South Africa's problems in the post-apartheid age can only be solved through the destruction of capitalism. Taking the longer view, it may be that in seeking to create a new orthodoxy the Marxist writers are preparing a ready-made history for the new society of the post-apartheid age. Every society needs its

6

'foundation myth', as Moodie has said of modern Afrikanerdom (Moodie 1975) but not many are so fortunate as to have it made ready in advance.

To that extent, therefore, academic discourse is relevant to the future course of events. This is not to say that in the post-apartheid age a correct historical analysis of the strength of the apartheid state, of how and why whites acquired their dominant position and what forces helped them to maintain it, will offer direct guidance to the new leaders as to how they should solve the problems which will beset them. Nor will debate over whether the transition from apartheid to socialism will take place in a single stage, or via an intervening national democratic revolution, if, indeed, the socialist phase is achieved at all. But although such debates are unlikely to influence the course of events in the short term, the intellectual tendency favoured by the future rulers will have a great influence both on their internal policies and on their dealings with the outside world. (It should not, of course, be assumed that the new rulers will all belong to the same tendency. For an example of complex ideological division one has only to look at ZANU in independent Zimbabwe.)

Nor can one be certain that the arguments about South Africa have been conducted in the right terms to provide the future leadership with correct perceptions of their problems, and so (perhaps) with appropriate policies. The danger is that they may turn out to be misperceptions and mistaken policies, because the real problems of South Africa (and, for Marxists, the conditions of class struggle) will be similar to those which already face what are sometimes called 'threshold countries' or Advanced Developing Countries. The experience of South Korea will be more relevant then than that of Angola or Mozambique.

CHAPTER 2

Separate Development

In this chapter, and the two following, I look at three of the approaches which have been adopted to South Africa's problems, namely separate development, liberalism and revolutionary socialism.

'Separate development' is the name officially given by white South Africa to the policy of keeping the races apart, and refers particularly to the policy's territorial base. Thus the old reserves, whose extent was finally determined at about 13 per cent of the country's surface area, have been turned into statelets, in which the 'Bantu' (as Africans used to be known officially) can 'develop along their own lines' uncontaminated and uncontaminating. These mini-states, nicknamed Bantustans in their early days, were later officially known as 'homelands', a designation which (inside South Africa) is now increasingly being used also by those who oppose the policy or are indifferent to it, and which I shall adopt here. The newest official name 'national states' seems to be little used, except by government and civil service.

This pure statement of the policy is now somewhat old-fashioned, but it has been of considerable importance in the recent past and cannot be ignored. Before trying to assess the policy's effectiveness we must specify the problem it is intended to solve.

The difficulty which has always faced white South Africa is that it has needed black labour power, (on this Marxists and capitalists have no difficulty in agreeing) whilst being desperate to avoid a permanent black presence or any direct ownership of significant assets in the white area. (Rich blacks could presumably become indirect owners by buying shares on the stock exchange, but there have never been enough rich blacks for this to become a serious consideration). The policy of separate development seemed for many years both to meet the demands of the white economy and to satisfy the belief of many white South Africans that uniting the races was socially dangerous and morally wrong.

On the other hand, the two races have been inextricably entwined in the development of the economy. South Africa's assets, minerals, agriculture, industry, commerce and finance have been created (or, in the case of natural resources, exploited) by a combination of black physical labour and white management, since blacks have until lately not been allowed access to managerial or even skilled positions outside the homelands. This

8

is not to say that all whites enjoy affluence and the absence of physical labour; there are many relatively poor whites, particularly Afrikaners, employed by, most notably, the railways. But the command posts outside the homelands are held by whites and in government, the civil service, the police and the armed forces, predominantly by Afrikaners. Since the white population is under four and a half million according to the census of 1980, the country's resources of high and medium ability manpower are severely stretched. At the top of the various pyramids in society the white personnel aspire to and appear to reach the highest international standards of competence, but lower down it seems likely that there are many whites under-qualified for their jobs, and even if they were all sufficiently qualified, there would still not be enough of them. (The same of course might be said of other countries where opportunities are confined to a minority, but some of those countries do not, perhaps, set their sights as high as does South Africa.)

Even if white South Africa could do without black labour, the homelands could not possibly support the entire black population. In the 1950s the Tomlinson Commission undertook a detailed survey of the reserves and produced an immense report, a one volume digest of which was published in 1956 (UG 1955). The Commission worked out the number of acres which would constitute an economic unit, capable of supporting a family of six and generating a gross family income of £60. (Naturally the figures varied considerably, according to the type of land, amount of rainfall, etc.) The Commission calculated further that although only 12 per cent of the land was set aside for Africans it had 20 per cent of the productive capacity of the total agricultural land in (what was then) the Union. They then made estimates of population and concluded that in the best case (that is, with the smallest black population) there would be room in the reserves for 70 per cent of the black population by the year 2000, if large sums were spent on developing the reserves. As a start they recommended expenditure of £104 million over ten years. (For a fuller account of the Tomlinson Commission see Hill 1964: Ch. II.)

As it turned out, the government rejected that recommendation and spent far less. At the same time, as current population projections show, the population has grown, and continues to grow, much more rapidly than Tomlinson expected. Nevertheless, after some years of ambiguity and uncertainty it became clear that the legal process of devolution of political authority to the homelands, which began with the Bantu Authorities Act of 1951 and continued with the Promotion of Bantu Self-Government Act of 1959, would culminate in independence for such homelands as could be persuaded to accept it. This was the policy's logical end, but many observers, in and outside of South Africa, had doubted if it would ever be reached.

The homelands are not apt candidates for independence, since, apart from being very poor, their territory is divided by 'white spots', that is, small pockets of land owned by whites. Even after a good deal of very expensive consolidation KwaZulu, for example, is still divided into numerous unconnected blocks.

The Transkei is the least fragmented of the homelands and received limited self-government in 1963, with a constitution weighted in favour of the ruling party (The Transkei National Independence Party) since 64 of the members of the first assembly were non-elected chiefs, most of whom supported the TNIP and its leader, Chief Matanzima. (The latter achieved a long-held ambition when he was raised to Paramount Chief, thus officially gaining equality of status with his old rival, Paramount Chief Sabata Dalindyebo of the Tembus, who has since been deposed and gone into exile.)

Matanzima has written his autobiography (Matanzima 1976) which is very short and naturally somewhat one-sided. Dirk Kotzé has written in detail and at length of politics in the Transkei and other homelands (Kotzé 1976). It is enough to say here that Matanzima had little difficulty in maintaining and consolidating his power when he was Prime Minister, assisted by his brother as Minister of Justice, and retains it now that he has become President (though for how long is uncertain) and his brother has succeeded him as Prime Minister. (For a valuable study of the new Transkeian élite see Southall 1977.) He gladly accepted independence when it came in 1976 and was disconcerted when no state other than South Africa recognized Transkei (the 'The' having been dropped) as an independent state. (The British Goverment's attitude, which it shared with its European Community partners, is discussed in Hill 1976.) There continues to be little likelihood of international recognition being granted, except perhaps after some major constitutional rethink covering the whole of South Africa, including the homelands.

Subsequently Bophutatswana accepted independence under Chief Mangope in 1977, Venda in 1979 and the Ciskei in 1981. KwaZulu (formerly Zululand) is judged ripe for independence by the South African Government, although its territory is still fragmented, but its leader, Chief Buthelezi, has, after some years of skilful ambiguity, rejected it. Buthelezi, his biographer (Temkin 1976) has suggested, may believe that in the future he may play some unifying role between the homeland leaders and the old banned parties. If that is correct, and his 'secret' meetings with exiled leaders suggest that it is, he needs to keep all options open and above all to avoid the odium which would follow the acceptance of independence.

For the homelands system is almost universally execrated, and in any case cannot be a success even in its own terms. Of course the policy can be pushed to its logical conclusion, which is that every black in the Republic (except immigrants from Zimbabwe etc.) would receive the citizenship of whatever homeland he was judged to hail from and lose his South African rights. This has already happened in the cases of the Transkei, Bophutatswana, Venda and the Ciskei, and their leaders' acquiescence in the arrangement contributes greatly to their unpopularity. Much governmental thinking is now being devoted to the question of citizenship, fuelled by the report, presented to Cabinet in May 1980, of a commission chaired by Professor Charles Niewoudt of the University of Pretoria. The report, which was not published and remains confidential, was thought to have recommended some form of combination between South African citizenship and homeland nationality, loosely on the model of the (formerly British) Commonwealth, and it appears that such an arrangement would be accepted by Bophutatswana and Venda, but not Transkei, and perhaps not the Ciskei. Hints of this line of thought have filtered through in official pronouncements, but the issue remains somewhat confused. What is clear is that the leaders of the non-independent homelands are determined to retain South African citizenship in some form, whatever line is taken in the 'independent' territories.

The loss of South African citizenship does not in itself render the position of blacks in black townships in white South Africa less secure—since their permission to reside permanently there is gained under section 10 of the Urban Areas Act, and is not revoked by the Acts of Parliament associated with the independence of the various homelands. The Ciskei Commission, which advised the Ciskei Government on the advisability of accepting independence was also assured by officials that '. . . the fact that Ciskeians outside, as well as inside the homeland would cease to be citizens of South Africa is stated to involve no loss of the existing rights of anyone either to reside in urban areas . . . or to acquire property there on a 99 year lease' (Ciskei Commission 1980: 114). However, children born after 'independence' will not, it appears, inherit permission to reside in a town, and this complicates the issue of leasehold tenure, which blacks are now allowed for up to 99 years. The problem of how a person is to proceed who inherits the unexpired portion of a lease, but has not the right of residence which is necessary if he is actually to live in his house is to be solved 'administratively'. This will presumably be done under the housing regulations contained in Government Notice R 1036 of 1979, which allow officials to grant a residence or site permit to people not qualified under the Urban Areas Act (SAIRR 1980: 401-2).

Nor are the 'reforms' proposed by the Riekert Commission (RSA, 1979a) affected by the citizenship question. The reforms have the effect of improving conditions for workers who are safely in the white area, but of controlling 'influx' more severely than before, partly through the labour bureaux, supplemented where necessary by labour agreements with foreign states and homelands. Employment is also controlled more effectively than hitherto via a series of measures, such as heavy fines for employers who employ unauthorized labour. Such labour is simply redirected to the homelands, where land and employment are inadequate to support even their present populations.

The effect, therefore, of the rigid control of labour is that Africans can only be employed on contract, unless they have been granted permission to reside permanently in white South Africa. The need for the contract to be renewed, say once a year, does not in itself prevent continuity of employment, since firms may simply arrange for their employees to travel back to, for example, the Transkei annually, whence they are re-engaged through the system of labour bureaux. This is a thoroughly inefficient system, except for workers who have family in the homeland with whom they wish to spend a holiday, and it maximises the worker's feeling of insecurity. Despite its irrationality in economic (not merely bourgeois capitalist) terms, it is likely to persist, if only because a large number of jobs in the white bureaucracy would be lost if it were abandoned. (For an elaboration of this point see Adam & Giliomee 1979: ch. 8).

Though it is as easy for white South Africa to deport blacks to reserves within the Republic as to nominally foreign countries, there is clearly a difference, at least on paper, between removing South African nationals and deporting foreigners. The loss of full South African citizenship by blacks would, if pushed to its limit, define the 'black problem' out of existence, because if all blacks in the Republic are eventually to be foreigners they will have no right to complain about their treatment there, or, if they do, their remedy, in the government's view, is simple. In sober fact, however, whilst many blacks do preserve links, of varying extent and intensity with the rural homeland (well discussed by e.g. Mayer 1962), for the many who have been born and brought up in the towns it has little meaning—any more than a man bred in London is particularly interested to learn that his great-grandfather was born in rural Cumberland. In any case the homelands are far too small to carry anything approaching their imputed populations and efforts to industrialise them would not, even if successful, keep up with the natural increase of the local population and, *a fortiori*, they could not possibly accommodate further inflow of nominal citizens from outside. It may be noted here that these efforts to industrialize have taken different lines as the ideology of apartheid has developed: before independence became the unambiguous object of policy the emphasis was on *border* industries, that is, placing the industries just outside the homelands, with the workers commuting from inside. With independence the emphasis shifted to the promotion of industrial growth within the homelands (see e.g. Hill 1964: Ch. II, Bell 1973 and Curle 1978): now it has shifted again to thoughts of regional co-operation between homelands and white areas.

To the inability of the homelands to provide a living for all the Republic's Africans must, as we have seen, be added the fact that the white economy would be unworkable without the presence of black labour. Of course many of the labour force may be migrants, particularly in the mines, but migration is decreasing in importance for a number of reasons. First, many migrants return again and again to the same job on what is in law a series of contracts, but in fact is virtually continuous employment. Secondly, the governments of some neighbouring states seek to discourage migration to the Republic. Thirdly, although a migrant labour force is likely to be docile and therefore easy to control, its attraction for some employers is diminishing, because the increasing use of expensive and sophisticated machinery and equipment necessitates the development of at least semi-skills among the labour force, and this in turn calls for career, instead of casual workers. Hence the need for workers to be accommodated in permanent housing with their families, instead of the barracks considered suitable for 'single' migrants. Finally, despite the many obstacles to the legal establishment by Africans of urban residence, there is now a large settled urban black population.

Though the policy of separate development is unworkable and does nothing to solve South Africa's underlying problems, which are those of any third world country with a galloping rate of population increase, it has many devotees in South Africa. Afrikaners, in particular, stress the rightness of the various African peoples standing on their own feet and achieving their own development; the observation is constantly made that this is what the Afrikaners have done since they finally got away from British colonial domination in 1910. There are Afrikaner businessmen (in both private business and state corporations) who recognize full well the need for an improved supply of skilled blacks and therefore for the extension to them of training and job opportunities hitherto reserved for whites; nevertheless, some of them are so convinced of the rightness of ultimately self-sufficient separation that they will at the same time insist that this training will only temporarily be used in the white economy. Eventually, the argument goes, the Bantustans will become industrialized and it will then be the skilled black's duty to go 'home' and use his skill for the benefit of his own people. Others will justify the existence of a large settled African population in, say, Soweto by suggesting that Soweto should be given the status of an independent city state. Alternatively it might be divided into ethnic segments, each of which would be constitutionally attached to the appropriate 'parent' homeland.

Whilst Afrikaners tie themselves in these knots, English-speakers, particularly businessmen, whose attitudes in other respects need not be especially liberal, (business attitudes of both white language groups will be considered further in Chapter 6), tend to dismiss the homelands policy as nonsense. Outside South Africa the policy is condemned by the banned black parties, whose leaders naturally dream of one day taking power in an unfragmented South Africa, not a series of poverty-stricken labour reserves surrounding a prosperous, if embattled, white core. Inside the country a few blacks say all they dare to oppose the policy and many of them are in consequence banned: others, like Chief Buthelezi, remain precariously at liberty.

International organizations, like the United Nations, take their tone from the African parties, particularly the ANC, as do third world and Soviet bloc countries. In the industrialized west, though many leaders and officials may have no great interest one way or the other (and some sections of public opinion may even see the white South Africans as Ladies Bountiful who are to be congratulated for 'doing something for the Natives') there is nothing to be gained except trouble from, for example,

13

recognizing the Transkei as an independent state. It is an area which few could locate on the map and which has no natural resources of interest to the industrialized world, nor had the South African Government anything to offer in exchange for international recognition at the time when the possibility was a live issue, except perhaps increased co-operation over the solution of the Rhodesia/Zimbabwe and South-West Africa/Namibia questions. In short, so far as South Africa is concerned, the policy of separate development has few friends.

SEPARATE DEVELOPMENT IN NAMIBIA

The policy is, however, not confined to the Republic: something similar has also been pushed forward in Namibia following the Odendaal report of 1964 (RSA 1964), which gave the detailed blueprint for the division of the territory into ethnic blocs. The policy, in its Namibian application, was extensively discussed in the International Court hearings in 1965 and has been universally criticized since. (For an early critique see Mason 1964.)

The Namibian population is too small, estimated at 955,000 in 1977, (see Thomas 1978: 19) for a series of independent states to be seriously contemplated, except perhaps in the case of the Ovambo people, estimated at 396,000 in 1974 (of whom 84.8 per cent lived in Ovamboland) or 46.5 per cent of the total population (*Ibid*: 18 & 21). Ovamboland achieved a limited degree of self-government under Pastor Ndjoba—a development which has been bitterly opposed by the largest black political party, SWAPO (South-West Africa People's Organization). SWAPO, which has, however mistakenly, been recognized by the United Nations General Assembly (not the Security Council) as the sole authentic representative of the Namibian people, has considerable support among the Ovambos and is probably growing in popularity elsewhere. How much support it has will be difficult to gauge until an election is fought under conditions which the United Nations, SWAPO and South Africa can agree.

Although full-blown homelands, apart from Ovamboland, were out of the question in Namibia, the establishment of local ethnic organs of government was sufficiently advanced for all groups (except the Bushmen, whose representatives were chosen for them) to select delegates to the Turnhalle Conference (Cowley 1976: 190–6). This conference, which started work in 1975, laboured long to produce a constitution which, by proposing three tiers of government, managed both to retain separation of the races in most matters, whilst keeping the South African Government's promise that the new Namibia would be a unitary state. Out of that conference grew a new party of all races, the Democratic Turnhalle Alliance, which decisively won the elections of December 1978 (in which SWAPO refused to take part) and under whose control the territory has proceeded to the virtual exercise of internal self government. However, those elections gained no international acceptance and did nothing to soften opinion at the United Nations. The UN's objective is now, through the 'contact group' of the five western powers which were members of the Security Council when the negotiations

14

began in 1977 (Britain, Canada, France, West Germany and the USA) to arrange elections which would be supervised by the UN and in which SWAPO would therefore be unable to refuse to take part. The negotiations made slow progress for a number of reasons. First, western politicians and officials were for much of the time preoccupied with the question of Zimbabwe. Secondly, there has never been a settled determination in South Africa to bring Namibia to an independence blessed by the United Nations; rather there have been conflicting threads of opinion and advice, of which now one and now the other has gained the upper hand. Thirdly, both South Africa and SWAPO have been determined to drive a hard bargain. The negotiations nearly foundered for good at the abortive Geneva conference of January 1981, but after a long pause during which the policy of the new American administration began to take shape, they were resumed and seem likely to come eventually to a succcessful conclusion, and be followed by elections which SWAPO will win.

In that case, neither the apparatus of Ovambo self-government under the home-lands system nor the 'second tier' of ethnic government which was instituted in terms of the Turnhalle agreement will survive in their present form, though the size of the country, coupled with poor communications and low population, make probable the *de facto* retention of a large measure of local autonomy. If, on the other hand, the negotiations were finally to fail and South Africa granted independence to Namibia unilaterally, much of the present apparatus might be expected to survive.

SEPARATE DEVELOPMENT IN THE 1980s

My purpose in the previous section was to show that separate development does not solve South Africa's and Namibia's problems, even in the terms of those who advocate the policy. I turn now to some recent modifications to the pure, and now out-dated, Verwoerdian conception of separate development.

Currently it looks as if Pretoria's reliance on the homelands policy in its traditional form is markedly decreasing. The new trend can usefully be discussed in the context of the report of the Ciskei Commission (to which brief reference has been made above) commonly known as the Quail Report, after its chairman. This Commission, although it was concerned solely with the pros and cons of Ciskeian independence, necessarily discussed broader issues and its thinking can now be seen as the logical precursor of subsequent developments. Indeed, it would not be fanciful to identify the Commission's report, in retrospect, as a turning point, poor, small and encumbered with unwilling and unwelcome immigrants though the Ciskei is. A further remarkable feature of the Commission was that a minority of its members was Afrikaans speaking, whereas in white South Africa it is rare to find a member of an important Commission who is anything else. It even included three foreigners, a former British Ambassador to South Africa (Sir Arthur Snelling) and two American Professors. The presence of non-South Africans on such a commission is perhaps the clearest signal that the Ciskei's Prime Minister, Chief Sebe could have given of his determination to demonstrate independence (without at that stage necessarily being prepared to accept formal political independence) from white South Africa.

In fact, of course, the Ciskei was only semi-autonomous at the time and the Commission was appointed in August 1978 to advise Sebe on whether he should accept independence; in the event it finally advised that he should not, unless far better terms could be negotiated than those previously accepted by the Transkei, Bophutatswana and Venda. Nevertheless, Sebe conditionally accepted independence in October 1980: as will be seen, the conditions are significant.

In supporting their recommendation against independence the Commission rehearsed the arguments for and against and, in a wide ranging discussion, considered the other available options—the *status quo*, full internal autonomy, federation and confederation, the 'constellation of states', (as the Prime Minister's envisaged closer association between South Africa and its neighbours is known—See Ch. 16), a unitary state and amalgamation with the Transkei. The Commissioners considered the *status quo* valueless; they thought full internal autonomy somewhat better, since it would 'help meet the desire for political progress' without endangering Ciskeians' rights to citizenship, residence or employment in white South Africa. Furthermore '. . . it would give the Ciskei greater political experience in preparation for independence or for some other change in status' (Ciskei Commission 1980: para. 274). A unitary state covering the whole of South Africa was the option most favoured by respondents to the Commission's attitude survey, but seemed to the Commissioners an unrealistic hope at present, because of its unpopularity with whites; amalgamation with the Transkei was rejected, largely because of the latter's record since 'independence' so that only a con/federal future or membership in the constellation of states remained to be taken seriously.

The principal argument against independence was that it would weaken the Ciskei's chance of negotiating satisfactory terms for entrance into a con/federation, which the Commission believed to be very much on the cards. The advantage of federation would be that '. . . It would avoid the painful issues of citizenship and nationality inherent in independence . . .', it would provide a framework within which economic inequality could be reduced, and would preserve Ciskeians' access to employment in white areas. It would also:

> . . . facilitate consolidation and boundary adjustments, which are undoubtedly easier to accomplish in a single country than between two independent countries. It would remove the ground for white fears that independent homelands could become a threat to South Africa's security and bases for terrorism (*Ibid*: para 278).

The South African Government, on the other hand, favoured independence first, followed by negotiations which would lead to some kind of coming together between those who decided to join, and it appears

16

that Sebe has accepted the government's view. The Commission believed, however, that the Ciskei would be ill-advised to take the risk of accepting independence and then negotiating the best deal it could with its powerful neighbour:

> Undoubtedly, the South African government would be in a stronger negotiating position, and the Ciskei in a weaker one, if the homeland had first taken her independence and in so doing accepted a position in which she had lost these rights. The logic of the matter seems clear: if the Ciskei values, as we think she should, the advantages which federation could secure, she would be well advised not to run the risk of losing them by first accepting independence and hoping subsequently to win them back in negotiations for some form of confederation or other loose association of states. A confederation should, in our view, be accepted only if its terms can be settled simultaneously with the negotiation of any independence (*Ibid*: para 282).

Rather similar considerations surrounded the notion of a constellation of states, which had been promoted by the South African Prime Minister in 1978 and 1979. But the details of the constellation remained unclear, though it seemed that Mr Botha saw it as a stage which would follow the acceptance of independence by the homelands. This interpretation of the Prime Minister's thinking, if correct (and the Commission did not believe it was universally held in National Party circles) would expose the Ciskei and other homelands to the same dangers as were presented by independence before confederation:

> It would be imprudent to abandon any prospect of securing more acceptable citizenship arrangements, a large measure of land consolidation and the prospect of economic benefits solely in order to benefit from the hoped-for, but as yet ill defined, advantages of membership of a hypothetical constellation (*Ibid*: para 287).

The case against independence was succinctly summarized:

> . . . blacks are not properly consulted about whether they want it; the loss of South African citizenship is unacceptable; the homelands are too small and fragmented; their inhabitants could suffer important economic disadvantages and there is no prospect of international recognition (*Ibid*: para 307).

Blacks, the Commission said, had never been properly recompensed for their part in generating South Africa's wealth; now, at last, white South Africa was beginning to accept the justice of the black case. This was no moment to leave South Africa, and be dependent on charitable 'aid' to a nominally foreign country, rather than participating by right in the prosperity of an undivided South Africa:

> Opponents of independence argue that South Africa is modernising—and especially in the way the modernising process affects its ethnic policies. The more it modernises the more it is in the Ciskei's economic interest to remain inside South Africa, maintaining real claims on future economic growth and substantial and growing claims to political benefits. These may be as large as they are now incalculable. In short, this is not the time to leave South Africa. It is the time to stay, to take part, and to prosper (*Ibid*: para 321).

The Commission had a positive recommendation to make, and resonances of it may be detected in much subsequent thinking. The

Commission believed that a non-racial 'condominium' should be created, which would consist of the Ciskei, the white areas earmarked for incorporation in it, and the white corridor to East London which divides the Ciskei from the Transkei; the Commission also hoped that East London would become a free port with an export-oriented manufacturing zone surrounding it. The condominium's form of government, in which power would be shared between blacks and whites, would be for negotiation, as would its share of general South African taxation.

This recommendation, revolutionary though it may sound to specialists in South African affairs, has been overtaken by recommendations from a source close to the heart of the Afrikaner 'Establishment' (Professor Jan Lombard). It is possible to see now that the shift of emphasis from the old Verwoerdian image of separate development to a preoccupation with consolidation of the homelands was itself only a stage on the road to a new regionalization which would cut across homeland boundaries; we shall discuss the recommendations in a later chapter, since their importance extends beyond the homelands policy into the question of the whole constitutional future of South Africa.

It remains to consider Chief Sebe's surprising rejection of the Quail Commission's advice and his conditional acceptance of independence, announced on September 30 1980, which suggests that he decided to do precisely what the Commission had warned against, namely to take on trust whatever conditions of future association with the Republic could be negotiated with the South African Government. This attitude contrasts strikingly with that of Chief Buthelezi, and other homeland leaders, like Dr Phatudi of Lebowa.

Homeland leaders, like politicians elsewhere, wish to stay in power and Chief Sebe is no exception. He clearly had no intention to allow moves towards greater autonomy for the Ciskei if they would further weaken his rather shaky political base and an essential *quid pro quo* for the acceptance of independence was further territorial growth. Sebe apparently believed that a satisfactory agreement had been reached with South Africa on land consolidation, which would triple the territory's area by ceding to it all the white land between the Great Fish and Great Kei rivers (it had been expected that King William's Town would be handed over to the Ciskei, but in the run up to the election of April 1981 the whites of King William's Town were assured this would not happen), as well as on a confederal arrangement which would protect Ciskeians' South African citizenship, and on the rights of Ciskeians to live and seek work in white South Africa. (*The Times* 5 December 1980). Armed with these assurances Sebe felt confident in proceeding to a referendum on the independence issue, which he duly won with a very large majority, which according to some observers was to be accounted for by a combination of fear and boycotts. (The figures were 295,891 in favour, 1,642 against and 2,198 spoilt papers in a 59.5 per cent poll; see SAIRR 1981: 407). Subsequently, however, it became clear that Sebe's confidence was to a large extent misplaced.

The position of Chief Buthelezi, who has steadfastly resisted moves towards independence for KwaZulu, is rather different since he has behind him not only the homeland government, but also the Zulu cultural movement, Inkatha. Despite his outspoken attacks on the Pretoria Government and his contacts with the ANC, and perhaps also the PAC, he is vilified by some urban leaders and radical blacks at home and in exile for consenting to play any part in the institutions of apartheid. Nevertheless, Inkatha, despite its faults (notably the lack of other significant leaders and its shortage of non-Zulu members) attracted the favourable attention of President Kaunda, who sent his own aircraft to bring Buthelezi to Zambia to study the workings of the United National Independence Party, with the result that Inkatha's constitution is modelled on that of UNIP.

Despite their differences both Sebe and Buthelezi have contributed to the evolution of the policy of separate development in ways which emphasize the irrelevance of the traditional version of that policy to the real problems of South Africa. Sebe, by insisting on citizenship safeguards would, if he had been successful, have removed one of the policy's main planks. Buthelezi, by refusing independence, has removed its corner stone. The South African Government seems to be in the process of accepting that the old homelands policy is dead, whilst of course proclaiming that it is alive and well. At the political level this acceptance shows itself in the movement towards a confederal arrangement which will unite white South Africa and the homelands in a single constitutional structure; at the economic level it is manifested in the new vision of South Africa as a set of regions and 'joint venture areas' including both black and white areas, in which homeland boundaries will be of greatly reduced significance. (For an elaboration of the new policy see RSA 1982.)

CHAPTER 3

Liberalism

There may be many people who wish that liberal attitudes would lead to actions which in turn would lead to solutions of South Africa's problems, but it must be doubted whether there are many who actually believe anything of the kind will happen. Not only has liberalism come to seem a lost cause—it has also become a dirty word, in the mouths of both the illiberal left and the bigoted right.

A typical view from the right is Dr J. D. Vorster's: 'Liberal Christians, liberal Jews and liberal-minded universities have, down the years, rendered the greatest assistance to communism' (Quoted in Midlane n.d.). From the left the accusations are more varied: for example, liberalism does not generate testable hypotheses but instead tends to be presented in abstract, sometimes highly abstract, form; liberals are incapable of devising a programme of action, but have to fall back on identifying liberalism as a state of mind; liberalism is not just compatible with capitalism, but is compatible with no other mode of production; it has even been held that liberalism was thought up by capitalist *ideologues* with the conscious purpose of justifying, or legitimating capitalism. South African liberalism is accused of failing even to ameliorate the condition of blacks in South Africa; on the contrary things have got steadily worse for them since the National Party came to power in 1948.

To take first the attack from the right, it is in a sense true that liberals assist communism, though hardly in the sense intended by Dr Vorster. But it is an essential liberal belief that, even if liberals had it in their power to destroy beliefs with which they disagreed, there is a positive value in toleration and therefore a duty to allow rival beliefs to flourish. The difficulty for liberals is where to draw the line. Is there for example a duty to allow a belief, like Marxism, to flourish, which in most formulations is incompatible with liberal beliefs and which would, if successful, seek to destroy them?

By a normal definition of communism it seems extremely improbable that liberals have assisted it, except in the limited sense already noted of preaching the general duty of toleration. However, Dr Vorster's definition was unlikely to have been normal, given the very wide range of beliefs, which official South Africa labels 'communist'. (For a detailed account of the Suppression of Communism Act see Naudé 1969.) Given the meaning

Dr Vorster probably attached to 'Communism' his statement becomes true, indeed tautologous.

The arguments of the left also contain some truth. It is perfectly correct to say that liberalism does not generate testable hypotheses, but to say this betrays a misunderstanding of one of the main functions of political philosophy, which is to present a systematic set of statements about what ought or ought not to be the case. Most philosophers, and laymen, but not those Marxists who believe that a correct analysis leads necessarily to correct action, would agree that there is a fundamental logical difference between statements about what is or is not the case and ones about what ought or ought not to be the case. (Hudson 1969 is an invaluable collection of papers on this subject.)

Thus, the liberal might answer that it does not matter if his beliefs yield no testable hypotheses, because he, like all political philosophers (including Marx) is concerned with prescription. He would, I think, go on to say that liberalism more readily yields negative than positive prescriptions. For example, it might be held wrong to withhold from any properly qualified person the civil right to vote, without there being any certainty about what constitutes a proper qualification. Should it be simply the age of majority (which itself has to be decided) or should there in addition be a property or educational qualification?

It must therefore be accepted that much liberal discourse, like much Marxian discourse, is highly abstract. We may even with Minogue (1963) admit that it is more a state of mind than anything else. Furthermore, if we now turn to the various connections that have been made between liberalism and capitalism, we can accept that the two are at least compatible and that classical liberalism began to be formulated at just about the time that early capitalism showed itself. But to go further and say that i) liberalism is the only ideology compatible with capitalism; ii) capitalism is the only mode of production compatible with liberalism; or iii) that liberalism has been devised by ideologues *with the intention* of justifying capitalism is much harder to sustain. Before examining these propositions we should consider some of the characteristics of classical liberalism.

There is a general liberal principle, deriving in modern times from Locke, that government is a trust which should be exercised by the government only to the extent necessary to protect the individual's wellbeing. (The rights to freedom of speech and assembly, freedom of movement, etc., can be derived from this principle.) In recent times, when the range of services which some governments are called upon to provide has grown enormously, the proportion of citizens' resources which government must control if it is to meet those demands has grown also. The liberal cannot realistically resist in its entirety this extension of the range of governmental actions, though he will certainly keep a weather eye on it and seek whenever possible to reduce it, or at least prevent further extensions of the government's role. To the growth of legislation and the multiplication of

21

socially determined goals he will oppose individual liberty and the belief that only those aspects of life which must be regulated should be. However, since the balance between individual and group responsibilities is constantly changing, the liberal will find it difficult to say precisely where the line should be drawn, though he will have little difficulty in identifying at least some countries, for instance South Africa and the Soviet Union, where the extent of government power is unacceptable and, though this is a different point, the manner of its exercise brutal. People will rebel in both socialist and capitalist countries against the government's arrogating to itself excessive powers, though the definitions of 'excessive' will naturally differ. Though capitalists will, on the whole, insist more strongly than socialists on the principle of governmental abstention from extending its scope, capitalists will not invariably insist. They are unlikely, for example, to resist interference with the free market mechanism if that interference protects their interests.

Liberals in any society will, if they dare, deny the claim made by authoritarians of right or left, that they have certain and indubitable knowledge of how human affairs should be conducted, of whom should be appointed to conduct them and of how these guardians should be selected (e.g. a qualification may be party membership or race). Furthermore, the liberal will react with scepticism to the view that, if people cannot be brought to want what their leaders know they need in South Africa, separate development 'along their own lines', in Tanzania, Ujamaa villages) they must be forced, for their own eventual good. He will doubt claims to certain knowledge; he will have noted (though he may not commit himself to a belief in 'human nature') that most men are corrupt if given a chance and will distrust those who wish to behave like Plato's Guardians; he will resist the kind of thinking which is prepared to sacrifice the present good of this generation for the expected eventual benefit of the next. If deprived of free speech or association 'for the common good' he will want to know who has decided what the common good is, and on what grounds.

The liberal believes, on the contrary, in the value of individual human beings, a belief which is often linked with the profession of Christianity. In the South African context Archbishop Hurley, not surprisingly, makes the latter connection (Hurley 1966) whilst Hobart Houghton does not (Houghton 1970). Colour is irrelevant to the value of human beings; so is class membership. Nor will the liberal accept an analysis of society which sees the economic variable as governing all others.

Liberals believe in rational discussion and shrink from violence. Naturally, a person of liberal disposition may engage in violent acts from time to time, (some South African liberals, who were members of the African Resistance Movement in the 1960s did so) but I do not think he can be said to be acting liberally on those occasions, any more than I can accept the view put forward by some theologians that loving your neighbour is consistent with shooting him. (For an argument that it *is* consistent see Herbert McCabe, who says:

22

. . . participation in the class struggle is not only compatible with Christian love but is demanded by it . . . there are circumstances in which even violence itself—by which I mean killing people—is not only compatible with Christian love but demanded by it.

(McCabe 1980: 156)

However, just as the Christian does not invariably act in a Christian way, so there is no reason to expect the liberal always to act as such.

Capitalism implies property, and the right to own property (I am concerned only with civil rights since the notion of 'natural rights' seems to me valueless; see Hill 1969: Ch. 1) is one to which any liberal would subscribe, particularly if he adopted Locke's very wide sense, or rather senses, of 'property' (Locke 1690). However, though the right to property is certainly a cardinal feature of capitalist societies, it is not confined to them; moreover, in virtually all societies, whether capitalist or not, it is subject to restriction, either by regulations which prohibit accumulation or by taxes which take away part of what has been accumulated. Thus the right to property is not peculiar to capitalist societies, though it is essential to them.

To conclude the first part of this very short account of liberalism, the liberal will not favour rapid change even if the current state of affairs is certainly bad and a better one seems possible of attainment. Though this kind of caution is not peculiar to liberals, they distrust blue-prints for the future and insist that change must be orderly, controlled and regulated. Finally, though they believe in the basic rights of man, they do so more in the manner of Edmund Burke than of Tom Paine. Rights are discussed further in the next section.

LIBERALISM AND HUMAN RIGHTS

A further set of arguments against liberalism centres on the lack of practicality of the liberal concern for the maintenance and extension of human rights; similar arguments are frequently used to rebut those who urge the need to respect Western democratic values in third world countries which are in fact ruled by single parties, army officers or dictators and it may be useful to look at these arguments in some detail.

The Universal Declaration of Human Rights was eventually completed in 1947 after long negotiations which covered fundamental differences between the Western and Soviet blocs. Some of the difficulties are concealed by careful drafting, but there remains a number of 'inalienable' rights in the list which would certainly not be permitted in the Soviet bloc. The rights incorporated in the list fall into two categories (it does not matter for our present purpose whether they were believed to be natural, or whether the rights listed are merely those which the compilers thought ought to be guaranteed universally as civil rights). The first category includes the liberal freedoms, such as freedom of speech and assembly, which some Western statesmen habitually urge third world countries to respect. The second category contains some which are patently absurd if demanded universally;

23

for example, the assertion of a right to a paid holiday reads like a sick joke in a world one thousand million of whose inhabitants are starving and where many barely subsist and have no use for money.

However, it is the propagation by liberals of the first category of human rights which is so much resented in the third world. At least four kinds of argument are used. First, to try to spread human rights is decried as 'cultural imperialism'—some remarks by President Marcos of the Philippines provide a good example (*The Times*: 29 August 1978). The argument is that 'human rights' are a Euro/American concept, which the west has no right to seek to propagate elsewhere. Secondly, the *tu quoque* argument is, perhaps justifiably, used: e.g. Britain has no right to comment adversely on other countries' practices whilst abuses continue in Northern Ireland. In the third place, it is sometimes said that to guarantee human rights in a poor country struggling with the problems of development simply cannot be afforded. To entrench e.g. freedom of speech would, so the argument goes, encourage division where unity is desperately needed, by encouraging opposition politicians to gather a following when they should be loyally supporting the national leader in his attempts to cope with the problems of poverty. This kind of argument does not deny the desirability of human rights, but counts the cost.

Finally, the fourth kind of response is that rights are all very well for the rich, but of little use to the poor, whose interests are limited to avoiding starvation and with luck finding employment. The argument is spurious, *unless* it can be shown that by safeguarding e.g. freedom of speech the chance that crops will be grown, employment created, population controlled, etc. will be reduced.

In South Africa variants of all four of these arguments are used by apologists for the government (or, more generally, the system) often as part of an attack on liberals. The first argument (cultural imperialism) presents some difficulty, since on the one hand, white South Africans are anxious to claim membership in the western Christian community, whilst on the other they are coming more and more to insist on the characteristics South Africa shares with countries of the third world and the unsuitability therefore of, for example, the 'Westminster Model'. Secondly, the *tu quoque* response to foreign reproaches is very frequently used and in some countries would be difficult to answer if it were taken seriously. Thirdly the denial of rights to political prisoners, banned persons, etc. is justified by reference to the overwhelming national need to combat communism, though, since this is a goal set by whites, it is probably not of much interest to blacks. Finally, there is some tendency to say that human rights are less important than bread and butter.

The broad accusation that all blacks are systematically deprived of rights is simply denied, with the assurance that in their own areas Africans (but not coloureds and Indians) can enjoy full rights, including that of national independence. This view has a certain attractive symmetry, which is wholly misleading, since, as we have seen, the homelands are quite inadequate for

24

the populations ascribed to them, and cannot survive without continuing to export labour to South Africa.

LIBERALISM AND ECONOMIC AMELIORATION

The view that economic forces will bring the end of apartheid, which was briefly mentioned in Chapter 1, is usually identified as liberal. It is linked with the name of Michael O'Dowd, a Director of the Anglo-American Corporation of Johannesburg, and one of the view's most persuasive advocates (O'Dowd: 1974) and is shared by many businessmen, including Harry Oppenheimer, lately Chairman of the Anglo-American Corporation, and some academic economists (e.g. Horwitz 1967).

Briefly, it is held that, as the population of South Africa grows, the white percentage of the total will fall and it will be impossible for whites to continue to occupy all the responsible positions and provide most of the skilled labour which the economy requires. It will then become apparent that such practices as job reservation are incompatible with the rational operation of the economy and, having been exposed in their full absurdity, will fall away. The need for black labour at all levels in the economy will in turn lead to the improvement of black education; the rules governing the mobility of labour and the right to live in the white area will be scrapped and at that point South Africa will 'take off' on the road to self-sustaining growth.

The reference to Rostow's notion of economic take-off complicates the argument but is not essential to it (Rostow 1960). As a metaphor it is compelling and easy to understand, but the difficulty is that actual countries have not passed through the various stages of growth which Rostow believes to be necessary. Nevertheless, some countries have taken off, (e.g. Brazil, Hong Kong, Korea; indeed according to Bozzoli (1978: 42) South Africa itself did so as long ago as the 1930s) and there is no reason not to use the term, provided it does not imply that those countries have taken exactly the Rostowian path.

On the other hand, if one ignores that aspect of O'Dowd's thesis something very important is left—namely the insight that the myriad regulations of apartheid inhibit the rational operation of the economy. (I leave on one side for the moment the Marxists' objections to this use of 'rational'.) It does not, however, necessarily follow from the fact that the rules are recognized as hindrances that they will fall away, because businessmen may simply resign themselves to having to live with inconveniences. Alternatively, they may press for the removal of some black disabilities, but only those which directly affect efficiency, leaving much of the present system as it is. We shall see in the section on the Wiehahn and Riekert reports that this is what is happening in fact.

A different view, which is not necessarily incompatible with O'Dowd's, has been put in an influential article by Blumer and is constantly put also by spokesmen of multinational corporations (Blumer 1965). Blumer believes that businessmen do not seek radically to change the systems within which they operate, but instead adapt to their surroundings, even if this results in somewhat lower profit than might be made in optimum conditions. The maximisation of profit is, therefore, not their only goal; on the contrary, they are prepared to sacrifice something to avoid brushes with authority and in order to function harmoniously in the society where they happen to be. It would be consistent with Blumer's view, though he does not go on to say this himself, to add that if local conditions are too uncomfortable a business may simply withdraw, or perhaps put its operations on to a care and maintenance basis in order to keep competitors out of a given territory, but without any expectation of making a profit unless conditions improve.

A line similar to Blumer's is taken by many multinational corporations, which point out that it would be impossible, and wrong, for a company which operates in, say, a hundred countries, to seek to correct the injustices it perceived in all of them—therefore it should not seek to correct any. The conclusion does not strictly follow, but it is easy to see that in many countries it would be impossible for a company to involve itself very deeply in social issues without incurring the wrath of the host government; if it did this it would at best divert much of the energy which should be devoted to the commercial aims of the company, and at worst be put out of business. Furthermore, multinationals' spokesmen will often take the moral point that it is positively wrong for a business to seek to impose on the receiving societies, with all their diversity, a single standard of moral behaviour which commends itself to the central planners at the London headquarters of, for example, ICI: this is the 'cultural imperialism' argument reversed. Thus non-interference in politics (which itself is a political decision) is justified by business on both prudential and moral grounds, in a way consistent with Blumer's thesis and, it is argued, if the arguments are valid for one country they are valid for all.

Blumer's view that inconveniences may simply be accepted is to some extent contradicted in a study by Feit and Stokes (1976), who formed the hypothesis that Afrikaner workers would continue to favour the retention of barriers to prevent blacks acquiring skills, even if they realized that the barriers were economically irrational. They tested the hypothesis with evidence from an attitude survey and asked their sample whether they would vote for a candidate who professed himself in favour of African advancement. To their surprise they found that '. . . economic perceptions are the most direct cause of a projected vote in favour of a candidate who supports the use of African artisans'. They deduced from this and further questions that '. . . culturally generated racial antipathies do not necessarily constitute an impermeable barrier to change in racial policy . . .' and found that the better informed the Afrikaner artisan, the more likely he was to support the admission of Africans to skilled jobs. The authors add the warning that '. . . racial antipathies play a major role in shaping economic perceptions'. Nevertheless, the labour shortage is seen as a good reason for improving black opportunities, which led to a conclusion closer to O'Dowd's point of view than to Blumer's: 'As the labour shortage is a consequence of industrialization and not its cause, the assumption that forces can be unleashed by the process that will induce change does seem warranted'. (Feit & Stokes 1976: 497–501)

O'Dowd surely is right in some respects. Black wages have increased, and even before the Wiehahn and Riekert Commissions were appointed, the labour shortage was obliging private business and state corporations to allow blacks to occupy positions and perform tasks from which they were previously barred. Thus, within the economic system there is movement—and since the economic and the political are inseparable the movement has some political significance. The questions are how much, and where will it lead? O'Dowd believes that economic rationalization will lead to the eventual extension to blacks of full political rights.

Of course it would be ridiculous to expect him to demonstrate the conclusion—one cannot demonstrate the unknowable future—but the weakness of O'Dowd's thesis is that he fails even to make it remotely plausible. Whereas the advantages of purely economic liberalization are obvious except, as Feit and Stokes say, to people whose perceptions are distorted by racial antipathy (and of course to non-liberals), common sense suggests, and experience confirms, that among significant sections of the whites (sections which cannot be identified solely in class terms) the fear of extinction is such that they would never give up their present political advantages in order to achieve a future economic goal. Their doubt that they would live to enjoy the goal is too strong. Thus, though economic development will stimulate black demands for political rights, there will be nothing automatic about the process of acquiring them; the blacks will still have to struggle.

Though O'Dowd's conclusion seems to me wrong, his insight that the system contains potential for improvement (from a very low base, admittedly) is obvious. From the left, however, his thesis is attacked, not only because it cannot be proved or disproved, only experience will do that (and to some extent has done so already) but because it is essentially capitalist. From that point of view one does not have to be interested in South Africa to attack O'Dowd; to be opposed to capitalism is enough and improvements achieved within a capitalist society either are not really improvements at all, because they distract attention from the long-term goal, or are certain to be neutralized by skilled corrective action on the part of the bourgeoisie.

The O'Dowd thesis is undoubtedly a comforting one for capitalists, for it allows them to be humanitarian and self-interested at the same time. From the socialist point of view, the belief that capitalism can be reformed, in the process avoiding both the nationalist victory and the subsequent socialist revolution, may be more repugnant than a capitalism which makes no effort to reform, and a more dangerous enemy.

LIBERALISM, CAPITALISM AND APARTHEID

O'Dowd can hardly be accused of having concocted an incorrect theory merely because he wishes to justify immoral capitalist practices. It has, however, often been suggested that his predictions not only have not worked out, but cannot, because capitalism needs apartheid in order to survive. Before examining this assertion (which is one of the most important dividing lines between liberals and Marxists) one must distinguish various elements in apartheid; geographical separation, repressive laws, and 'petty apartheid'. Clearly the last is inessential, except in so far as it facilitates the major goals of white domination and prosperity, but it is often said that South African capitalism cannot do without geographical separation, and therefore also needs the laws which so regulate urban residence that a large portion of the labour force is obliged to migrate to and fro between the homelands and industrial white South Africa. The argument proceeds from the true statement (though not all economists accept it fully (see, e.g. Kantor and Kenny 1976)) that capitalism has in the past benefited, and continues to benefit now, from the apparatus of apartheid, which provides an ever-ready supply of labour at low cost, with little obligation to provide housing, schools, etc. in the white area, to the conclusion, which cannot be proved either true or false, that without these benefits capitalism would collapse.

It does, however, seem far more likely that, deprived of their present opportunities to 'super exploit' labour, capitalists would continue to find ways to exploit it to an extent which they would find worth while even if more of the normal costs of housing etc. had to be accepted, either directly or via taxation. (Indeed some companies have already successfully insisted to the South African Government that they must be allowed to accept them, even if this requires exemption from certain laws.) Thus, the detailed historical work on e.g. the mining industry and the control of labour, which shows that the interests of capital and state in South Africa have been intimately connected in the past, and that the laws made by the state have, at the least, been highly convenient for capitalists, tells us a great deal about the past, but nothing about the future; the past relations between capital and state (about whose precise nature there is in any case much disagreement among Marxists), by no means entails that any such relation need persist in future. Nor can the extent to which the apparatus of apartheid will be retained or modified be known *a priori*, since it depends on decisions which have to be made in specific situations. David Yudelman has made the point about the contingency of events:

> The degree of coercion initially required to bring black labour into the industrializing economy is still, moreover, a moot point . . . Even slightly better conditions and pay could conceivably have brought sufficient labour voluntarily to the mines and obviated the need for the undoubtedly coercive system which did develop. This is merely to argue that there is no necessary and *logical* connection between industrialization and coercion of labour.
>
> (Yudelman 1975: 92)

Earlier he says '. . . The liberal-reformist claim that the racial order will be transformed by industrialization is seen by the radical-revisionists as being at best a pipedream, at worst a self-serving rationalization.' In a foot-note he adds: 'They (the radical revisionists) refer of course to 'capitalist industrialization', as do the liberal-reformists. Comparisons with other modes of industrialization would, however be illuminating and tend to expose the constricted form of the debate so far' (*Ibid*: 91). Guelke reinforces the point that we cannot foresee the future:

> '. . . it would be foolish to make any prediction, since we cannot know in advance what course the South African Government will *choose* (Guelke's emphasis) . . . In this sense, the debate about the compatibility or incompatibility of apartheid with industrialisation and economic growth is an artificial one.'
> (Guelke n.d.: 114)

There is a remarkable degree of agreement among writers of very different ideological persuasions that capitalism in South Africa would operate more efficiently if some of the apparatus of apartheid were removed, though on the left the discussion is made difficult by highly complex theoretical debate. But whatever one's particular inclination within the broad Marxian mode of discourse, and whether, for example, one takes the view that the state is autonomous, or that it is the servant of capitalism in South Africa or even synonymous with it, there seems to be fairly general agreement (with some notable exceptions, like Legassick and Innes, p. 6 above) that a process of reform is in progress—though the reforms are variously categorized as illusory, irrelevant, destructive, etc.

We should note in passing the view held by many non-liberals that liberalism is a justificatory ideology thrown up by capitalism. This view has been powerfully propounded by C. B. MacPherson (1962) in relation to Hobbes and Locke in England, and adapted to South Africa by the Marxist 'school', sometimes known as 'neo-Marxists' or 'radical revisionists'. It is held that, just as capitalists are the dominant class in South Africa so liberalism is the dominant ideology. (Furthermore, until the relatively recent efflorescence of Marxist analyses, liberalism had dominated much academic writing about South Africa.) For the sake of brevity I do not discuss this view, nor the related views that liberalism is the only ideology suited to capitalist society, or that the latter is the only kind of society to which liberalism would be appropriate; nor do I ask how one identifies the dominant ideology in a given society.

It is, however, worth making the general point that there must be *some* relation between ideology and environment. It is trivially true that what people believe cannot but be influenced by upbringing, experience and surroundings—unless one imagines a believer who is not a believer at all, but merely a builder of abstract models. In this trivial sense, liberal theorists, like all theorists, do construct theories which relate to the conditions of their own society, which may be capitalist society. There is also a trivial sense in which liberals are necessarily apologists for the capitalist class, or capitalism as a system, namely if the author of the assertion goes on to say (probably in a roundabout manner which at first conceals the sense) that any theorist who is not such an apologist will not count as a liberal theorist. This makes the original assertion true by definition. It may however also be claimed, non-trivially, that liberal theorists seek to justify conditions in capitalist society, perhaps in a way which other kinds of theorist living in that society do not.

It is not always easy to pin down exactly what is being claimed (see e.g. Legassick (1976) on the work of R. F. A. Hoernlé) but, leaving on one side the logical difficulties, it must be admitted that the central point is of great importance and value. This is that liberals are wrong if they formulate the problems presented by South Africa solely in racial terms, at the expense of economic and class factors. Many modern liberals would accept this, but they would disagree with the neo-Marxists over the emphasis they place on class, and instead would argue that both race and class are essential explanatory factors. To argue this does not tell us why race, as opposed to, say, eye colour, came as a matter of historical fact to have such extraordinary importance in South Africa. But that is a separate question, for which there is not space here.

It is certainly the case that 'race relations' (which for liberals need not be placed in inverted commas) have been the chief preoccupation of members of the liberal and multiracial tradition. This tradition has run from missionaries like Philip and Livingstone through the Natives Representative Council and the Joint Councils Movement, to such early bodies as the SAIRR (mooted in 1926, founded in 1929) the Location Advisory Boards Congress (also founded in 1929) the Institute of Administrators (for brief details of the last two see Davenport 1969: 108–9) and the National Union of South African Students (NUSAS), and to more recent foundations, like the Liberal Party itself, the Black Sash and the Christian Institute. (For a general historical account of South African liberalism see Robertson 1971.)

It is also undeniably the case that Cape Liberalism did not achieve much, though such a view would naturally be contested by people who have devoted their lives to liberal causes and it must not be forgotten that great fights were made, though unsuccessfully, to preserve the Cape's non-racial franchise. The Churches (excluding the Dutch Reformed) remain strongholds of liberal thinking and outside them liberal minded men and women, particularly English speakers, are to be found in the professions and elsewhere, but virtually no organization with overtly liberal objectives (unless one includes the parliamentary opposition) has survived. Those which do are shadows of their former selves, like NUSAS or, like the courageous women's organisation, Black Sash, are little more than a nuisance to the government. That is not to deny the great value of the Sash's legal advisory service for blacks, nor the moral courage of their public statements of principle, but they are never going to undermine the state, nor would they wish to. Thus the charge that liberalism has achieved little in South Africa is, broadly speaking, well founded, though of course it is impossible to say how much worse the condition of the majority would be now if there had been no liberals in the past.

One of the charges most frequently made against liberals is that they do not only work for amelioration within the system rather than its overthrow (and even that unsuccessfully) but they do not really want anything more. Liberals, in other words, are not even working for power sharing between the races, and even less for handing power over to blacks.

Much depends upon the route (particularly whether it will be travelled violently), as well as the destination, but to an extent the accusation is just. Liberals (like people of other persuasions in other countries) must often have seemed patronizing, self-righteous, insensitive and ultimately committed only to themselves. As so often, Archbishop Hurley puts his finger on it: 'There is always that paralysing fear that a benevolent attitude towards non-whites must culminate in black Government, and the end of the white man in South Africa' (Hurley 1966: 15). The Archbishop had no answer to this, except to urge the need for changed moral conviction to precede political change. 'Political change is impossible without a moral revolution'. He might have added that human frailty is not confined to liberals. The reluctance (to which further reference will be made in the next chapter) of many white socialists to admit the validity of black nationalism may be soundly based in theory, but it fulfils the same function as does liberal half-heartedness; that is, to protect white participation in the future.

RACE, CLASS AND AFRIKANER NATIONAL IDENTITY

Marxists do not direct their attacks only against liberals, but also against each other. There is much internal debate within the Marxian school of thought about South Africa and one of the more wounding charges one Marxist can make against another is that he is 'straying perilously close to liberalism'. But whatever their disunity, Marxists have surely done a service to the study of South Africa by moving away from the excessive dependence on race, national identity, Afrikaner identity and so on as explanatory variables. However, most of them run the risk of throwing the baby out with the bathwater—for common sense (a common sense conditioned, to be sure, by the petit bourgeois class position which intellectuals cannot escape) powerfully suggests that race, in everyday South African life, is a category constantly present in people's minds. Naturally it may be so as a result of class problems which have produced class solutions, but to insist on class and class struggle as the sole determinants of ideology does not help us to deal with the fact that race is implanted in the minds of most South Africans, black and white, functioning at the very least as a means of classifying people and usually of evaluating them. The consciousness which attaches such importance to race may (to follow Marxian usage) be false, but it cannot be ignored by any commentator on South African politics.

Another variable which is frequently rejected as appearance rather than reality, without any explanatory value, is 'Afrikaner identity', and again, to reject it is to deprive oneself of an essential category. Of course, Afrikaner identity does not explain everything about the rise of Afrikanerdom. That is a complex story, first of cultural and then of economic advance. But to

31

concede that it fails to explain everything is not to admit that it explains nothing. It may be that economic advance was not possible without cultural self-realization, and even that leading Afrikaners promoted the latter in order to achieve the former; in that sense it may be that the Afrikaner's feeling of identity has been artificially created for ulterior ends. But even the acceptance of that rather extreme hypothesis does not allow us to ignore the feeling that Afrikaners undoubtedly have that they have 'an identity' which is somehow valuable. Nor should we be led into denying that the consciousness of, and attachment to, this identity leads Afrikaners to behave, in order to protect it, in ways in which they would not behave if they did not believe they had it, or if they did not believe it was in danger.

None of this reduces the value of a class analysis, provided only that the latter's adherents will admit that theirs is not the only legitimate and useful method of analysis. To admit this does not mean that they need enter into scholastic debates about whether there actually is 'such a thing' as Afrikaner identity. The proposition is untestable, unless 'identity' is held to be equivalent to 'culture', and it is not difficult to establish that an Afrikaner culture exists. However, the two are not equivalent. The difference lies in the element of self-awareness incorporated in the concept of identity, which need not be present in that of culture. The importance of 'Afrikaner identity' is that it forms part of the belief system, or mental furniture of Afrikaners and as such influences their actions.

At the same time it is possible to discern the classes within Afrikanerdom which benefited particularly from the Afrikaners' material advance. O'Meara does this in his study of the Broederbond, where he suggests that certain classes had a special interest in the success of this and other Afrikaner cultural organisations. But to go on to say (O'Meara's formulation is not absolutely clear) that the purpose of the Broederbond's founders was solely, or even primarily, to further a particular alliance of classes in the Transvaal, with cultural interests in a subordinate position or none at all, seems to go beyond the facts into the economic reductionism which many Marxists decry (O'Meara 1977).

Indeed, the Broederbond is a useful body upon which to focus a discussion of Afrikaner identity, because it displays in an extreme form the determination of Afrikaans speakers (to whom membership is confined) to further their national interests, both cultural and economic. Perusal of Broederbond documents, which is now possible thanks to certain journalists (Wilkins & Strydom 1978) shows a continual preoccupation with cultural and ethnic issues and comparatively little with economic. It may be that such evidence should be treated with reserve, either because the leaders were systematically deluding their followers (and perhaps themselves) or because all fundamental interests of their very nature are ultimately economic, and therefore to be fully understood only in the context of class struggle and class alliances. It seems to me, on the other hand, more consistent with the facts of life in South Africa to acknowledge that a consistent and successful drive has been made to advance all aspects of Afrikaner interests in the past half century, and that one of those interests has been the achievement of national advancement and power. The nation, thanks partly to the conscious efforts of the late Dr Diederichs and others to neutralize individual class interests, cuts across class to appeal to a wider loyalty, so that 'I am an Afrikaner' has a meaning independent of the class position of the speaker. If that is correct, it need not follow from the fact that, as O'Meara has shown, most members of the Broederbond are bourgeois or petit bourgeois, that their exclusive purpose is to benefit members of those classes.

To use the notion of Afrikaner identity at all has been referred to as 'colonialist tripe'. One recent work which uses it to great effect, whilst not rejecting any of the factual (as opposed to theoretical) discoveries of the Marxists, combines an understanding of the need for structural analysis, to lay bare the economic bones of South African society, with due regard for culture and ethnicity. This work, *The Rise and Crisis of Afrikaner Power* (its title in South Africa; in Britain it was published as *Ethnic Power Mobilized*), has the considerable advantage that one of its authors, Giliomee, lives in South Africa and, as an Afrikaner, has a rare opportunity to interpret his fellow Afrikaners to the English-speaking world. The book, by combining approaches from the liberal tradition with those of the newer and, in the case of South Africa, still inchoate Marxian tendency, may mark a turning point in South African social science and therefore in our understanding of that society. It will not, presumably, be popular amongst Marxists, precisely because it incorporates so many of their insights without adopting their total approach.

By way of summing up, it may be suggested that liberalism has, on the face of it, achieved so little in South Africa that it should perhaps be consigned to the dust-bin of history. On the other hand, liberal attitudes have done something to see that notions of justice have been kept alive in South Africa; they have until lately done little or nothing to improve the system, but they have helped to ensure that it has been administered fairly within the rules laid down by the National Party government. Ideas of 'human rights' have been maintained in Parliament by such courageous individuals as Mrs Suzman, for many years the sole member of the Progressive (now the Progressive Federal) Party and outside by such bodies as the Institute of Race Relations. When the future of South Africa is eventually settled, it is reasonable to hope that liberals will come into their own again.

Even to use the word 'liberal' in Afrikaans-speaking company is to invite disapproval, because of the word's associations with the old colour-blind franchise of the Cape, the battles that were fought to keep some Africans and coloureds on the common roll in the Cape, and more recently the activities of the Liberal Party. This is not to say that notions of human or civil rights are alien to Afrikanerdom, nor that liberalizing measures are not in train. The point is simply that another word must be found, which will not carry with it reverberations of the Westminster model, one man

33

one vote, and the rejection of cultural diversity. In this anti-liberal attitude there are echoes, too, of traditional anti-English feeling, a feeling which is not solely to be explained in terms of class struggle (the antipathy of poor for rich) nor of the conflict between imperial and national capital. The anti-imperialist is not only complaining about economic domination, though that may be part of what he is doing.

In the end the difference between liberals, white nationalists and Marxists is a difference about what is rational. The liberal will not necessarily reject the values, motives and social structures found in capitalist societies—though he may. (In either case, if he is a scholar, he will, like his Marxist colleagues, be a member of the petty bourgeoisie and presumably conditioned by that class membership.) The Marxist, however, will reject the 'rationality' of the capitalist market as intellectually inadequate and morally worthless. He will therefore reject, except perhaps in the short term, any reforms (which he may well characterize as self-serving rationalisations) which do not touch the underlying relations of production. For the Marxist, South Africa is a case study in the struggle for socialism; it may indeed become socialism's last laboratory in Africa.

CHAPTER 4

Revolution

In recent years the view that the 'solution' to South Africa's problems will be violent has become very widespread, both among outside commentators and among whites inside the Republic. What blacks within South Africa think is less easy to discover, because it is almost impossible to meet non-homeland blacks for any sustained conversation and they are in any case circumspect. Nor, because of the many laws governing the content of publications, can much be gleaned from such black publications as are published in the Republic, though opinion polls provide valuable insights. It is impossible to tell how far the exiled organizers and rank and file of the banned black political parties represent or are in touch with black opinion at home—though a pamphlet from the recently dismissed editor of *Workers' Unity*, the journal of the South African Congress of Trade Unions, argues that the effectiveness of SACTU itself is minimal within the Republic (The Workers' Movement, n.d.) The parties abroad certainly accept that violent revolution must be the outcome and believe that eventually the blacks must win, an opinion shared by many other outside observers. The 1976 riots suggest that many young people are prepared to meet force with force, but those events do not seem to have been directly linked with either party (though credit has naturally been claimed, no doubt reasonably, for the influence, rather than direct participation, of both parties, particularly the ANC). It is true that large crowds attend the funerals of old ANC members, but impossible to gauge the extent to which the participants' image of the ANC corresponds with that of the party in exile. The parties' names are also kept in the public eye by the many trials of ANC and PAC members, but these trials, though they indicate that the parties at least have a 'hit and run' capability, do not reveal any mass public support; nor of course do they provide evidence against it. (It might be said that, from the Government's point of view, it is unwise so to focus attention on the parties, thereby perhaps helping to keep them alive; on the other hand, the trials do, by linking the parties with communism, reinforce the average white's fear of black nationalism. This is important, because many whites have already been directly involved as conscripts or regulars with fighting black nationalism in the field, mostly in Namibia, or indirectly as parents of servicemen.) We may guess, intuitively, that in any free election the ANC would sweep the board, but, again, it is impossible to say whether

35

the voters' conception of the party would be at all close to that in the minds of the leaders abroad.

The fact that young blacks who leave South Africa join the PAC or ANC or align themselves with Black Consciousness (radical young whites join the ANC) proves little about opinion in South Africa—there is, after all, nothing else to join. Some evidence, however, suggests that knowledge of the parties is limited; for example, Archie Mafeje interviewed South African black students in Botswana, and found that they knew the parties' names but virtually nothing about their programmes. On the other hand, the parties can hardly produce counter evidence without revealing details which they would wish to protect (Mafeje 1978: 25). Within the country it is clear from the campaign for Nelson Mandela's release which started early in 1980 that he, if no others among the leaders then on Robben Island, is a popular hero, but whether as a party leader or as a great man who is now above party it is impossible to say. The growth of Black Consciousness may indicate a search for something new; on the other hand, as ANC supporters constantly point out, Black Consciousness has no clear programme and so provides no real guide to action. Nor, so far as one can tell, does it extend beyond the intellectual élite. The fact, however, that black consciousness is a state of mind does not mean that it need be inconsistent with the major parties' programmes. From the point of view of the ANC it is suspect because it seems to lead more readily to the PAC; ANC members who adhere to the socialist traditions within the party have an additional reason to disapprove, since black consciousness seems bound to be closer to the black nationalist than to the socialist strand in the party's ideology and so to make non-blacks' membership precarious.

'Socialist' in the context of the ANC must be understood as the revolutionary socialism of the Communist Party, rather than the evolutionary kind which at least does not rule out of court the possibility of peaceful progress. E. S. Sachs, a former Communist (expelled from the South African Communist Party (SACP) in 1931) showed this attachment to peace when, having asserted that 'Not all the terror and chicanery of the imperialists and white settlers . . . can stop the irresistible march of history', he added, two paragraphs later, 'Owing to the mulish obstinacy of the whites, the prospect of a peaceful solution in southern Africa does not seem very promising at present. Yet such a solution is not impossible' (Sachs 1965: 7–8). Sachs believed that the South African Labour Party, whose support came mainly from British artisans, could have weaned large numbers of Afrikaners away from the National Party if only its leaders had:

> . . . gone to the 'Poor Whites' on the land and the Afrikaner workers in the towns with a clear challenging socialist policy . . . Above all the Labour Party should have made it clear to these workers that their enemy is not the black worker but the grabbing land-owners and rapacious mineowners; that the Colour Bar does not protect them, but on the contrary will only drive them into poverty. Instead, with some honourable exceptions, the leaders of the Labour Party failed to find a bridge to the Afrikaner workers, supported the Colour Bar, entered into coalitions with reactionary parties and could not be bothered with

the national, anti-imperialist sentiments of the Afrikaners. The Nationalist demagogues on the other hand, exploited the national feelings and poverty of the Afrikaner people in typical Nazi fashion and secured much support from Afrikaner workers in urban areas in 1948 election (*Ibid*: 230–31).

Despite the worsening state of the 'non-white' peoples Sachs thought it '. . . fatuous to speculate when the clash . . . will come. It is far more important to consider ways and means of *preventing such a conflict*' (*Ibid*: 335). He believed that '. . . every possibility of legal work must be fully utilised.' Action could not be *confined* to the legal, but:

> There has been far too much glib talk about the use of violence and a number of sincere but confused people proclaim: "the policy of non-violence has failed, we must therefore pursue a policy of violence" (*Ibid*: 338).

Instead the African parties must be urged to sink their differences, the international labour movement must show solidarity by refusing to handle South African goods and by assisting the African trade union movement. 'It may take a year, five years, certainly not more than a decade for the whole of the African continent to become liberated' (*Ibid*: 339).

Though this judgment now seems optimistic, as does the very similar verdict of Donald Woods in his book on Steve Biko (Woods 1978), at least most non-revolutionaries would join with Sachs in *hoping* for peaceful change in South Africa, even if they reluctantly believe it unlikely to occur. However, from the point of view of the Communist Party and many others on the left, peaceful change is not merely unlikely, but positively undesirable, since the creation of better relations between the races is only an interim goal. The real objective must be a radical rearrangement of the social and economic order based on the overthrow of the (largely white) exploiting class by the (black) exploited class—or classes—of proletarians and peasants and this can only be done as a result of revolutionary upheaval. As No Sizwe puts it '. . . the "racial" oppression of the black people is understood as a function of the capitalist system itself' (No Sizwe 1979: 178).

The racial complications of South Africa do however present problems for orthodox Marxist-Leninists. First, the white working class does not behave as a working class should and recognize its exploited position. This failure, which is not confined to South Africa, occurs because it has become the ally of the white exploiting class, or even been absorbed into the white power structure. (As Turok puts it '. . . they have also been incorporated into the ruling capitalist class and have a stake in the *status quo* in a way that ensures their loyalty, for at least the foreseeable future' (Turok 1974: 12)).

This question of the persistence of racial, as opposed to class, loyalty has preoccupied the CPSA almost since its foundation in 1921. (At that time it was the SACP. In 1951, just before the Suppression of Communism Act came into force, it dissolved itself. However, shortly thereafter it reconstituted itself underground as the CPSA, though no public announcement of its rebirth was made until 1960.) On the one hand the ultimate objective of a socialist society must not be lost to sight, but on the other the

Africans' desire to improve their condition seems obstinately rooted in a black/white scheme of things.

The 'national' question, in other words the Africans' conception of themselves as black first and exploited second, had always been a cause of dissension in the party, but it came to the fore when in 1928 the Comintern in Moscow took the part of the nationalist faction in the CPSA and said that the first objective must be the establishment of a Native Republic of South Africa. It appears that, although the Comintern had been briefed in the previous year by South Africans, it knew little about the special conditions of South Africa and tended to assimilate it into the wider 'Negro question' (Johns 1965: 423). Nevertheless the CPSA, though understandably disconcerted by a policy which might have been interpreted to leave little room for CP members, loyally followed the line developed in Moscow.

It was not that too large a proportion of the membership of the CP was white, since of its 1,750 members in mid 1928, 1,600 were said to be 'nonwhite' (*Ibid*: 399). The Comintern, however, believed that too much energy had been spent on trade union and similar work directed to raise the level of political consciousness of white workers, and too little attention given to African advancement.

Over the years this dispute has continued to produce tension in the party and sometimes to split it apart. It has played a similar part in the history of the ANC. In 1958 the Africanist wing of the Youth League (a radical ginger group which had come to the fore in reaction against the party's inactivity in the '30s) split off in protest against the ANC's multi-racial policy and against the influence of communists in its counsels, and in 1959 named itself the Pan-Africanist Congress. The PAC still holds that Africa is for black Africans, whilst the ANC and CPSA say there is a place for all who share their beliefs, and still rails against Soviet imperialism, indeed against the imperialisms of the two superpowers. Nevertheless, it has established close relations with China and professes great admiration for its people and principles.

The CPSA and ANC have maintained a fruitful co-operation over the years. The CPSA acknowledges the ANC as the leader of the South African revolution and regards itself as a junior partner in the Liberation Movement. This involves tactical sacrifices, such as condoning the adoption by the ANC in 1969 of the highly nationalist Morogoro programme of action. At the same time the CPSA realises that it must constantly study and refine the guiding principles of its ideology, in line with the basic Marxian imperative to unite theory and practice. Thus, the Party, despite its accommodation with nationalism, sees itself as the guardian of ideological purity and as the vanguard of the masses.

The national revolution is, as Slovo makes clear, only the prelude to the socialist revolution, which can only begin once the liberation struggle is won. The end point therefore is the attainment, through further revolutionary struggle, of a republic where socialism reigns. The debate about

38

whether or not the revolution is to be in two stages (national democratic, followed by socialist) is unnecessary: one should rather see revolution as a continuing process, not a series of stages (Slovo 1977). A similar point is made by Ruth First when she says 'The national and the class struggle are not part of some natural order of succession, but take place coterminously', though she qualifies the statement by adding that 'national demands cannot [I think this is a statement of *logical* impossibility—CRH] be met under capitalism' (First 1977: 98). (Whatever their ambiguities, Joe Slovo's formulations deserve respectful attention, since he is regarded as the master tactician—directing operations from Luanda—of the militant wing of the ANC, and is credited by the South African Government with responsibility for the sabotage of oil stores at Sasolburg in mid 1980.)

No Sizwe (to whom reference has been made above) is like many other writers in 'solving' the national question by selective use of definition and assertion. He even concludes that 'nation' cannot be precisely defined but that the approach to a definition must be in class terms. 'Such concepts as "nation" . . . can only be related to *changing* (emphasis in original) forms of state formation. [Nations] . . . consist of antagonistic or potentially antagonistic classes [and therefore] . . . cannot be a community of culture' (No Sizwe 1979: 167–68). 'The content of the term "national" is dependent on the level of political consciousness attained by the classes of people concerned and their representatives' (*Ibid*).

The ANC has, however, not lived up to this class-based formulation, nor has it always been committed to drastic solutions. No Sizwe makes this point in quoting some of Nelson Mandela's replies to prosecuting counsel at the Treason Trial, where Mandela states his own preparedness to advocate refraining from civil disobedience, stay at homes, etc. in return for gradual extension of black representation in Parliament. No Sizwe is hard on these replies, which he sees as representative of:

. . . the views at the time of many of the old guard (but, ironically not necessarily those of Mandela himself, despite his explicit statement to that effect) . . . the typical liberal bourgeois point of view which was held by most of the Congress Movement at the time and which is still held by many 'leaders' who now operate in the 'opposition' parties in Bantustan legislative assemblies and even in the Black Consciousness Movement (*Ibid*: 176–77).

This old-guard view is, of course, nationalist rather than socialist. No Sizwe emphasises that this tendency within the movement will not achieve liberation, but acknowledges that it is still influential:

. . . (it) not only continues to have a resonance among the people but, because of the singularly difficult military problems faced by the South African revolutionary movement, it will continue to be the greatest danger to it, assured as it is of the full support of all the imperialist states . . . The ideological dimension of a social formation always lags behind its political and economic dimensions. Prejudice ingrained over centuries will not evaporate overnight. But to the extent that the property relations are radically restructured the question of the nation is resolved in principle (Ibid: 180–81).

This passage raises a number of questions. For example, the reference to 'prejudice ingrained over centuries' suggests that the prejudice (which appears to mean 'nationalist feeling') originated before the development of a capitalist system in South Africa; in that case it seems necessary to explain how, why and under what economic conditions it came about. Again, it appears that to resolve the question of the nation 'in principle' is really not to resolve it at all, since ancient prejudice may long outlast the restructuring of property relations and, presumably, prevent that restructuring from achieving the elimination of the national tendency from the liberation movement.

The tension within the ANC and its associated bodies is not confined to theory, but often has repercussions at the level of politics. One recent example of dissension which attracted considerable notice has been the suspension for 'factionalism' of four members of the ANC following circulation of a memorandum written by one of them, Bob Petersen, the then editor of *Workers' Unity*. This last is the official journal of the South African Congress of Trade Unions (SACTU), which is closely allied with the ANC; it is, however, not identical with it, so that the four were able correctly to riposte that the ANC was acting improperly for suspending them for activities not carried on in their capacities as ANC members. (The memorandum and associated documents are reprinted in *The Workers' Movement, SACTU and the ANC*, the pamphlet which was mentioned at the beginning of this chapter.)

The memorandum had argued that SACTU '. . . should be built underground as an organization of militant workers in their tens of thousands, in the mines, factories, docks, offices and on the farms (*Workers' Movement*: 1). However, 'The present exile leadership of SACTU, the ANC and the CP is opposed to the building of SACTU for this task'. On the contrary, Petersen and his colleagues were convinced (though they nowhere show why it should be necessarily true) that:

> National Liberation for the black majority can only be secured through the overthrow of capitalism . . . But the leadership of the ANC, SACTU and the CP are opposed to a socialist programme, holding out the perspective instead that it is possible to achieve national liberation on the basis of capitalism. . . . The leadership . . . is torn between the policy of guerillaism, which is incapable of securing a revolutionary victory in South Africa, and leaning towards the pro-capitalist Buthelezi (*Ibid*: 2–3).

These quotations give the essence of a wider debate. Much of the memorandum itself is devoted to the analysis of the place of trade unions in the liberation struggle, and the part SACTU should play:

> . . . for more than 15 years SACTU has been confined almost entirely to an exile existence . . . 'Workers' Unity' was started up as the official paper of SACTU from January 1977 mainly in order to become an organising weapon for underground work in South Africa . . . But the struggle to take these tasks forward in SACTU has unfortunately encountered serious opposition . . . the leadership is unwilling to take up the tasks that are its responsibility: of building SACTU as a genuine, independent, underground trade union organisation inside South Africa (*Ibid*: 19–20).

40

In fact SACTU is out of touch:

Well over 50,000 copies (of *Workers' Unity*) have been printed in all—yet the number which have been transported *through our organisation* into South Africa *cannot total more than a few hundred copies over these two years*! . . . we have not received a single contribution from any SACTU machinery which may exist in South Africa . . . The content has become increasingly abstract and . . . Our news reporting on factory and township struggles is drawn *entirely* from already published material—and almost always *from the South African bourgeois press* (*Ibid*: 25–27; emphasis in original).

The reforms in, for example, trade union legislation are valueless under capitalism:

The economic struggle is thus doomed to frustration unless it is linked to the revolutionary struggle for state power, the destruction of apartheid, the expropriation of the capitalists and the building of the foundations of socialism (*Ibid*: 38).

This is not to say that workers have a duty not to join trade unions under these conditions, nor that the trade unions are irrelevant or trapped irrevocably in reformism, but:

The trade union movement can only fulfil its responsibility to the working class, and indeed to the whole of society, by consciously linking the struggle for better wages and conditions to the revolutionary struggle for the overthrow of the apartheid regime and the expropriation of the capitalist exploiters (*Ibid*: 44–45).

Bodies, therefore, whether in South Africa or abroad, which push for reform without linking it to class struggle and the need for an underground 'vanguard' party are mere allies of the capitalist system, as of course are foreign governments which take a reformist line. The authors assert, and here they have probably read correctly the mind of the bodies referred to:

The heightened interest and intervention in South Africa by leading officials of such bodies as the ICFTU and the AFL-CIO have as their aim to ward off the danger of revolution through the cultivation of reformist leadership and policies in the black trade unions (*Ibid*: 46).

The nub of the matter is that, under capitalism 'not a single serious and lasting improvement in the conditions of life of the mass of our people is possible while this system remains' (*Ibid*: 47). (One may remark, in parenthesis, that it is difficult to know how seriously to take this observation. On the surface it appears plainly false, unless of course such words as 'serious' and 'lasting' are so defined as to make it necessarily true.) The memorandum continues that the 'basic rule' therefore '. . . is to put forward demands which are supported by the workers as clearly right and reasonable, but which . . . cannot be conceded by our enemy' (*Ibid*: 48). This seems a logical enough strategy, within the logic of revolution, though it is weakened by the list of demands which immediately follows. For example, the demand is made for a national minimum wage of R50 for a 40-hour week, which *could* be accommodated by South African capitalism, though of course not all at once.

Petersen's memorandum concludes with a list of fundamental questions

41

which, Petersen believes, had not been confronted by SACTU. It is indeed surprising that they had not, for the list includes matters which must be basic for a trade union organization, like what its attitude should be to the Wiehahn Commission, which was then sitting and whose subsequent report led to reformist legislation.

Faced with such root and branch criticism it is perhaps not surprising that the ANC's Regional Policy Committee suspended Petersen and his three associates (Ensor, Hemson and Legassick) from all ANC activities and units, on the grounds that they had:

> . . . seen fit to attack the policies and leadership of the revolutionary alliance led by the ANC in public and have thereby sought to weaken the position of our movement among the general public at home and abroad (*Ibid*: 67).

The response by the four to their dismissal both encapsulates many of the issues which preoccupy the left, and broadens the attack. Not only, they assert, is it the case that 'within the ANC, working-class and middle-class interests struggle for dominance' (*Ibid*: 71) but its bureaucratic centralism stifles discussion. They acknowledge that discipline is necessary, but:

> The harmonious combination of democracy and discipline—which can only find its complete expression in a revolutionary workers' organisation—is democratic centralism (*Ibid*: 73).

The CPSA is also attacked, among other things for its failure to organize in South Africa and for its attachment to the two stage theory of the South African revolution. Its leadership's main fault, however, is that:

> . . . having gained effective control of the ANC apparatus it conspicuously fails to use its power to transform the ANC into an organisation promoting the revolutionary socialist aims of the workers' movement in a struggle for workers' power. Instead it helps to prop up and defend within the ANC the influence and interests of the middle class . . . (*Ibid*: 74).

But, as the authors conclude, no doubt correctly, their suspension will not remove Marxist influence from the movement:

> . . . Marxism can only grow in influence . . . It is no accident that our enemies, whose main fear is the power of the working class, point day after day in their press and journals in South Africa to the danger of the ideas of Marxism (*Ibid*: 75).

Since the demands of a race (or 'national') and of a class analysis cannot be reconciled, the debate (until the liberation struggle has been won) concerns the emphasis which should be placed upon the rival principles, both of which are frequently enunciated in the same document. Another method of bringing the two approaches together, but at the political, rather than the theoretical, level has been for members of the CPSA also to join the ANC, and *vice versa*. A famous example is Moses Kotane, who was for many years general secretary of the CPSA and a leading member of the ANC. According to his biographer (Bunting 1975) his transparent honesty convinced all doubters that when acting as a member of one organization he acted solely in the interests of that organization—though the interests of the two were of course complementary. There is no reason to disbelieve this assessment, any more than one need doubt the word of the business man who sits simultaneously on the boards of a number of public companies.

Though the CPSA and ANC have often been wrong or misled, for instance in their adulation of Stalin and the Soviet Union, the CPSA has often hit the nail on the head. For example, in the early days of World War II the Party pointed out the absurdity of expecting Africans to fight for democracy when they had so little of it at home, and argued that in any case the war was between the rival imperialisms of Britain and Germany, which were morally indistinguishable. The ANC, on the other hand, though making similar points, also insisted that Africans should be allowed to take an equal part in the war. The different lines cannot have been altogether easy to accommodate, though the CPSA did its best by arguing that the defeat of Fascism in Europe would contribute to the eventual defeat of Fascism in South Africa. Nevertheless, the logical position became easier when Germany turned on the Soviet Union in 1941. Thereafter to fight against the Axis was to defend the land of freedom. The CPSA was, again, surely right to insist that the Japanese should not be less passionately opposed because they too were 'non-white'. What mattered was that the Japanese were allied with the Fascists of Europe.

The ANC committed itself to violence only after the Emergency of 1960, when it finally became clear to the leadership that peaceful efforts towards change would simply be repressed with all the force and brutality the state could muster. Thereafter, with the ANC underground and its newly formed violent wing Umkhonto we Sizwe (Spear of the Nation) beginning a campaign of sabotage, little is known in detail about their operations. The exception to that generalization is the trial records from the trials of captured activists. Feit has done a study (1970) of Umkhonto entirely from these records, showing that in its early years the movement achieved little. (Feit fully acknowledges the inadequacy of trial records as the sole source of evidence; nevertheless, South Africa is especially rich in such material, since even magistrates' courts are courts of record, and their proceedings become public documents.) Turok also admits that the sabotage undertaken by Umkhonto did not have a demonstration effect; 'it failed to ignite the prairie fire as many had hoped' (Turok 1974: 45). To the outside observer this is hardly surprising; it appears obvious that poor people who have not been subjected to continuous political education are unlikely spontaneously to imitate acts of sabotage, particularly if the explosions cause no great damage and the guerrillas are promptly caught.

It is clear however that in recent years the ANC has had no shortage of volunteers, nor of training facilities and weapons. Incursions into the Republic of small bands (they discovered the folly of trying to move large numbers in the abortive operation by 100 or so guerrillas from Rhodesia in 1968), have been reported, though whether their operations are of the hit and run type, or whether the guerrillas merge into the countryside is not publicly known. Presumably, however, there exist cells of loyal ANC supporters inside the country, if only to man the escape routes which the 1968 experience showed to be essential. Presumably, also, some parts of the organization have been penetrated by informers. It has never been difficult in South Africa (nor in many other authoritarian states) to enlist spies, since the rewards for co-operation and the penalties for non-co-operation can be great. One might however hazard the guess that as the eventual victory of the liberation movement begins to look more likely, spies will be less easy to find, and some of those who are recruited will try to reinsure by becoming double agents.

Whilst the activities of the liberation movement in the field are naturally known only to as few people as possible, scholars continue to produce quantities of supportive literature, much of it written by Marxists. It is tempting to see the minute, and often tedious disagreements of the left as the disputations of medieval schoolmen writ new, providing students with a useful training in neo-scholastic argument, but of little other relevance to the real world, but this would be a mistake. For one thing, the 'real world' is not a set of given data; everyone constructs his own view of the world, so that one man's fantasy may be another's reality. For another, Marxist scholars are, as we have seen, trying to replace the dominant liberal or bourgeois paradigm (or set of assumptions) within which the country's history has been written. Armed with the broad outline provided by Marxism, they are engaged in the detailed working out of a new interpretation, which will eventually produce a full scale Marxist history of South Africa. But this cannot be done all at once; once the bold artist's impressions of the edifice have been accepted a great deal of detailed work has to be done on the architect's plans and then on laying the foundations.

Furthermore, political action is constantly subjected to scrutiny in the light of theory. For activists the burning questions (whose answers need to be backed up with theory) are, for example, who is to organize the workers inside South Africa and should the strategic emphasis be on armed struggle or strike action? Mafeje asks 'Is there a chance that the people at home have gone ahead on their own and have thus rendered the movements outside irrelevant' (Mafeje 1978: 25). '. . . Soweto . . . showed unequivocally how irrelevant discussions at the top can be if not prompted by popular action on the ground.' The ANC, he adds, though it has an urban base, seems to have no coherent theory of guerrilla warfare: '. . . which should not be confused with mere bravado of opening up with machine guns on a few policemen, as some ANC are reported to have done in the aftermath of Soweto' (*Ibid*: 27).

Mafeje believes that the commitment to armed struggle should be reviewed and the emphasis shifted to political methods. But whether the ANC or the CPSA is to organize the workers presents a problem:

> It is the right of the petit-bourgeois nationalists to organise the workers on their terms in a national democratic movement. On the other hand, it is the duty of the

Communist Party to protect the interests of the workers at all stages of the revolution (*Ibid*: 29).

The veteran CPSA leader Ruth First reacts strongly against all this, attacking Mafeje for his lack of a programme, his 'attentisme', his mechanical use of class categories and consequent failure to emphasize class struggle and above all his '. . . revolutionary puritanism with its abstract theoretical reservations and its record of abstinence rather than engagement' (First 1977: 97). This revolutionary puritanism is counter-productive because it:

> . . . fails to make connections in political practice between immediate demands which mobilise, or more spontaneously ignite mass struggles, and the longer-term programmatic conception of the revolutionary alternative society (*Ibid*).

The theorist, in other words, must not lose sight of real events, and should turn them to advantage.

However, even if the future unfolds in broad conformity with the expectations of the revolutionary left, it is impossible to forecast when the liberation struggle will be won, and whether the subsequent (or coterminous) struggle for socialism will be successful. There are in South Africa flourishing black capitalist and petty bourgeois classes, whose members can be expected to oppose socialism to the last (though their leaders increasingly use the language of the nationalist wing of the ANC) and there are well over three million Indians and coloureds, many of whom hold on to what they have despite the identification which many of their young and better educated people make with Africans. The whites must be expected to stand together (in this respect the CPSA is surely correct in seeing the white workers as an integral part of the white power structure) and even if they can bring themselves to accept some form of power sharing with blacks, will hardly consent to do so within a socialist framework. But if they want to stave off socialism they will have to move fast, for it seems likely that the 'normal' ANC leadership is moving steadily to the left, and may be expected to continue to do so.

We may now try to sum up the potential of the revolutionary path to change in South Africa. A revolution occurs when one class loses control of the means of production and another gains it. As we have seen, there is a considerable body of literature devoted to the analysis of South African society in class terms, but rather little about when a decisive change in class relations is likely to occur. There are claims, whose substance is impossible to judge, that small groups are active underground—but, even if they exist, little is known about their ideological bent. There are also claims that SACTU (and, by implication, bodies associated with it) is virtually inactive in South Africa. What is known is that there has been considerable industrial unrest in recent years and that, despite the Victorian attitudes of many employers, workers have been gaining in courage and maintaining strikes (some of which are discussed in a later chapter) which even ten years ago would have been unthinkable. Such a state of affairs obviously offers opportunities for action by the ANC (whether of the nationalist or socialist tendency) and PAC, provided organization can be achieved and adequate theoretical instruction and tactical advice be given to the workers without the details of the organization becoming known to the police. The extent to which advantage is in fact taken of these favourable conditions is unknown, though the South African Government appears to think that the ANC was actively involved in the 1980 disturbances. Similarly, it is difficult to know what groups took part behind the scenes in the Soweto uprising of 1976, though numerous claims to having played a part have subsequently been made and it would be surprising if the older members of the community did not look back with nostalgia to the days when the political parties were legal and draw inspiration from the memory.

But to remember the ANC is not necessarily the same as preparing revolution, and from the demands made by strikers in South Africa it appears that many are simply seeking proper wages and representation through trade unions chosen by themselves, rather than revolutionary upheaval. Similarly, the growth of a black bourgeoisie and petty bourgeoisie, though it does nothing, according to Marxist authors, to mitigate the evils of the capitalist system, is, according to some of the same authors, to be taken seriously as a threat to revolutionary action. The 'co-optation' of part of the African people may, in other words, do exactly what it is intended to do, namely to give them a stake in the capitalist system. That, however, is not the same as winning them as supporters of the system of apartheid, nor of leaving them content to forgo political rights. They may be dissuaded from socialism, whilst remaining nationalists.

The victory of socialism in South Africa, though likely, is not inevitable. Some form of negotiated accommodation between black and white is increasingly being seen as essential among the Afrikaner rulers, and the settlement will, no doubt, be reached (as in Zimbabwe) against a background of increasing violence. But there may be little to comfort the left in that settlement, because once it has been reached it is perfectly possible that most of the parties to it will combine to prevent the subsequent victory of socialism. It is the fear of that outcome which motivates the continuing struggle between the nationalists and socialists within the liberation movement and which informs the eternal vigilance of the CPSA.

CHAPTER 5
The Background to Change

The process of change now going on in South Africa has its roots in the recent past, and can only be understood in the light of conditions a few years ago. In this chapter, therefore, I offer some observations on industrial relations, and on the broader economic and political scene, as they appeared in the mid-seventies.

Suckling, writing in October 1977, gives a valuable account of contemporary thinking about reform in business and government and of industrial relations legislation then in force. He found that in 1975 there was a shortage of 7,916 white male artisans and 425 black in the metal and engineering, electrical, motor, building and printing sectors. These sectors were chosen because they included:

> . . . those occupations in which employers have considerable influence on employment trends; and those skilled occupations over which trade unions have more control in that via the artisan/apprentice training scheme the predominantly white, skilled workman can exercise his option *not* to train Blacks.
>
> (Suckling 1977: 1).

During the period 1969–75 the number of Africans in managerial and administrative posts had increased at 44.7 per cent per annum, though the absolute numbers were very small—3,806 blacks in 1975, or a small fraction of the black work force.

African real wages grew at 3.9 per cent per annum from 1960–1970, but the absolute difference between black and white average wages also increased. In 1970–75 the gap decreased slightly, (from R 2,815 to R 2,724) and the ratio fell from 1:13 to 1:11. Suckling adds that:

> Breaking down these aggregates suggests that the most marked changes have taken place in central government where the real absolute wage gap between Black and White has dropped from 1:6 in 1970 to 1:3 in 1976. The ratio in the manufacturing sector has stayed roughly constant over the same period. . . . money incomes originating in the predominantly English speaking private sector have kept better pace with inflation than money incomes in the public sector, against a successful drive to increase real Black wages across the whole economy (*Ibid*: 3).

It follows, (though Suckling warns that the generalization is very broad) that, given that Afrikaners dominate the public sector, such redistribution of income as had occurred had taken place from Afrikaners to Africans rather than from English speakers. This had not been particularly noticeable at first, because the improvement in black conditions had taken place in an atmosphere of growth and optimism: but in the economic downturn of 1976 white attitudes had hardened.

Foreign pressure and growing black awareness played their parts in producing improvements, but Suckling rightly points out that increased wages would not have been paid if employers had not been able to absorb them, though part of the price to be paid was increased concern by employers with productivity. In a period of growth employers see no contradiction between rising wages and a higher level of employment: however, '. . . much of the technology used by South African firms is imported from overseas and reflects the cheap capital, expensive labour factor availability in those overseas countries' (*Ibid*: 6). In such sectors higher wages will have little effect on employment.

There were four main economic reasons for the wage gap. First came the inferior education of blacks, which to an extent could be corrected by employers operating under the *Bantu Employees in Service Training Act* (No. 86 of 1976). However, training to skilled levels demanded white assistance:

> . . . the Apprenticeship Act of 1944 does not bar the training of Blacks via apprenticeship schemes, but the mechanics of the Act require that any potential apprentice's registration has to be approved by a board on which White trade unionists are in a majority (*Ibid*: 8).

Secondly, although legal job reservation only affected 2.9 per cent of the work force in 1977, social and political factors powerfully inhibited black advancement. The principal necessity if white self-esteem was to be preserved, was (and still is) to avoid whites being bossed by blacks; the latter can attain positions and salaries superior to those of some whites, but they must be in separate racial pyramids.

The third reason for the wage gap was, and to an extent still is, the restrictions placed on black labour representation. The most notorious disability was the provision of the *Industrial Conciliation Act* (No. 28 of 1956) which, by excluding Africans (but not coloureds or Asians) from the definition of an employee, precluded them from forming trade unions that could be registered; thus they could not be directly represented in Industrial Councils, whose agreements had the force of law. They could form unregistered unions, but agreements reached with them were not enforceable under the Act. Instead a system of works committees and liaison committees was set up under the *Bantu Labour Relations Regulation Act* 1953 (and its 1973 amendment). Works committees tended to be relatively unpopular with companies, since they could be composed entirely of employees whose chairman would negotiate with the employers. Liaison committees, on the other hand, were joint bodies, which tended to be dominated by employers. At the end of 1975 there were 2,042 of these, but only 287 works committees. (By the time Wiehahn reported in May 1979 these figures had risen to 302 works committees, representing 74,000 black workers and 2,626 liaison committees, representing 690,000 (RSA 1979b: para. 3.19)). (The Act of 1956 replaces those of 1924 and 1937).

Suckling observes that some companies had successfully set up bargaining systems drawing both on the Industrial Councils and the African committee structure. He concludes that:

> . . . enlightened employers can utilize even the existing system of legislation to open up acceptable links with the Black labour force. A crucial point is whether such links will be opened up fast enough to defuse growing Black demands for real trade union representation as opposed to the more dilute works-liaison committee system.
>
> (Suckling 1977: 11)

The conclusion of the majority of Professor Wiehahn's commission, (whose recommendations will be discussed in Chapter 9) that black unions should indeed be allowed to register, suggests that the previously available links were not sufficient. This is not to say that Wiehahn's reforms are judged adequate by black trade unionists, but they do, as we shall see, radically alter the industrial relations system. Until the confusion induced by the recession of 1976, the South African Government was deaf to appeals for 'liberalization' in the fields of wages and jobs. In that year, however, a series of Commissions, adding up, in the words of one economist, to a whole 'constellation of uncertainty' was set up to look into various aspects of the economy. The most important were the Wiehahn and Riekert Commissions, which were specifically concerned with legislation affecting industrial relations and the labour supply. In setting them up the government was both recognizing economic reality and making a significant gesture to organized business. Indeed, it seems that the economic thinking of business and government was not far apart.

However, business men do not regard it as their duty to make constitutional proposals, and in that field the government was ahead of the industrial and commercial organisations. The constitutional proposals of 1977 were produced by a committee chaired by the Minister of Defence, Mr P. W. Botha (who, after he became Prime Minister, continued as Minister of Defence until August 1980) and were endorsed by Mr Vorster (then Prime Minister) and his cabinet. They proposed a measure of 'power sharing' with the coloured and Asian communities in a complicated way, which in fact safeguarded continuing white power. There were to be three parliaments, white, coloured and Indian, each of which was to deal with matters pertaining exclusively to its own racial group. They were to be linked through a Council of Cabinets, presided over by a State President elected by an Electoral College on which the three racial groups were to be represented, in rough proportion to population, in the ratio of four whites, two coloureds, one Indian. Since the College was to be elected by majority vote of each parliament, its members would naturally be members of the dominant parties in the parliaments. The Council of Cabinets would consist of Ministers from each of the three Cabinets, in the same ratio of 4:2:1. (For a fuller account see SAIRR 1978: 7–8.)

From the outside the proposals appeared hopelessly timid, though in South African terms they verged on the radical. They have since been superseded by the proposals of the Commission on the Constitution (Schlebush Commission) and subsequent legislation, though Mr Vorster himself remained committed to them. Although the 1977 proposals were inadequate and have been severely criticized, both within and outside the Republic (see e.g. Slabbert & Welsh 1979), they are worth a mention because they represent the beginning of a continuing process, which just possibly may result in a new constitutional dispensation acceptable to the people of South Africa as a whole. [*See note on p. 56].

The objections to the proposals were, however, very strong. To start with, the whole notion of 'power sharing' is unconvincing: it would be far more realistic to talk about the *division* of power which the new arrangement would have initiated. Secondly, the new constitution, involving three separate Parliaments, would have been enormously expensive and cumbersome, and probably would not have worked. There were also vast areas of ambiguity, though it seems clear enough that ultimate power would have remained in white hands. Finally, and most serious (in this very incomplete list of objections), the proposals made no mention of the urban Africans. The Shlebusch proposals are open to some of the same objections, particularly the last, as we shall see later.

Reactions to the proposals, among businessmen and the white community at large, illustrated the varying Afrikaans and English speaking approaches to politics. By English-speaking members of the opposition parties they were denounced root and branch. By Nationalist Afrikaners they were far more readily accepted as a big step forward, because many Nationalists, including business men, have so fundamental an ideological commitment to separate development that they believe the problems, including that of the urban Africans, will be solved within that framework. One should also not forget that the senior Afrikaner business man may well be better informed than his English-speaking counterpart. He is likely to be in intimate touch with trends of opinion within the National Party and to have a good idea of, for example, when a plan for the urban Africans will be made public and with what backing.

It would be over simple to relate all this activity solely to the depressed state of the economy, but without the recession much of the incentive for the new political and economic thinking would have been lost. In 1976 South Africa's recession, which it shared with much of the rest of the world, was combined with inflation, then down to 11 per cent from a peak of 14 per cent. The annual rate of growth was well below the 5 per cent upon which projections were based in the *Economic Development Programme 1976–81*. Indeed the EDP insisted that, despite its use of 5 per cent, no forecast was implied that such a rate of growth would actually be achieved. On the contrary, it stated that it was highly unlikely.

Meanwhile, black population and black unemployment were growing. The EDP projected a total population of 29,744,000 in 1981, of whom

50

21,260,000 would be black, with a total economically active population of 11,348,000 in 1981, of whom 8,689,000 would be black. Black unemployment (excluding agriculture in the homelands) was estimated at 492,000 in 1975 and projected to 552,000 in 1981, with the *caveat* that measuring black unemployment involved special problems (unofficial estimates range between one and two million). (There has even been an eccentric attempt to show that there is no involuntary unemployment in South Africa, on the grounds that if there were unemployment wages would not have risen as they have. See Ellis' (1980) attack on this view, refuting Kantor 1980.) The EDP foresaw a growing need for skilled and semi-skilled workers, particularly outside the mining sector, leading to drastic adjustments in the development pattern of the South African economy and a need for continuous adjustment of training programmes. It warned that in narrowing the wage gap between the races the wage cost per unit of GDP should not be allowed to rise in relation to the capital cost. If it did there would inevitably be a movement towards capital-intensive development.

In the boom years, South Africa's current account was kept in surplus by the high price of gold. Thereafter the reduced gold price, together with vastly increased Government expenditure, notably on defence and such projects as the two new harbours at Richards Bay and Saldanha, forced the Government to adopt ruthless import controls and to go all out for an export led recovery. By 1979, of course, South Africa was once again in an extremely strong economic position, thanks to the much higher price of gold, though in 1981 and 1982 conditions became less easy, with gold less than half its all-time high of $860 per ounce.

If economic factors alone were relevant, there would have been much cause for optimism in South Africa, even without the subsequent dramatic rise in the gold price. The new harbours were beginning to make a contribution, which could be expected to become considerable, to the current account. In the view of one very senior official, who thought the surface of South Africa's new mineral wealth had barely been scratched, 'a whole new mineral province' had been discovered in the north western Cape. Its products, too, were to be exported through Saldanha. Naturally, officials are well aware that customers for minerals may, on political grounds, look elsewhere for their supplies, but they are confident that no insuperable difficulties will be encountered. They point out that probably no other country possesses as wide a range of minerals, that South Africa has an excellent record as a reliable supplier and that she has never threatened to nationalize the mines. Furthermore, in some cases the USSR is the only alternative source of supply and on the whole it seems likely that the western countries would prefer to depend on South Africa.

However, such optimism had to be tempered by political judgments. Strong pressure from the UN, the OAU and individual Governments, combined with a loss of business confidence abroad, had led to a reluctance in foreign companies and financial institutions to commit new funds in South Africa, whether in the form of loans to Government or state corporations, or in new investment of any kind. This, of course, does not mean that capital investment had dried up completely, but it was being largely financed from retained profits, and far less than before from abroad. The March 1977 budget increased the incentive to reinvest profits by changing the rules governing their remittance overseas; formerly it had been possible to remit profits accumulated from as far back as 1960, but now they must have been earned within the past two years.

Capital deprivation, now a thing of the past, was a most urgent problem, since in 1977 capital was leaving the country, much of it illicitly, at about R100m a month, whereas as recently as 1974/75 there had been an inflow of R2,780m, 80 per cent of which was long term.

Of course, the bankers and business men responsible for the capital shortage required different reassurances from those demanded by the UN or the OAU. White South Africans' attitudes to these bodies and to the USA hardened perceptibly in 1977. Many now believed (perhaps reasonably in the light of our earlier discussion of some of the Marxist literature) that whatever changes were made, they would never satisfy 'international opinion' and there was much talk of tightening belts and resisting to the end whatever pressures might be applied. Such talk was in a sense contradicted by the continuing and growing illicit movement of capital out of the country; nevertheless, white, particularly Afrikaner, national pride did seem to have been stiffened by recent events. This trend has continued and intensified; white power matches white stubbornness and can, at a price, withstand any likely pressures for the foreseeable future. There can be no doubt, however, that provided the government is not seen to be weakly giving way to pressure, it will, in fact, and preferably in private, give way in certain limited areas. These areas of 'give' will extend if the electorate comes to share the perception of large sections of the élite that the game being played now is the politics of survival, no longer the politics of domination.

Overseas investors are not 'world opinion' and are not necessarily concerned about one man one vote in a unitary state, which most whites insist is completely off the cards, but about stability. Many of them would no doubt agree with those white South Africans who say that such a major shift of power would lead to such chaos that South Africa would no longer need foreign capital, because the economy would no longer have the capacity to absorb it. After the Soweto riots, or uprising, of 1976, the four main reasons for overseas investors' lack of confidence were, first, their doubts about the political situation throughout southern Africa (except Namibia, about which they seemed reasonably happy); second came the internal situation, where South African officials on tour overseas had gained the strong impression that some positive move by Government was hoped for, particularly in relation to urban Africans. Thirdly, in Europe, there was a good deal of uncertainty about the Carter administration's intentions; clearly no banker was likely to make loans to South Africa if the American intention was to strangle the Republic. (In America, it appears, bankers are less worried about their Government's intentions than are their European opposite numbers, perhaps because they are better informed, perhaps because they do not take kindly to Government interference.) Fourthly, and to a much less important degree, shareholder groups, the churches, students' protests and other pressure group activity were judged to have contributed to a climate of unease and so to have had an indirect effect on investment decisions. Despite all these causes of unease, in 1977 it was believed in Pretoria that relatively minor internal changes would satisfy the foreign institutions.

The climate of change affects society as a whole and it may be useful to look back, not only at thinking about political and economic matters, but more generally at the social atmosphere as it seemed at the time. The Soweto events, which were paralleled, though on a less dramatic scale, in other cities, now appear to many observers to mark the turning point in modern South African history, and provide the obvious point of reference. I noted then (in a privately circulated paper—Hill 1977a) that South Africa had changed greatly in the past ten years. On the one hand there was the extreme thoroughness of the separation of the races. One met virtually no blacks (except in the Transkei, where one meets few whites) apart from servants, and with the rising cost of living many of the less well off white families, which might previously have employed at least one servant, could no longer afford to do so. The result was that many white children and young adults had not had even that degree of experience of contact with the majority race.

On the other hand, changes of a different kind were occurring. Black wages were increasing; job reservation, formal and informal, was being broken down, though not systematically; blacks looked less downtrodden and more confident, which was hardly surprising since Mozambique had demonstrated that European power could be broken. The least important change, which was also the most frequently quoted, was that whites could now lunch with blacks at such places as the Carlton Hotel in Johannesburg: this is true, but irrelevant to the vast majority of the population.

The difficulty was (and remains) that there was no programme for change: the electorate was by no means agreed that change was necessary—nor is it now; nor, indeed, were all members of the Cabinet aware of the mood among blacks, and among those who were there was disagreement about how to deal with it, though this has diminished since Dr Treurnicht (the powerful *verkrampte* leader of the National Party in the Transvaal) was expelled in March 1982. Some Ministers seemed, as one 'moderate' African put it, to believe that small changes in the towns, made in response to such manifestations as the Soweto riots, plus major constitutional changes in the homelands would satisfy Africans. In fact, however, most Africans were uninterested in the homelands and determined, above all, to obtain better treatment in the urban areas. 'Until you give us something to lose in South Africa you can forget about peaceful change'. This determination now seems much better understood in the

South African Government and has contributed to the shift of emphasis away from the original version of the homelands policy which was noted in chapter 2.

During the riots it was impossible for the ordinary white in Johannesburg to visit Soweto or to gain much hard information about what was going on there. Despite press and television coverage it was very difficult to remember that these extraordinary events were going on just a few kilometres away, and not in another continent: it was possible to have a far sharper feeling in London than in Johannesburg of the reality of Soweto and with arrival at Jan Smuts airport unreality descended.

Nevertheless, it was possible to gather a strong impression of the heightened precariousness of township life. Africans who went to work in defiance of strike orders were liable to revenge on return in the evenings. Taxis would only take them to the edge of Soweto and, if they went by train, the police could only protect them at the railway station itself. Although employers were allowing employees to leave early to get home in daylight, the walk from the perimeter of Soweto could be very dangerous and stories of narrow escapes were common. It appeared, too, that many Soweto families were sending their children away to relatives in rural areas, and some servants in white households were bringing their children out of the townships to the safety of the 'quarters' provided by their employers.

The generation gap which appeared between 'moderate' black adults and their teenage and even younger children, has been widely noticed. The difference between the generations was well summed up in the remark of a black youth of sixteen to his father (passed on to me by a white student): 'All I care about is my race and my people. If you die in the riots it's just too bad.' This new mood of the young (which previously had only shown itself in the black universities, especially Turfloop and Fort Hare, and occasionally in senior forms of schools) must be the principal obstacle to any form of gradual improvement. The latter (provided there were a definite programme) which was inconceivable in the state of white opinion in 1976, but might not be so now, might also be accepted by moderate adult blacks; indeed, readiness to accept gradual change is a large part of what is meant by 'moderate'. The difficulty is that no reliable means exists of finding out how many blacks fall into this category, though the proportion seems almost certain to be declining as the number of very young black adults increases with the continuing growth of the black population. It should also be noted that, according to the Quail report, dissatisfaction is far from confined to the young (Ciskei Commission 1980: 244).

Among whites, too, there was, and remains, a feeling of precariousness. On the surface the extraordinary wealth of the northern (largely English speaking) suburbs of Johannesburg seemed secure enough; but the habitual obsession with politics was so intense that politics and the state of the economy were virtually the only topics of conversation among whites. There seemed to be a strong body of opinion that the riots signalled a qualitative change in relations between the races, and there was even some

54

talk among white parents of leaving South Africa to save their children from butchery in the coming conflict. No doubt, however, such talk was to be heard in 1960 after Sharpeville, but if so it died down fairly soon. This time, uncertainty about the future was far more deeply rooted.

In 1976 South Africa's economy was in crisis: high imports and very high Government expenditure, for example on defence, combined to produce a debit on both current and capital accounts which at then current prices could no longer be met by gold sales. There was growing black unemployment, continuing difficulty in finding competent whites to fill the managerial and other positions which law and custom reserved for them, and growing difficulty in attracting overseas capital. This last was a direct result of diminishing political confidence, caused by the deteriorating internal situation. (As has been noted above, sentiment has in this respect since changed significantly, at least so far as the short term is concerned.)

Among prominent English speakers there seemed to be a feeling of despair, based on the conviction that the future lay with the Africans, that change, if it came at all, would come from within the Nationalists, and that meanwhile all the English speaker could do was try to lead a decent life outside party politics, or perhaps, if he was in business, exercise some indirect influence on the political process through business associations.

There were a number of *verligte* Afrikaners, mainly in the professions, who advocated change within the limits that Afrikanerdom could tolerate, though it was very difficult to specify those limits, or to establish the degree of influence that the *verligtes* had over the *verkrampte* majority. Nevertheless, it was possible to make some informed guesses: it seemed likely that all *verligtes* would be prepared to give up most aspects of petty apartheid, like segregation in trains and buses, restaurants, lavatories, and so on, and to jettison job-reservation. Some, but not all, would have done away with segregation in hospitals and cemeteries; rather few would have forgone separate schools and separate residential areas and fewer still would have scrapped legislation forbidding marriage or sexual relations across the colour line. Now the position is rather different, for as Afrikanerdom prepares to sacrifice much of its traditional privilege in the interest of survival, the attachment to cultural symbols, especially education and language, grows correspondingly stronger. At the same time it appears that many more Afrikaners, particularly among the élite, would now be prepared to abandon the regulation of marriage and sexual relations, but with the passage of time such 'concessions' have become decreasingly interesting for Africans, except for the minority who are personally affected.

The English speakers' conviction that meaningful change must come from the Nationalists, and especially from within Afrikanerdom, seemed well founded and still does. The question is, how much change, and at what speed? The cultural bonds of Afrikanerdom are so strong that it would be unreasonable to expect changes to be advocated which would cause their supporters to become anathema to fellow Afrikaners. There are a few Afrikaners who will risk that sacrifice, but they are very few.

We shall examine in a later chapter the range of new thinking among the Afrikaner élite, focussing most closely on the academics in the National Party, especially those at the University of Stellenbosch, and on Nationalist Members of Parliament. It is sufficient to say here that the élite of the National Party is certainly far from monolithic in its thinking about relations between the races. The 'ferment of ideas', of which so much has been made in recent years, really exists; even such subjects as the release of Nelson Mandela can be discussed without the proponents of such ideas being suspected of disloyalty to the *volk*. But, just as in 1976, it is still difficult for the outsider to avoid the feeling that Afrikanerdom is fiddling while Rome burns. The difference is that the knowledge is now far more widespread that the city is indeed alight, but there can still be little hope that the fire engines will arrive in time.

---

* In 1982 new constitutional proposals emerged, remarkably similar to those of 1977, which have been mentioned on pp. 49–50. The new proposals are briefly discussed in Chapter 18, postscript.

CHAPTER 6

Business Pressure Groups

Since I share the general view expressed by the Marxists (whilst rejecting most of the assumptions associated with it) that business interests have played a considerable part in bringing about change in South Africa, I now proceed to examine the groups concerned and the changes they have sought. This chapter considers particularly the events and attitudes of the mid seventies when the pressure was at its most intense. (An earlier account may be found in Welsh 1974. See also Greenberg 1980).

Pressure has been exerted upon the South African Government by a variety of business interest groups, to promote the removal of social and economic discrimination. At national level the three main bodies are ASSOCOM—the Association of Chambers of Commerce of South Africa, the Federated Chamber of Industries (FCI) and the Afrikaanse Handelsinstituut (AHI). Pressure has also come from state corporations such as ISCOR (The Iron and Steel Corporation), which may act alone, or through SEIFSA (The Steel and Engineering Industries Federation of South Africa) or through the Iron and Steel Producers Association, whose membership largely overlaps that of SEIFSA.

At local level there are many, some say too many, chambers of commerce in South Africa. The most important of the English-speaking local bodies is the Johannesburg Chamber of Commerce (JCC); others in the first rank are Port Elizabeth, Cape Town and probably Durban, followed in the second rank by Benoni, Bloemfontein, Pretoria and many others. Each of these cities also has its Sakekamer (Afrikaans for Chamber of Commerce).

Another body is the Urban Foundation, founded by South Africa's 'hundred top business men' in December 1976. It is of considerable significance because it brings together business men of all shades of political opinion (Africans, Afrikaners and English speakers) with the shared 'non-political' objective of improving the quality of life of all non-white groups, particularly in the urban areas. It was initially distrusted by blacks, but seems now to have achieved a rather better image, at least in the Transvaal.

In varying degrees all these bodies seek to modify government policies. Their objectives in 1977 (with some of which progress has been made since) included the removal of job reservation, statutory, administrative and customary; movement towards the elimination of the wage gap between black and white; the examination of a wide range of legislation which had the effect of inhibiting the labour supply, in the hope that much of it would be jettisoned; practical measures to improve the quality of life in black urban areas. Some, but by no means all, hoped for a redefinition of 'employee' in the Industrial Conciliation Act, so that blacks could be recognised as employees and hence become members of registered trade unions. This was duly recommended by Wiehahn. Others wished for the removal of the unions' right to agree 'closed shop' arrangements with their employers, which confined certain jobs to employees as defined in the Act, and so had the effect of excluding blacks. (This change, too, was recommended by Wiehahn, with the proviso that already existing closed shop agreements should be allowed to stand.)

There was another group of changes desired by the business lobbies, towards whose realization no progress has yet been made. Some business men (opinions vary as to how many) wanted the abolition of separate 'Bantu Education', though without necessarily thereby urging that schools should become racially integrated. A few went so far as to urge the removal of residential segregation, though those who did this realised that there were few blacks who could afford to live in even a 'poor white' residential area; in any case, they were themselves rich enough not to be disconcerted by the thought of having a black neighbour. There were even some business men who described the whole apartheid system as drivel and who would have gone so far as to remove such notorious, though in a sense peripheral, features as the Immorality Act (Section 16) and the Mixed Marriages Act, which respectively forbid inter-racial sexual intercourse and marriage. Antipathy to these last Acts was shared, perhaps surprisingly, by some very senior Afrikaner industrialists, on the ground that there could be few individuals who were tempted to transgress them. One of the more *verkrampte* Ministers said some years ago that, although these Acts could not be removed from the statute book, if they did not exist already no modern South African Government would be so foolish as to invent them.

Very few whites, English or Afrikaans speaking, in 1977 or now, would contemplate a future which includes one man, one vote, in a united South Africa—though of course universal suffrage does already exist in those fragments which have become 'independent homelands'.

The overriding desire of all businessmen was to restore the flow of foreign capital to both public and private sectors. This meant creating an environment in which the fears of potential investors (based on political assessments rather than the economic fundamentals) would be allayed. In theory this could have been done by even more thoroughgoing suppression of dissident elements than occurred already, though businessmen who hankered after such a solution recognized that it was no longer a serious option, especially since western countries had begun to take seriously the Nigerian ultimatum that the west must choose, sooner than later, between black and white Africa. In some quarters it was argued that, if only foreigners were not misled by the media of communication, they would realise that South Africa was essentially stable; for these the answer was to ensure that the right information was put across to the right people. The majority, however, realised that some positive changes, which perhaps need not be very great, provided they were effectively presented, were necessary if foreign confidence was to be restored.

There has been, naturally enough, considerable resistance to measures of this kind. It comes as much from relatively sophisticated white trade unionists, who fear the removal of privilege and security, as from the white man in the street, for whom any kind of equality with blacks is almost inconceivable. However, the intensity of these political difficulties has greatly decreased since 1977, thanks to the slow softening up by the government to which Robert Davies refers (see p. 94). There are, of course, great differences about the desirable pace and extent of reform, but, as Hanf has shown, they are least in the general area of jobs and labour relations. Indeed, the electorate tends to be rather ahead of the politicians (Hanf *et al.* 1981: 240).

A number of arguments are commonly used to persuade white public opinion that change must come. There is, first of all, the argument from enlightened self-interest, used, for example, by Mr Harry Oppenheimer in a televised discussion, in which he argued that substantial donations to the Urban Foundation were in the interest of shareholders in the companies whose funds had been used. The argument directed at the trade unionists and general public is very much the same. Its gist is that at present the white man is to a considerable extent protected against job competition, but the only way he will be able to survive in future is on merit—otherwise the forces of frustration and even hatred unleashed by his unfair access to job security and high wages will crush him. Enlightened self-interest, sometimes also presented as an appeal to a sense of fairness, therefore demands that the doors be opened now, without delay. This assessment of the white trade unionists' future is often softened by the observation that the South African economy increasingly demands skilled and semi-skilled labour, so that, provided growth is resumed and that some whites will accept retraining (ignoring for the moment those who are not capable of benefiting from retraining) there will be enough work for all. Furthermore, at least in the minds of Afrikaner businessmen, if not of English speakers, the homelands are, as we have seen, not dead, and they eventually will absorb much of the new black skilled labour. There is a duty, it is added, to anticipate that day by undertaking generous training schemes now.

Of course, these arguments may not be understood in detail by the average voter: he may not appreciate the precariousness of South Africa's membership of the international trading community, nor know much more about foreign affairs than that his son is serving, and earning danger money, on the border (between Namibia and Angola). But the voter, particularly the Afrikaner, respects his leaders—and where they lead he will follow. (For a valuable study of white élites see Van Der Merwe *et. al.* 1974.)

The methods and style of the business interest groups vary considerably.

ASSOCOM (and the JCC) tend to be abrasive and confrontational, whilst the FCI and AHI rely far more on behind the scenes pressure and advice. Since much of their contact with Government is confidential, there are problems for the researcher in assessing how effective they have been—or even in finding out exactly what objectives they have had in view in the past. Members of their staffs are, however, happy to talk to enquirers.

1. THE ASSOCIATION OF CHAMBERS OF COMMERCE

This is the largest body, with about 16,000 members (many of whom are small businesses) organized in about 100 local chambers. About 40 per cent of the members are industrialists who choose to work through commerce; some members also belong to one of the other national organizations. There are good informal relations with AHI and FCI, but they seldom make formal joint submissions to Government (indeed, there appears to be no recorded instance of all three signing such a submission and only a few of joint action by FCI and ASSOCOM) partly, no doubt, because each must justify its separate existence to its members. Representatives of the three bodies do however meet on various committees, there is some exchange of policy documents and at local level there has been active co-operation. For example, the JCC, the Johannesburg Sakekamer, the Transvaal Chamber of Industries (TCI) and the National African Chamber of Commerce (NAFCOC) have worked together over Soweto. The lack of co-operation at national level, though in some ways unfortunate, does carry with it the advantage that ill-wishers cannot represent that business as a whole has 'ganged up' to confront government. This matters in South Africa, where government is peculiarly unwilling to be seen to give way to pressure.

Each of the 'big three' has its own balance between public and private pressure, though even ASSOCOM, the most outspoken, does a good deal behind the scenes. ASSOCOM's Executive Director, unlike his predecessor, is expected by his members to react swiftly to events, often without consultation. He would not, however, be as outspoken as, for example, the Chairman of a local chamber like the JCC, since he has to remain close to the shifting 'centre of gravity' at national level. An important part of his evidence for determining where the centre of gravity lies comes from the speeches of local Chambers' officers.

It is perhaps unfair to blame these interest groups for their rather low public profile, given that the issues to which they address themselves are of such fundamental importance, particularly to the white population, and that in South Africa there is virtually no chance that power will shift to the opposition. Nevertheless, ASSOCOM was publicly rebuked in October 1976 by Mr Vorster, who in opening its annual congress bluntly told businessmen to leave politics to the politicians. Subsequently, however, in a letter to the then chairman of ASSOCOM, Mr Goodwin, dated 14 April 1977, he took a substantially different line. After a brief review of current economic conditions, he said:

The view is frequently expressed in business circles that in order to restore the confidence of foreign investors we should do all we possibly can to ensure stable political conditions both in our own country and in the sub-continent as a whole. My reaction to this is that we should of course pursue these objectives, and are indeed doing so, but in the first place because they are worthy objectives in themselves, rather than to impress potential investors. I agree however that the degree of our success in pursuing them will have an effect on the perception of South Africa by foreign investors.

He went on to outline the limits of possible action, and to warn against the illusion that internal changes of a kind acceptable to white opinion would be sufficient to satisfy South Africa's less moderate opponents. Points on which 'no-one should expect us to yield' included:

. . . the right of our white people to retain control of their own destiny, the maintenance of law and order, and the determination of the kind of economic system under which we are to live and work . . .

He mentioned in passing efforts to involve Asians and coloureds in decision-making, whilst:

in respect of the Blacks the decentralisation of political autonomy to the Homeland Governments will continue, while the intention of the Government has already been announced to provide for a meaningful role for Blacks in their local affairs in the metropolitan areas.

In an important passage he said:

In the economic as in the social sphere the Government has clearly expressed its intention to do away as fast as possible with restrictive measures which discriminate on the basis of race and colour.

Obstacles to Asian and coloured job mobility had been all but eliminated and:

Blacks have been moving increasingly into more sophisticated jobs in terms of negotiated agreements between employers and the registered trade unions. It has already been announced that Coloured and Asian industrialists are to have free access to industrial areas outside their own group areas (and consideration was being given to) the extension of business rights for Blacks in Black townships outside the Homelands.

He referred approvingly to the efforts being made, in consultation with the Urban Foundation, to devise a suitable form of land tenure for blacks in these townships, warned that because of existing interests and established procedures progress could not be expected overnight, and assured private business that it could '. . . play a valuable role in identifying areas in which further adaptations can be made, and devising methods by which this can be done'.

The ASSOCOM line is usefully illustrated by some of the motions which were unanimously passed at the October 1976 congress. These included urging Government to move more purposefully towards the elimination of discrimination; to recognise the *de facto* permanent presence of Blacks in urban areas; to allow permanent ownership of property by all racial groups *in their own parts of the urban areas* (my italics); to phase out one year contracts and replace them with a system of employment quotas; to allow migrants to be regularly visited by their families and to facilitate the provision of improved housing for migrant workers.

Perhaps the most notable feature of these resolutions is their moderation: there is no suggestion that group areas or migrant labour should be scrapped—only that the existing system should be more rationally operated. That ASSOCOM's reputation for abrasiveness hides a genuine moderacy of demands may also be learned from some of its Executive Director's speeches. Addressing the Midland Regional Chamber of Commerce Conference on 12 June 1977 he complained that:

> . . . decisions on economic policy do not seem to be co-ordinated in the shape of a total 'package'. We are also prone to the 'too little, too late' syndrome in making the necessary changes. These often appear to be piecemeal, fragmentary and diffused. The result is that the country neither gets the full benefit nor credit for the movement which is, in fact, taking place and which, if added up, could show a significant pattern of change in the Republic.

He went on to urge the preparation of a five year socio-economic plan, which would not only constitute:

> . . . a vital weapon with which to defend and promote South Africa, but could also be the basis upon which to raise foreign capital for the very objectives of the Plan itself.

Mr Parsons went on to specify that what was needed was to improve blacks' economic opportunities by removing legislation which discriminated against black businessmen and workers and 'the removal of any friction points arising out of the system of separate development', for example in transport, training facilities and education, and in streamlining the pass laws. He asked also for the *phased* (his italics) improvement of social opportunities, better lighting and housing, improved property rights; better provision for recreation and (again) education; better consultation and communication procedures; local government autonomy for blacks, etc. Thus, the concessions government was asked to make were ones which it had already in most cases announced that it intended to make. The requests were for changes within the existing system, since it would be useless yet to urge government to abandon the system itself; yet from another point of view, these same requests could be seen as the start of a process to which, once begun, there is no logical end, except to dismantle the whole edifice of apartheid. The line taken by ASSOCOM may, therefore, be attacked from two very different angles: by people, on the one hand, who reject gradual amelioration as inadequate, and, on the other, by those who see any concessions as the thin end of the wedge.

A further extract from a speech by Mr Parsons (4 August 1977) may serve to sum up ASSOCOM's thinking at that time. Once again, though pungently expressed, it is not inconsistent with the official thinking expressed in such documents as the *Economic Development Programme* or the annual report and speech by the Governor of the Reserve Bank. Mr Parsons said in part:

We are getting the South African economy into a 'vicious circle'. This is related directly to the difficulties experienced on the balance of payments. Lack of foreign capital has necessitated a continuance of stringent economic policies. This has caused a deepening recession with a concomitant increase in Black unemployment: the unemployment creates the risk of more unrest, which, in turn, leads to a further deterioration in foreign investor confidence, resulting in a reduced capital inflow and thus further strains in the balance of payments.

In 1975–7 ASSOCOM exerted pressure in an energetic and positive manner. Since then, however, it seems to have concentrated more on the bread and butter of its role as an association of Chambers of Commerce, and to have confined its part in the broader socio-economic issues largely to reaction and comment, rather than initiation. Many of the numerous speeches made by the Executive Director and his various annual Presidents have been, to a great extent, though not exclusively, concerned with such matters as: taxation, and the need to make it attractive to outside investors; inflation; the balance of payments; the state of the economy and business confidence; monetary policy and the budget.

Some of the Association's main preoccupations were the benefits of the free enterprise system and the need to make them apparent to all racial groups; the need to recognise that South Africa's economy was one and indivisible, and after 300 years of interdependence could not be unscrambled; the intrusive nature and excessive extent of state intervention in the economy, which prevented employers from employing whom they liked, when they liked, where they liked and correspondingly prevented labour from moving freely to wherever work might be available. Towards the end of the period there has been a feeling of regret running through the documents that governmental aspirations and policy have been insufficiently translated into legislation.

There have, of course, been other themes, more directly related to relations between the races, sometimes contained in comments on Government reports and draft legislation, or in confidential reports on meetings with Ministers. These have included: the need for growth, both as something desirable in itself and as a means to absorb black unemployment; the shortage of skilled labour and the need for the private sector to involve itself in education and training, in particular by making better use of the eight In-service Training Centres established by commerce and industry; black housing and the need to provide more of it; occasionally education.

ASSOCOM's main beliefs may be readily summarised. It believes that all discrimination based on race or colour should be eliminated, especially in the economic sphere, and supports the SACCOLA (South African Employers' Consultative Committee on Labour Affairs) Code of Practice, one of whose main objectives is the removal of racial discrimination in employment. It advocates the removal of all restrictions on black business men. The Bantu Education Act should be repealed, and education for all racial groups controlled by the same Department of State; universities should be open to all on a multi-racial basis; Africans should enjoy freehold

63

tenure, rather than 99 year leasehold, in black townships; Community Councils (organs of African local government) should be responsible to Provincial Councils, in the same way as white local government; the trade union system should ideally be non-racial, though black unions are acceptable as a second best; all unions should be registered, though it may be necessary for employers to deal temporarily with unregistered unions. There has been a general feeling that over the years too much has been done by government *for* blacks, whereas the accent should be on consultation with them. Too high a proportion of South Africa's total manpower has been engaged in the public service, largely because of the unwieldy apparatus needed to administer the racial groups separately. Black labour bureaux should be abolished and employment services for all races centralized under the Department of Manpower Utilization.

ASSOCOM welcomed the intention of the Wiehahn and Riekert reports, though it regretted their watering down in subsequent legislation, draft legislation and regulations. In particular, the association commented adversely on the draft bills (known as the Koornhof Bills) which were published in December 1980 and intended by Dr Koornhof, the Minister of Co-operation and Development (though not, it has been suggested, by his more *verkrampte* officials) to put Riekert into effect. ASSOCOM, having, like many other bodies, commented unfavourably on the short time allowed for submissions, pointed out that the bills were riddled with ambiguities. Some substantial points were that Section 10 rights under the Blacks (Urban Areas Consolidation Act) might even be removed from Africans hitherto allowed to live in the white area and that a wedge would in any case be driven between rural blacks and those allowed to live in town, necessarily promoting increased unemployment among the former; this prospect was particularly serious in KwaZulu and of international significance because that homeland abuts on Mozambique. The association reiterated its belief in freehold tenure for Africans and in the provision of opportunities rather than the exaction of penalties as the means to deal with urban migration, which was in any case unlikely to be successfully controlled by regulations.

Internationally, ASSOCOM emphasises the regional importance of South Africa: 'From an economic point of view, if South Africa sneezes, then the rest of southern Africa catches cold.' But the dependence is not all one way: South Africa, too, needs water and energy from its neighbours and will need to import food by the end of the century. In the broader international context ASSOCOM still adverts to the danger of sanctions and stresses the need for foreign capital if growth is to be achieved. It is necessary therefore to bear in mind the effect of internal conditions on potential investors; their perceptions of South Africa may well become more favourable if the task of making the benefit of the free enterprise system accessible to all population groups is successfully undertaken.

One of the most interesting international contacts was with the International Labour Office, where the Secretary of ASSOCOM took part in the South African delegation to the annual meeting of the ILO's Tripartite

Committee on Apartheid, consisting of representatives of governments, workers and employers. The two former furiously attacked South Africa and said that such reforms as had occurred were cosmetic, while the employers' representatives (even black delegates from African countries) thought they should be taken seriously as steps in the right direction. The South African delegation was present only with observer status, to brief the employers' side, but the intemperate arguments of the governmental and workers' representatives do seem to have sunk into the mind of ASSOCOM's Secretary, judging by submissions which he made later in the year to the National Manpower Commission. (*Assocom Circular REG 865* of 4 November 1980.) In this representation ASSOCOM urged the Commission to '. . . examine ways and means whereby registration of Trade Unions can be made more attractive and whereby the existing stigma and suggestion that Government wishes to 'control' the Unions can be removed.' The Association also submitted that freedom of association was an absolute right and that the racial composition of a Union should be entirely a matter for the Union and not for government. There should be '. . . no right of veto with regard to membership of Industrial Councils. This is a subject which has caused considerable criticism both within and without the Republic and it is difficult to defend.' Finally, ASSOCOM urged that the changes proposed by Wiehahn and adopted by government should be incorporated in legislation rather than administrative regulations.

All these points had been forcefully made at the ILO meeting. The fact that ASSOCOM's Secretary chose to repeat them in a Circular to members suggests that his attendance at Geneva had not been fruitless, and so, by extension, that there is a case for allowing South African delegates to attend international gatherings.

This sketch of ASSOCOM's thinking in recent years supports the suggestion made earlier that there has been little new thinking in the business lobby since its heyday in 1975–7. Rather, its energy has been devoted to technical matters, to maintaining pressure along lines already established and to commenting on such results as have been achieved.

2. THE JOHANNESBURG CHAMBER OF COMMERCE

Sometimes, it appears, the JCC needs to assert its independence from ASSOCOM. For example, the outgoing President, Mr Smale, said in his end of year speech on 9 August 1977:

> At times we had had to act independently of Assocom and a case in point is the Black, Coloured and Asian Affairs Committee. We found that when this was a joint committee with Assocom, our members were involved in national issues at the expense of the problem that had to be solved at local level. This led to the dissolution of the Committee and the formation of a Joint Action Committee (to which reference has already been made) with the Sakekamer, the TCI and NAFCOC.

Mr Smale did not pull his punches. Referring to Mr Vorster's letter of 14 April, he said:

65

The promise to eliminate restrictive measures which discriminate on the basis of race and colour in the socio-economic field was the building block that we so badly needed. Regrettably there has been little, if any, progress in bringing about the desired change.

He went on to cite, as an example of action contrary to what had been promised, the recent statement on black shop managers in white areas. This referred to the refusal of the Department of Bantu Administration (whose Minister, Mr M. C. Botha, was not among the more *verligte* members of Cabinet) to allow ten black shop managers trained by Topcentre (a subsidiary of Truworth's, a leading chain of clothes retailers) to be appointed to manage shops in white areas, although those shops were almost entirely directed towards black customers.

It appears from Mr Smale's annual report that the JCC had only lately begun to take a firm political line. He said:

> ... this Chamber is made up of members of many shades of political opinion but if the politicians are unable to provide a business environment in which we can operate, then it is our duty to play an active role in correcting the situation: the Chamber has had no alternative but to shed its traditional reluctance to involve itself in political issues ...

The Black, Coloured and Asian Affairs Committee's report had identified the main restraints on trade as the Physical Planning Act, which prevented commerce and industry absorbing the natural growth of the labour force; the provision of the Industrial Conciliation Act which allowed Trade Unions to limit the employment of blacks; job reservation and influx control. Assistance towards home ownership was urged, even before conventional freehold terms had been granted, and the point made that '. . . since the economic process of a country was indivisible, equal opportunities should be given to all.' This acceptance of the unitary nature of the South African economy is of some interest, since it has often been argued (see p. 4 above) that it should more properly be regarded as dual, rather than as an integrated whole—and this view is still held by some influential South African economists.

3. THE FEDERATED CHAMBER OF INDUSTRIES

Opinions differ as to the relative effectiveness of ASSOCOM and the FCI. Although the latter's members are largely English speakers, it took the decision some years ago to move to Pretoria and appoint an Afrikaans speaking Director, in the belief that lobbying would then be made more effective. Now only one member of FCI's staff is an English speaker; the Federation appears to be well regarded by Afrikaners and to have good access to civil servants, whereas ASSOCOM, it is said, often finds the same doors closed in its face. FCI has a large office and conducts extensive research, so that the bureaucrats correctly feel that it does not merely make demands, but also has something to give. It is thought to understand the Government's problems and be willing to forgo publicity in favour of private pressure, having understood that the National Party government is instinctively averse, to a quite abnormal extent by international standards —or even by opposition South African standards—to be seen to change its mind or give way to pressure. It prefers rather to make changes without announcement, once it has divined, by what one sharp observer called 'a process of osmosis' that it can carry the voting public with it.

FCI and AHI together have about the same number of members as ASSOCOM, 16,000. AHI has seventy local chambers, but FCI is differently organised with only eight. FCI seems able not only to co-operate with Government, but also with other bodies, like AHI and SEIFSA, more easily than does ASSOCOM, and whereas FCI's strength appears to lie in its links at official level, AHI is acknowledged to be most influential with politicians.

The FCI has pushed for the enfranchisement of the business community as a political entity; the reduction of government interference in the operation of the market; the acceptance of high growth and a relatively free market as answers to South Africa's problems, of which the foremost is employment creation to absorb a rapidly expanding population.

The Prime Minister's Carlton Centre Conference in November 1979, when the entire Cabinet attended a meeting with top level business men, symbolized the acceptance by government of business as a partner, by contrast with the wary approach of earlier generations of nationalists, who had perceived business as a threat. That conference symbolized the government's intention to allow business to run its own affairs and to take primary responsibility for some matters, such as trade unions, which hitherto has been seen as suitable areas for governmental control. The intention to reduce governmental interference was, in part, put into effect by the Prime Minister's streamlining of the civil service, a process which included reducing the number of Departments of State to eighteen. Business could henceforth be seen as a shield between government and the rapidly growing urban black population. In the field of industrial relations, for example, government had set up a framework of negotiation, but then dropped out of the front line, leaving its operation to business. In this new atmosphere of openness, it is, of course, vital to business that it should work out means of speaking with one voice in its dealings with government, which suggests that there will have to be increased emphasis on liaison (already effective in some instances) between the various groups.

Government accepted the need to open the industrial relations system to blacks on an equal basis as a result of propaganda by the FCI and others and because it had become convinced of the need to increase supplies of skilled manpower beyond the capabilities of the white group. Mr S. P. Botha, the Minister of Labour, drew attention to this need in his speech at the 1979 annual conference of FCI, the same speech in which he announced his intention to extend union rights to migrants, including those from the 'independent' homelands.

One of FCI's principal contributions to liberalization has been in respect of trade unions, where it has had to crush a right wing revolt by its own members. SEIFSA (The Steel and Engineering Industries Federation of South Africa), for example, had wanted unions to register before employers would consider recognition, whereas FCI has come to the view that it is less dangerous to bring conflicting bodies together than to keep workers out of the industrial relations system by rigid insistence on registration. The role of government is, in other words, being reduced (in this instance by by-passing the registrar) and the discretion of the individual employer being correspondingly increased.

The FCI's 'Guidelines for Industrial Relations in the 1980s', in which companies are urged to be flexible and pragmatic in their attitude to unions, were published in January 1981, and are of the greatest importance. The Chamber reaffirms its support for the SACCOLA Code of Employment Practice 'for an equitable and non-discriminatory industrial relations system'. In this period of transition, when three million blacks have swiftly to be brought into the system, there is an essential need for employers to develop consultative skills and accept risks in order to promote improved conditions through consultation and negotiation. Both sides of industry should accept the Industrial Council system, because it gives a clear legal status to the outcome of negotiation. However:

> Legislative frameworks to guide the evolving labour relations structure must not be permitted to obstruct the democratic development of workers' organisations or to disrupt bona fide collective bargaining between representative employee and employer groups. As a corollary individual employers face the possibility that at this fluid stage of development they may have to enter into agreements falling outside the established industrial council system.
>
> (*Guidelines*: para. 4)

It is possible, the Guidelines continue, that issues may come up which are not normally regarded as subjects for industrial bargaining, but the parties should try to avoid the politicization of labour relations and stick to traditional subjects of negotiation. On the other hand, it is important to dispel any feeling among black workers that the new reforms are, in fact, intended as means of establishing closer control:

> Situations have to be judged on their own merit. It is therefore accepted that in a voluntary labour relations system there will be instances in which employers find it necessary to negotiate with unregistered worker groups which are representative of workers' interests, albeit on a conditional basis.
>
> (*Ibid*: para. 7(e))

Registration is only a mechanism, though a desirable one; the point is to promote freedom of association and to find out, through the process of negotiation, whether a group is indeed representative, and, since workers are wary of registration, to streamline the process and make it simpler. It is also necessary to find out what workers think of their official leaders and of their works/liaison committees; it may be necessary to conduct parallel negotiations both with a union and through a committee. It is not the business of management to foster or prevent the growth of any particular workers' group, though it may legitimately express a preference for broadly-based non-racial unions.

In addition to this enlightened stand on trade unions the FCI has been a prominent advocate of settled urban African communities (and therefore of the 99 year leasehold system) and of a new approach to black urban housing. By the year 2000, 90 per cent of the coloured, Indian and white communities may be urbanized (the Chamber eschews any suggestion that they may by then live in non-segregated housing) and perhaps 50 per cent of the black population. Much more needs to be spent on black housing—the FCI suggests an additional appropriation of R300m—but it is important that it should not be spent on contract-built undifferentiated housing units. Instead, encouragement should be given to home ownership, which motivates people 'to maintain security over their premises in times of unrest', and to home improvement, which bridges the gap between undifferentiated units and a developed urban community. Improvement requires the right of permanent residence, or at least the development of a market in housing, so that the improver may capitalize on the work done, by selling his 'sweat equity' if he wishes. Encouragement should be given to people wishing to build their own homes, which, in turn, will lead to desirable development of the informal sector, and to participation by the community in planning development and administration. It will be necessary for the state, or the private sector, to provide the infrastructure and make possible the purchase of low-cost building materials, and guidance may be needed if an unacceptably low standard of self-built housing is to be avoided. (See SAFCI 1980 for a fuller exposition.)

Though at one level the FCI's views on housing accord with common sense, and draw on the experience of poor African countries like Zambia and Zimbabwe, yet in South Africa commitment to the growth of settled urban African communities is highly political, if only because it undercuts the homelands policy, and the FCI has not shirked the political implications in this and other areas, as may be learned from, for example, the speeches at its annual conference in 1979.

In particular the speeches were concerned about whether the free enterprise system, whose prospects were so much improved in the new relationship between business and government, could be 'sold' to the black population. The FCI's President said:

> It is an open question, however, whether an advance towards prosperity for our Black fellow countrymen can be achieved through unbridled capitalism.
>
> (SAFCI *Annual Report 1979*: 12)

The Executive Director asked whether the black population had staked their future on the free enterprise system, and went on:

> Clearly in this area we, Government and subject alike, will have to devote much more attention to one of the basic tenets of the system, viz. equality of opportunity for all—regardless of race, colour or creed—to participate in economic endeavour and to be part of the process of the creation of wealth and to share in the rewards of such participation. To what extent do Blacks really

enjoy equality of opportunity? . . . We do well to take cognizance of the feeling among some Blacks that this system is to blame for the plight in which they find themselves.

(Ibid: 14–15)

The FCI, perhaps wisely, does not commit itself to a view of the extent of change which would go with non-discrimination and equality of opportunity, but the Chamber is clearly much influenced by the economic liberalism of the O'Dowd thesis (discussed in Chapter 3) which holds that the economic improvements brought about by the demands of the economy will lead also to social and political amelioration. If asked to specify the limits of change, the FCI would probably say that they are impossible to forecast, but that the direction of change has been firmly established and that an irreversible process has begun.

4. THE AFRIKAANSE HANDELSINSTITUUT

AHI's membership is limited to Afrikaners, because when it was founded in 1942 the other business interest groups objected and Government only allowed it to go ahead on that basis. Although in recent years it has been somewhat more vocal, in general AHI prefers to rely on private pressure and to limit itself to putting before Government views argued on strictly economic grounds—though its officials recognise that the distinction between the economic and the political is in some senses artificial. However, AHI's Executive Committee has a settled disposition to operate within the framework of Government policy, not, one would expect, an easy line for a body whose members are not all Government supporters and who come from all sections of commerce and industry, including gold. Furthermore, the AHI is explicitly against the abolition of the Physical Planning Act or of influx control and explicitly supports decentralisation of industry and homeland development. Nevertheless, it favours the end of job reservation (except in the army and police), partly because it believes that there is a Christian duty to train blacks for eventual service in the homelands, and partly because a larger skilled workforce is required than can be supplied by the white population. Nor, perhaps surprisingly, does AHI object to blacks bossing whites.

In the eyes of some English-speaking business men, the relationship between AHI and politicians and between FCI and government officials is essentially tribal—though it should be noted that some Departments, like the Treasury, are less prone than others to enter into this type of relationship. Such observers accept the Afrikaners' view of themselves as a tribe of white Africans. Indeed, both English and Afrikaans speaking business men constantly refer to the Afrikaners' long history of struggle to establish themselves in an economy dominated by English speakers. Even now, one senior Afrikaner industrialist pointed out, they do not produce half the country's engineers, and though the absolute size of their share of the economy has grown, as a percentage it has not. They own about 30 per cent of private industry, measured by asset value, which includes 40 per cent of banking and finance, but still only 20 per cent of mining. Thus it is not surprising that bodies like AHI (or the South African Bureau of Racial Affairs (SABRA) in the field of race relations) will refuse to 'rock the boat'.

A further characteristic of AHI is that it is much influenced by the kind of economic thinking expressed by Dr Wassenaar, Chairman of the great Afrikaans-controlled conglomerate Sanlam, in a recent book which attacked as creeping socialism the very wide extent of state ownership and control of the South African economy. This line of thought strikes a chord in many business men and civil servants. (Wassenaar 1977). It should be added that Dr Wassenaar was strongly reproached by the then Prime Minister, Mr Vorster, for expressing views publicly instead of in a private conversation. He also attacked Dr Wassenaar strenuously in Parliament (*Hansard*: 4 February 1977: Cols. 783–790).

5. THE URBAN FOUNDATION

This body, founded in December 1976, is of great significance because it brings together business men of a wide range of political views and includes Afrikaners, English speakers and blacks, all dedicated to the improvement of the 'quality of life' of blacks. Its attitude is ameliorist and non-confrontational, which from the beginning gave grounds for hope (augmented by the favourable mention in Mr Vorster's April 1977 letter to ASSOCOM) that the Government would be able to work with the Foundation without thereby giving the impression to its supporters that it was 'giving way under pressure'. A further sign of official approval was that Judge Steyn, a prominent Afrikaner, was seconded to head the Foundation.

The UF is basically practical. It has subscribers rather than members, and Directors who between them represent 60 per cent of capital investment and employment in the private sector. On the regional boards (Transvaal, Western Cape and Natal) some of the same companies are represented and Africans who hold high executive (rather than Board) positions, or who are independent of business, have been brought in. Very soon after the UF began 12 out of 25 regional board members were black, which in terms of the capital they represented was an over-representation. However, the UF recognises that it needs as many black sources of information and opinion as possible.

The UF's first financial objective was to persuade companies registered on the Johannesburg stock exchange to donate 2 per cent of their post-tax profits, which, over five years, would have come to R64 million. (Alternatively, the Foundation asked for 0.04 per cent of turnover.) This sum was to be geared up by 100 per cent, or even 200 per cent, by raising private loan capital. It was hoped also to raise loans from local authorities, which, since the UF had governmental approval, might be given at slightly 'shaded' rates of interest. Thus the UF is not a charitable trust, but in some respects is more like an investment bank; for example, one of its tasks has been to get consortia together for black housing projects. It gives money outright

71

to some projects and lends to others, and insists on providing supervision and management, largely by specialist personnel seconded to the UF by subscribers.

The UF should not, however, be seen solely in enterpreneurial terms. It was, and is still, extremely interested in promoting black community support for its projects and hoped eventually to establish a community development unit. Meanwhile, its diplomatic problem has been how to deal with the Bantu Affairs Administration Boards (BAAB) and the Department of Bantu Administration (with which bodies it is necessarily in very frequent contact—the latter is now the Department of Co-operation and Development) whilst distancing itself from them in the minds of the people.

This is particularly important in Soweto, where the West Rand Administration Board is cordially hated. During the Soweto riots of 1976, buildings associated with the administrative authorities were destroyed, whilst those belonging to charitable bodies, like the South African Legion, TOC H, or the YMCA, were not. The UF naturally hoped to be included in the latter category and so far has not suffered any physical attacks.

The UF sees the components of 'improved quality of life' as (i) housing and related amenities; (ii) adult education and job-related training; (iii) provision of community facilities and (iv) promotion of community involvement in projects. The objectives which required a stand on principle (as opposed to the various projects which could be planned and put into operation without delay) were security of land tenure for blacks and a code of conduct for firms.

A considerable amount of work has been done on both subjects. A code of conduct was issued jointly by the UF and the South African Employers' Consultative Committee on Labour Affairs (SACCOLA) and a long paper on land tenure was written for consideration by the UF's executive committee. This paper was the result of a joint UF/Government working party and identified the many changes in the law which would follow a decision in principle to give blacks security of tenure in Soweto and other black townships. The point was to obtain the essential characteristics of freehold tenure (without its necessarily being so-called) which were identified as (i) the right to use a house as security for a mortgage; (ii) strong security of tenure; (iii) right of transfer, including inheritance; (iv) no removal from townships on administrative grounds, for in current practice township superintendents had very wide powers to remove blacks within their own discretion. Once these principles were adopted and made possible in practice by the many necessary changes in the law, Africans would no longer be tenants of the BAAB, but instead be in normal commercial relations with mortgage companies.

The UF recognised the technical difficulty that freehold is normally given after an accurate survey. Soweto has never been surveyed, and to have undertaken it would have imposed an impossibly long delay. There were, however, reasonable site diagrams and records of occupancy; the UF therefore hoped that no further survey would be insisted upon, and that an abbreviated form of conveyancing procedure would be adopted. Since then things have progressed slowly, but a start on allocation of plots under 99 year leasehold has been made.

The UF has certainly been successful in fund raising and by the end of April 1981, 293 companies and other bodies had contributed or pledged R33 million, well past the revised five year target of R25 million. The funds came largely from business in South Africa, though the London offices of Barclays and the Standard Bank also subscribed, and the West German Government made an unsolicited gift of R5000.

Expenditure on projects in the Foundation's first three years, to 29 February 1980, was R20 million, of which R15.5 million was spend on housing, education and training, and the budget for 1980/81 was over R20 million. Housing has always been seen as a main field of activity because it offers scope for individual self-reliance; it is a field in which the private sector can contribute more than it has in the past and '. . . the Foundation can play a co-ordinating and catalytic role in the whole process.' (Urban Foundation *Information Bulletin 8*, January 1980.) The UF also plays a direct role in housing projects, because the necessary housing agencies do not always exist, but its long term aim is to motivate other agencies. Perhaps its best-known area of involvement has been the infamous squatter township of Crossroads, where 106 of its houses were ready by the end of November 1980 (*Sunday Times*, Johannesburg: 18 January 1981).

The Foundation now believes that 99 year leasehold provides an acceptable basis for the development of a market in African housing, since it gives a sufficient security on which to borrow. Housing is a subject on which much passion has rightly been generated, because it cannot be separated from the Group Areas Act, which governs where individuals may live, according to their racial group. The UF's policy, however, is to defuse passionate issues and the Information Bulletin cited above provides an example of rigid restraint and masterly understatement when it says, in discussing the housing issue: 'Security of tenure for 'Non-whites' has always been in some doubt, owing to influx control and Group Areas legislation.'

Although the UF's style is restrained, it does not shirk issues, as may be seen from the following remarks by Judge Steyn:

Determined thrusts in this direction (swifter implementation of 99 year leasehold) are essential to establish that what the public and private sectors are about is not calculated to soften the edges of a discriminatory system, but are designed to bring about real structural change. This is indeed what the Foundation is seeking to achieve in stimulating social and economic progress. It would be fatal if the response to the admittedly good and useful work which is being done is merely perceived as The Urban Foundation making apartheid comfortable for a privileged group of Blacks. What is done across the broad field of the socio-economic system by way of social advance for all population groups must be seen as working towards an end position in society which conforms with certain basic principles. These would certainly include a system in which discrimination based on race or colour has been eliminated, in which equal opportunity is available to all population groups and in which the advantages of the free enterprise system are accessible to all.

(Urban Foundation, *Annual Report*, 1979/80, p. 6)

It is true that the notion of 'real structural change' has become fashionable and that its implications are not always clear, but from the executive director of an 'establishment' body, these are fighting words.

It is difficult to obtain solid information on what impact, if any, the UF has made on the man in the Soweto street but, as has been mentioned above (p. 57), its image is widely thought to have improved in the Transvaal. It must, given its insistence on working with the Government, have run the grave risk of being seen as yet another official agency, a not unreasonable view, although a mistaken one. On the other hand, within its very strict self-imposed limitations, it has proved an effective agency for those reforms which are acceptable to government, but which for political reasons, cannot be carried out by any of the other existing bodies, whether governmental or private. Its developmental objectives and the kinds of project it undertakes to improve the conditions of black life are little different from those of, for example, the long established South African Institute of Race Relations. But the history and image of the Institute, liberal and to a very large extent English speaking as it has always been, would have made any large scale co-operation with government unthinkable for both parties.

ATTITUDES EXPRESSED BY BUSINESS MEN

There appears to be a significant difference between English and Afrikaans speaking business men, in that the former are able to make clear-cut economic demands unqualified by attachment to apartheid ideology, whilst for the latter it is far more complicated.

Afrikaners in business (in which I include the State Corporations) do not appear to be as *verlig* as some of those in the universities, newspapers and so on. Nevertheless, they are just as aware as are the English speakers that the economy cannot develop if it has to rely solely on whites for its skilled work force. The dilemma will, of course, become far less acute if the new economic and geo-political thinking expressed by Professor Jan Lombard and others becomes dominant (see Chapter 14), because in that case the emphasis will shift decisively away from homeland development. Instead the homelands will be seen simply as rural areas needing development within a greater South Africa divided on regional, rather than racial lines. At the same time, however, many Afrikaners remain in the grip of an ideological commitment to the grand design of separate development, not in its crude Verwoerdian form, but to some extent modernised to fit current conditions.

Thus, there is an intellectual and emotional dilemma. On the one hand, the need, for example, to train blacks for skilled work in white areas is recognised, but this has to be reconciled with the very great emphasis placed by Afrikaners on the cultural differences between black and white

74

and their conviction that there can only be a safe future for both if the blacks are brought to regard the homelands as the areas to which they primarily belong. The ideological reconciliation may be made by, for instance, asserting that blacks will only be trained for work in white areas as a temporary measure until homeland development has reached the point where the available skilled blacks can be attracted there. Similarly, Afrikaners stress, far more than do English speakers, the need for decentralisation of industry, not only because it is seen as desirable on economic grounds, but also as part of the overall social and political pattern of separate development.

Many Afrikaans speaking business men express doubt about African ability to pick up western skills and values and believe the process must take several generations; at the same time (in apparent contradiction) they do not doubt that blacks would, given correct training, be able to fill any job in the homelands. This freedom from restrictions is indeed one of the most attractive features of the homelands, and provides a justification for job reservation in white areas, because those blacks who do not spontaneously act on their simple duty to return to the homelands will be pulled by the superior opportunities available there. There is a general appreciation that blacks must have political rights, but only in their own areas (the homelands) and, in most cases, there is an unwillingness to talk in detail about arrangements for urban blacks. In these respects the state of affairs has changed little since 1977. One exceptional interviewee did, however, give a detailed account of how, in the short term, Soweto could be greatly extended in area to become one, or preferably four, 'city states', with full municipal rights and attached (though not geographically) to parent homelands, which would decide what proportion of their revenues would be spent on the rural areas, and what in the city state. The new Soweto would, as a relatively short-term plan, accommodate three million people: in the medium to long term a further three million would be housed in a completely new black city, perhaps adjoining Bophutatswana or Lebowa. (Preliminary plans for such a city were announced towards the end of 1980.)

'Liberalization', with its overtones of the now dissolved Liberal Party, is no more popular a word with Afrikaner business men than with other Afrikaners. Business men did, however, emphasize that what needed to be done was to increase the supply of skilled labour (one informant called it 'civilized' labour). But increased wages could only be generated by growth; higher wages without growth would only push South African industry into capital intensive development: the latter was a trend which had not yet started, but very easily could. This argument has also, since the introduction of Codes of Conduct for firms by the European Community and others, frequently been used against the codes on the ground that they endanger the expansion of employment by pushing up wages.

One industrialist, who was typical in emphasizing the great cultural differences between black and white, saw close parallels between black and

Afrikaner development. 'We were an agricultural people, much like the black man.' The Afrikaners' problem had been to establish prestige for their people: similarly, the blacks would get nowhere until they could produce men of substance, not just politicians, for themselves. Such a view, which among Marxists is seen as mere 'mystification', does nevertheless appear to be genuinely and fairly widely held.

This informant had thought for years that job reservation must go. It was not merely expedient to give opportunities to the fifty per cent of blacks who lived outside the homelands: they deserved them. The principal difficulties were the attitudes of white trade unionists and (in this informant's view) the much lower efficiency of blacks than whites. The unions, however, were not monolithic: much depended upon the history of any particular plant. At one steel plant, started in 1924, the first employees had been poor whites and the hard core of attitudes was still not easy to shift. At another, started in the mid '70s in a border area, all the crane drivers (except those dealing with hot metal) were Zulus, and it was not unrealistic to press hard for blacks to be trained as artisans. The technique was to keep men of different races, but doing similar work, in different sections of the plant. It would be unfair to ask the white trade unionists to work shoulder to shoulder with blacks, but even the advances already made at the second plant would be unthinkable at the first.

Another senior Afrikaner industrialist was convinced that blacks would never attain white levels in jobs demanding anything more than repetitive tasks (at which they were often better than whites). Nevertheless, he saw the need for black apprentices and supervisors, though he was doubtful that they could ever make managers. Here again, the white unions presented difficulties: in boom times it had been simple enough to raise the floor level of white employment.

Like the others, this industrialist would not look outside the ideological framework provided by separate development, though he produced a new variant when he suggested that some urban blacks who did not respond to the call of their ethnic group might have to be accommodated in a 'non-ethnic' homeland. He also believed that the homelands must not only be consolidated, but even extended beyond the maximum areas laid down in the 1936 Act. (This line, which a few years ago was rather daring, is now being quite widely taken, not only by *verligtes*.) One informant went so far as to say that there would be no objection to including Richards Bay in a Zulu Homeland. No real threat would be presented by any such enlargement of KwaZulu, since the economy of South Africa would still be so inter-dependent as to nullify any danger of nationalization.

Other points on which there seemed to be a measure of agreement were that trade unions should be decentralized rather than national and that one good reason for removing discrimination was that it might go some way towards removing foreign investors' fears. One industrialist made the important point that perhaps overseas investors did not realize how effective a weapon capital deprivation was. But most felt that, whatever

South Africa did, western governments would never be satisfied. South Africa was the victim of propaganda by the United Nations and the Organisation of African Unity, whose double standards must simply be accepted as a fact of life.

To generalize—Afrikaner business men in 1977 had three main sets of objectives, towards the first of which some progress has since been made, whilst the other two are being seriously discussed:

(1) the end of job reservation, movement towards equal pay for equally productive work; improved training. The possibility of blacks bossing whites was generally seen as a problem but a soluble one, particularly in the homelands;
(2) homeland extension and consolidation;
(3) some solution of the 'urban black problem'.

As the earlier quotations from JCC and ASSOCOM have shown, English speaking business men are more outspoken than their Afrikaner colleagues, and in general are not burdened with the ideological ballast of separate development. Their objectives do not differ essentially, but their influence is limited by their non-membership in Afrikanerdom.

CHAPTER 7

A Case Study in Industrial Relations

I turn now to a short case study of a company which I shall call Smith.

Management at Smith said as long ago as 1977 that the company's objective (which they considered was very widely shared by business in general) was to do away with all job discrimination. Consequential objectives were, *inter alia*, to begin training black artisans (at that time possible in the homelands) which would involve change in the operation of the Apprenticeship Act, which in theory was colour-blind, though in fact it had been used to prevent blacks becoming apprentices. It would then be essential either to terminate the unions' right to impose closed shop agreements or to change the legislation to enable blacks to be members of registered unions. The difficulties in the way of progress were not only legal, but lay in official and social attitudes, both of individuals and of organizations such as the trade unions.

However, Government attitudes were changing; business (as we have seen in the previous chapter) was becoming more vociferous and was getting a better hearing. The appointment of the Wiehahn Commission was seen as particularly hopeful, and the subsequent appointment of Dr Riekert's Commission was seen as additional evidence of the Government's seriousness.

On the whole, Smith's employees at staff (white collar) level got over any reluctance to work alongside blacks fairly rapidly, once the blacks had been appointed. The more important barriers were erected (often unconsciously) at an earlier stage; for example, a job specification might include the stipulation that five years' previous experience was necessary, thus effectively excluding blacks' applications. However, 250 of Smith's 4,000 monthly paid employees were black and coloured, and management had thought it wise to suggest that all staff associations should examine their constitutions and decide whether to remove any racially discriminatory clauses. All but one had decided to do so, but there was now, unfortunately, a move among the blacks to establish their own staff associations.

However, the real problems in bringing about equality of opportunity were presented by unionized labour. Smith had a good Industrial Council structure, incorporating whites and coloureds (although the bulk of the coloureds, who belonged to one domestic union which was dominated by whites, resented the fact that all posts in the union's bureaucracy were, as the law stood, necessarily held by whites) but its council agreement did not cover employment conditions for blacks.

Formerly Smith had had five Liaison Committees for blacks at factory level. This separation of consultation had been intolerable for a management which sought to establish a rational (that is, non-racial) pay structure, because it was only possible to talk to one group at a time, yet negotiations with either affected the pay curve for both. Management therefore had sought a joint forum, to which the white unions' reactions had been to suggest that they, the whites, should negotiate on behalf of the blacks. For management this was hardly an improvement, since such a solution would do little to help white trade unionists to lose their traditional perception of their situation in racial terms, so that, if racial interests appeared to clash, the blacks would be likely to lose. At the same time management could not ignore the possibility of racial tension becoming overt, and had accepted the view put forward by the unions that this was more likely to occur at the level of a single factory than at national level.

Smith had, therefore, agreed to a compromise, whereby the existing negotiating machinery, in which management dealt with the races separately, would continue at factory level, but a joint (mixed race) co-ordinating committee would be set up at national level to iron out anomalies, without, however, encroaching upon the existing rights (protected by law) of the Industrial Council and of Liaison Committees. This (probably transitional) arrangement had still to be accepted by the black work force.

Smith in general was not in favour of craft unions and hoped that company unions, on the American model, would evolve. At the moment they saw Liaison Committees (whose powers, it will be recalled, are defined in the Bantu Labour Relations Act) as reasonable vehicles for black consultations, but they would have had no objection to blacks whose affiliation was with conventional unions serving on those committees, provided they were able to secure election. They thought a considerable number of businessmen, and the government, shared a preference for company unions, which would represent the interests of all employees, though they realised it might be interpreted as a policy, not of divide and rule, but of submerging black interests in an amorphous whole.

Smith management saw it as a major task to persuade white unions that black advancement would not entail white redundancies. For skilled work (where whites and blacks performed at the same level) parity of wages had already been achieved. In the unskilled categories there was also a rate for the job, but fringe benefits still differed racially and would continue to do so for a little time yet. The starting wage for an unskilled black was R145 a month, from which R22.40 was deducted for board and lodging when applicable. An average of a further R30 could usually be earned for overtime, shift and service allowances, bonus etc.

So far no whites were bossed by blacks. Smith's management gave the impression, however, that whilst some companies were not yet ready even to think about the problem, others, like Smith, were fully aware that this was the 'crunch' which could not be indefinitely avoided. One way to avoid the problem (but only temporarily) was to recruit for an entire category of jobs in a given factory or plant from members of the same racial groups; recently Smith had advertised, in black and white newspapers, fifty operator jobs; the best applicants were black, and were engaged.

It seemed then, and seems even more likely now, that eventually some whites are going to have to work under black bosses, though they can evade it for a time by accepting retraining. (In this connection it seemed a mistake by government to allow companies to claim tax exemption for black training schemes, but not for white retraining; the anomaly has since been corrected, though there are still complaints that the process of obtaining official approval of a training scheme is too slow). The difficulty of evading the issue indefinitely is illustrated by the labour structure in Smith's factories. Here there were eleven levels. All whites were in the top three; coloureds were to be found at every level; blacks went up as far as level ten—only one below the top.

It is worth noting, partly as an example of the extraordinary extent to which the hierarchy of colour is engrained in South African society, that it is much easier to prepare the way for coloureds than for blacks to boss whites. Much depends on the coloured man's personality and, if Smith's experience is any guide, it will be easier to bring in coloureds on a temporary basis at first, to do a particular specialised job, which does not require them to give orders to whites. Then, when the whites have become accustomed to them and accepted their expertise, it should be possible to integrate them permanently. In the opinion of a senior Smith manager who had been in the American deep south in the fifties, the South African labour situation in 1977 was very similar; but he did not detect in South Africa the hatred that had existed in the United States.

Finally, Smith were fully aware of the problems of migrant labour. Of their 10,000 black workers, 75 per cent were migrants, mainly from the Transkei and the Northern Transvaal. The company had never had to maintain a recruiting organization, because its migrants returned again and again. When returning to the same job they did not have to go through the labour bureau again, but simply obtained a signature from the Bantu Affairs Commissioner on a form provided by the company. This is the 'calling-in card' system to which companies make frequent reference in their reports under the European Community's Code of Conduct.

Over the years these long-service migrants had tended to keep their links with the company in the family, by recruiting their own relations. However an individual being employed for the first time, even if on the recommendation of his father or uncle, did have to go through the labour bureau before starting his first contract.

Migrant labourers in the semi-skilled and skilled categories were treated like ordinary industrial workers. For example, they were not allowed to take long periods of leave, for such purposes as bringing in the harvest, but had to confine themselves to four weeks' absence. Annual turnover among migrants was very low—5 per cent—which is natural enough, since if they lost a job all they could do was to go back to the homeland. Among urban employees, on the other hand, turnover was initially as high as 35–40 per cent; again the higher rate is understandable (though perhaps not this level) since urban workers have some choice of employment, provided they have obtained permission for urban residence in terms of the Urban Areas Act, or are skilled at evading the authorities' surveillance. This potential mobility is increased under the post-Riekert regulations, provided always that the intending mover has both job and accommodation at his disposal.

The company was deliberately phasing out its use of migratory labour, giving social conscience as the reason. This was going to be a slow process, however, for two main reasons. First the migrants resented losing their jobs; secondly the increased turnover mentioned above could not but lead to decreased efficiency.

Before turning to some of the views expressed by trade unionists, I shall attempt to sum up managerial attitudes to trade unions, as they were expressed in Smith and other companies and public corporations.

1. Dealing with white unions was a constant pre-occupation; they were a major, but not insurmountable, impediment to black advancement, particularly on the gold mines. Since 1977 this difficulty has diminished as the government has become more confident of its ability to retain the loyalty of the working class. This confidence is symbolized by the government's crushing of the mineworkers' strike of 1979 (see p. 195 below), but may have been severely dented by the large number of votes gained by the Herstigte Nasionale Party in the April 1981 elections, and by the 1982 split in the NP.

2. Employers on the whole would prefer to deal with company unions (US model) than craft unions (UK model). So far as white unions were concerned, employers had to deal with the ones that existed, but the situation was still flexible on the black side, because black unionism was so relatively undeveloped.

3. Employers preferred works committees or liaison committees to black trade unions. AHI policy was to have nothing whatever to do with black unions. Others did not object if they elected members to the works committees or liaison committees and some had no objection to dealing with black unions if they could demonstrate a reasonable following, and were interested in representing their members on what employers saw as 'normal' trade union interests rather than in trying to achieve strictly political goals. (There is clearly much room for disagreement here about the definition of 'reasonable' and the distinction between the economic and the political). Black unions could not be registered and their members were not (as we have seen) employees within the meaning of the Industrial Conciliation Act, but there was no legal barrier to employers negotiating with them.

81

Nor was there anything to prevent employers on an industry-wide basis agreeing to negotiate with unregistered unions. It might be difficult for all employers in a given category to agree to co-operate: on the other hand, those who were reluctant to take part might feel that they were thereby losing something.

4. If their black labour force must be unionized, employers preferred to deal with pure black unions, which at least were permitted by the law to affiliate with white ones, than with multi-racial unions, which were not. Whatever the union system, some co-ordinating machinery was needed to bring together the negotiations with all racial groups.

5. There was little incentive to deal with independent black unions— that is, ones which refused to affiliate. In any case, there were only 29 of them, with a total membership of 70,000.

WHITE TRADE UNIONS' ATTITUDES

The attitudes of white unions varied dramatically. On the right the CFL (Confederation of Labour) recognized the need for blacks to be trained 'so that they can look after themselves, in their own areas'. The CFL had no interest in black or mixed-race unions and was uninterested in overseas practice or example. Its President had, however, in his capacity as President of the Municipal Staffs Association, set up separate committees (each with a majority of white members) for black, coloured and Asian employees so that their views and grievances could be brought to his attention. This same President (Mr Artie Niewoudt) was later a member of the Wiehahn Commission and dissociated himself from virtually all its innovative proposals.

On the left (though the term is misleading) of the established union movement, the Trade Union Council of South Africa (TUCSA) unequivocally believed that all job and wage discrimination based on race should go: discrimination in favour of union members should, however, continue. Thus, the closed shop should on no account be abandoned, since TUCSA believed that no-one who was not a union member should be allowed to do work which it held to be the prerogative of its members. But this was not to say that blacks should be excluded; instead the Industrial Conciliation Act, which in other respects was regarded by TUCSA as a good piece of industrial legislation, should be amended to allow blacks to be counted as employees. (This recommendation of the Wiehahn Commission, of which TUCSA's Secretary General, Mr Arthur Grobelaar, was also a member, has of course been accepted by the government). TUCSA regarded as nonsense the claim, frequently made, that Africans are not trainable for sophisticated jobs. The same had been said in the past about Asians and coloureds.

TUCSA also believed in racially mixed unions, (where registration was recommended by Wiehahn and eventually accepted) though unions which were at present confined to whites or coloureds should not be prevented from so continuing, if they wished. Arrests and bannings had had a deleterious effect on the development of mixed unions, since some highly competent people had been removed from the scene. This, according to TUCSA, was a symptom of the government's panic whenever it identified anything which might grow into a mass movement. In fact, trade unions in South Africa made responsible use of their power, and would never seek to bring about the kind of disruptive stoppage which occurs in Britain. Nevertheless the fear of mass movements was, in TUCSA's opinion, shared by employers, some of whom put up liberal smoke-screens but, when tested, would not allow trade union organizers on their premises, nor in some cases even allow them to hold discussions with their personnel managers.

This traditional working class distrust of management was emphasized by a leading white trade unionist, who thought the stated wish of business to give the black workers a square deal concealed a more fundamental recognition that a mature economy could not be operated without black skilled labour. He thought it was basically a question, as in any industrial economy, of workers versus management and that the question to ask was 'why should this black man *not* have a union?' Why should any black have to rely on the Wage Act, which provided for the interests of blacks who had no negotiating vehicle to be looked after by officials of the Departments of Bantu Administration and Labour? (As so often this trade unionist and the Marxist commentators would find little to disagree about in the short term, provided Marxian terms were translated into everyday language).

This trade unionist knew at first hand of the difficulties of promoting mixed unions, and thought that much of the white readiness to 'extend the hand of friendship' to blacks, which had been growing in recent years, had been dissipated since the Soweto riots of 1976. His own union had been formed in 1924, with a constitution explicitly limiting membership to whites. At the TUCSA conference 'you might think you were not in South Africa' because of the multi-racial character of the assembly, but his own members would 'burst a blood vessel' if non-whites came to its annual conference or joined the executive committee. There was no hope of changing the constitution, and many others contained similar racial clauses. Nor should one forget that there were many low-paid whites, who earned as little as R200 a month, if they had done no apprenticeship.

By way of general comment it is worth adding that one problem for white South African unions is that they have little contact with fellow unionists abroad, and often the advice and exhortation they are given is of little practical value. A further problem is that South African unions are very fragmented, many are independent of TUCSA and the CFL (though some thought has been given to the rather quaint notion of a federation of unaffiliated unions) and their machinery is very centralized, so that there is little activity at factory level and little incentive for central officials to arrange training for activities away from the centre. Most unions have little

83

money and, in general, unions are at best unfashionable and at worst positively disliked by the public.

RECENT DEVELOPMENTS AT SMITH

By 1977 Smith, stimulated by the conviction that the shortage of white skills made it imperative to improve the training and conditions of blacks, had firmly laid the bases of its policy. Subsequent developments have occurred naturally within the guidelines then adopted, but there have been no startling changes in managerial thinking, nor major policy shifts.

Labour turnover continues to be a major problem, exacerbated by the trend in the company's manpower profile towards higher proportions of skilled and professional workers. So severe is the national shortage in these categories that Smith has been obliged to recruit overseas, without, however, succeeding in filling even half the vacancies.

At the level of apprentices, not enough whites were being trained to meet the demand and the process of persuading whites to allow blacks to be indentured was long and slow. There was disappointment that Wiehahn's recommendations had been watered down in practice; in particular, blacks were still not accepted in white training colleges, so that in-house training colleges had to be established for blacks. The company had, however, achieved a victory by 1980 in persuading the white trade unionist members of the apprenticeship committee to accept blacks for indentures, on condition that the number of white trainees was not reduced over the next five years and that the selection and entry qualifications were the same for blacks as for whites. The response from blacks had been enormous and four blacks had earned qualifications by the end of 1980, possibly at a standard rather above the national minimum. Smith congratulated itself on this breakthrough, especially as it was achieved at a time of white backlash, which itself was caused partly by reports of events in Zimbabwe.

A further cause for disappointment was the provision in the new legislation that all training bodies must be registered, which made it doubtful whether such bodies as the Institute for Industrial Relations would be able to continue. Smith's management was uncertain whether the government was interested primarily in policing training facilities, or in controlling the tax concessions made for training schemes.

So far as trade unions were concerned, Smith was considering requests for recognition from two unregistered unions which intended to apply for registration and recognized eight that were already registered, in accordance with its policy of recognizing unions backed by 'a significant proportion' of any group of employees. The system of internal consultation had developed in accordance with the established guidelines: in 1978 a co-ordinating committee had been formed of management and black representatives elected by the black members of the Liaison Committees in the group's various factories. Another new body was formed with equal numbers of management representatives, blacks from the co-ordinating committee and trade union representatives (who at that time were still all white) from the Industrial Council. This new body negotiates agreements which are then ratified by the Industrial Council and the co-ordinating committee.

By 1980 the proportion of migrant employees had fallen to 63 per cent from 78 per cent in December 1976, and it remained company policy to reduce the proportion further despite the greater propensity to strike of urban workers. However, since many migrants were long-serving employees their contracts would only be terminated through normal turnover. Smith was also mindful of the very limited employment opportunities in the homelands from which the migrant labour came. Furthermore, at one factory, where there was 60% turnover, it had proved impossible to obtain enough urban workers. There was little unemployment in the area, and potential workers were deterred by shift work and by thuggery at night.

The lowest basic wage in 1980 was R208.85 per month for a family of five which was above the 'lower datum levels' provided by the Johannesburg Chamber of Commerce (JCC), the University of South Africa (UNISA) and the University of Port Elizabeth (UPE), though below their 'higher datum levels'. However, with overtime and allowances the estimated average rose to R245, which was above the higher levels proposed by UNISA and UPE, though not quite up to the JCC's.

Another success with the white unions had been that management had succeeded in obtaining their agreement to promotion on merit rather than race. However, the policy was difficult to put into practice in the absence of integrated training. It was also difficult to get over the settled predisposition of white middle management to promote whites: to break this habit it might be necessary for the company to proclaim itself dedicated to black advancement rather than, as at present, to equal opportunity. In that case Smith might need to subordinate the principle of promotion strictly on merit by moving, however informally, to the establishment of racial quotas, in response to black discontent.

The industrial relations picture, then, at Smith in 1980/81 presented no surprises when compared with the background of 1977. Progress might not be as rapid as the more enlightened senior managers believed it must be if South Africa was to solve its manpower problems, but the direction of change was clear enough, and seemed irreversible.

CHAPTER 8

Trade Unions in South Africa

Since the Durban strikes of 1972/73 there has been a great advance in African trade union activity in South Africa. The unions have operated under considerable difficulties, some of which have been removed as a result of the Wiehahn Commission's first report (RSA 1979b). Despite those difficulties, the unions have been widely identified, both in South Africa and abroad, as the bodies most likely to achieve progress for Africans. Because they are not 'political' organizations and yet are judged the most likely vehicles of political progress, they have received considerable aid, mostly in the form of training, from foreign organizations, like the British Trade Union Congress, international bodies, notably the International Confederation of Free Trade Unions (ICFTU) and foreign governments. So great has the interest been that there has sometimes appeared to be competition between countries to offer overseas visits to the small number of African trade union leaders able to take advantage of them.

For the South African Government this foreign concentration on the economic, almost technical, aspects of trade unionism has made protests about foreign interference difficult. Displeasure has however been shown from time to time by the last minute refusal of passports to leaders invited overseas; at home they have frequently been arrested or banned and their white advisers live in a constant state of anxiety. These advisers have taken care to advise and not to lead; their best known contributions have been through such bodies as the Industrial Education Institute at Durban (and its publication the *South African Labour Bulletin*) and the Urban Training Project at Johannesburg.

Interest has focussed on African unionists, since they suffered until recently disabilities not extended to Indians and coloureds. African unions (some of which have non-racial constitutions) are generally called 'black unions' and I shall follow that usage.

Although in the pragmatic world of international action the concentration on trade unions seems the obvious way forward, it presents a great many difficulties to the left. Much of the literature is in little known journals produced outside South Africa, such as *Colour and Class* and *The African Communist*, but as the points made are of importance and need to be considered, I shall discuss them before moving on to an account of some developments in trade union activity in South Africa itself.

The major debate is about the conditions on which trade union activity should be recognised as 'progressive'. It is common ground that it is necessarily reformist in the short term, rather than revolutionary, but there is disagreement about whether this reformism can be turned to revolutionary account, and if so, how. The debate turns (as Hemson points out) on the relation between class struggle and racial oppression and the relations between trade union action and political struggle (Hemson 1978: 2. In the original publication he is incorrectly identified as Henson). In Hemson's view, black workers, through their struggles, develop revolutionary nationalism rather than a pure class consciousness. Failure to develop the latter means that class interests tend to become reduced to economic interests, and political practice is not based on a working class strategy.

Hemson is right to point out the danger of concentrating on economic interests if the purpose of working class action is indeed to advance the class struggle in all its aspects, not merely the economic. But it is at least doubtful whether that assumption should be made. However, Hemson merely walks round the difficulties; for, having indicated the possibility of error, he simply assumes that the special conditions of South Africa prevent the working class from falling into it. 'The possibility of reforms confusing working class action or of trade union practice becoming economistic is immediately negated by the revolutionary potential of African working class action.' Bourgeois theorists, on the other hand, insist on separating industrial from political action. 'They are determined to remove the revolutionary content from working class action' (*Ibid*: 5–7).

It is certainly the case that bourgeois or liberal theorists would not commit themselves to the view that workers who engage in 'working class action' must necessarily have revolutionary intentions, nor that such action must have revolutionary results. To make any such assumption without taking local conditions into account would be simplistic. However, Hemson is surely wrong if he thinks, as he appears to, that when liberal theorists distinguish between the political and the economic they are some way erecting barriers between the two. For the liberal the political and the economic are both aspects of social life, as for the Marxist they are facets of class struggle, and the distinction between them is made for the purpose of analysis. It may be added that, quite apart from the theoretical implications, Hemson appears to give no weight to the purely prudential arguments for concentrating on the economic aspects of trade union work.

He recognizes, and here again he is on common ground with liberals, that strikes by themselves will not produce fundamental change; indeed the point has also been taken by some white nationalists. There has been Afrikaans press comment to the effect that the white population should not be over-alarmed by strikes, which are only to be expected in industrial societies. But though strikes are not sufficient stimulus to fundamental change, they are essential to it. As Hemson says: '. . . no decisive challenge to the state is possible without this proletarian form of action to disorganize production and the state'. He rightly links reforms with pressures from such bodies as the British TUC for non-political trade unionism, but then goes on to assert, without any evidence, that 'It is debatable whether the ideology of trade unionism in the "unionism only" form is the dominant ideology of union members, much less of the black working class as a whole' (*Ibid*: 33–34).

The Durban strikes of 1973 '. . . were only possible through the leadership of the underground . . . undoubtedly spontaneous in the sense of not being planned from a political centre . . . but not unorganized' (*Ibid*: 22). Again, the evidence of organization is sparse, but the assertion is essential to Hemson's broad ideological position, since effective spontaneous action without underground organization would make the organizers redundant.

Hemson's way out of the genuine dilemma which has been posed is not to despise legal work, but to ensure that it is backed up by a revolutionary party. Unions must have a mass character. 'It is for this reason that Lenin argued that communists should support non-party unions, and distinguish the party from the trade union even in conditions of extreme repression'. The strategy must be to take advantage of the difficulty which faces the government if it is to grant demands made by legal bodies '. . . without enabling the advanced forces within the black working class to seize these opportunities as a platform to demand more fundamental concessions' (*Ibid*: 34 & 35).

In summary, Hemson quotes (from *Workers' Unity* 5, September 1977) the SACTU position on trade unions which take up a non-political stance in order to avoid being smashed:

> There are, of course, not a few reformists, opportunists, and even collaborators —but there are also many who walk a tightrope of personal danger in truly serving the struggle of the working class . . . our policy is to fight for independent trade unions and to give these new organisations our support—in as far as they advance the workers' struggle (*Ibid*: 35).

Thus, Hemson, who has also, as we have seen in Chapter 4, associated himself with the view that SACTU is largely ineffectual, nevertheless leaves the way open to bodies inside South Africa to continue the struggle, while leaving those bodies (as well as liberals and the South African Government) in no doubt as to the course the struggle will take in future if work within the Republic eventually makes possible the establishment of an effective revolutionary party. So the immediate objective of various organizations and individuals is the same, namely to promote black trade unions, but long-term hopes and intentions are very different.

Other authors have discussed the use that could be made of the official industrial relations system. The anonymous author of 'The way forward from Soweto' states that as a means to building up SACTU 'It is, for example, necessary to examine more closely the use that can be made of the factory and liaison committee system . . . The building of legal trade unions in fascist conditions calls for a flexible application of general policy'

(*The African Communist* 1977: 43). On the other hand, Douwes Decker, a lecturer in the University of the Witwatersrand who had advocated just such a policy, namely that available works committees should be used, and gradually absorbed, by unregistered trade unions, is attacked by Hemson because 'The strategy which he offered encouraged a particularly limited form of trade unionism, which blends in with, rather than challenging, the state apparatus'. Here, however, it seems likely that Douwes Decker is being attacked less for the strategy he recommended, which had the merit of being legal and feasible, but because of a deeper ideological division (Hemson 1978: 26).

The divisions within the black union movement in the Republic are to an extent reproduced among commentators outside, though on the left, as we have seen, no legal activity is considered adequate by itself. For example, Drake Koka, formerly of the Black and Allied Workers Union (BAWU) and now in exile, is attacked for approving a training project offered by the USA and accused of using the same white liberals' language as does Buthelezi; rather surprisingly, Koka's Roman Catholic upbringing is not mentioned in the attack. This aggressive attitude in turn relates to the fear among Marxists (which has been mentioned in Chapter 4), that the South African Government will be successful in detaching sections of the black bourgeoisie and petty bourgeoisie from the liberation movement (*The African Communist* 1977: 37), Thus, according to Hemson, BAWU is doubly disgraced, both for its reformism and for its links with the Black Consciousness Movement (Hemson 1978: 24).

Hemson distinguishes four 'tendencies' in the 'open' trade union movement. First, the Urban Training Project (UTP), which is explicitly 'non-political' and seeks accommodation within the works committee system. [These characteristics explain Hemson's disapproval of Douwes Decker, mentioned above, who was associated with the Urban Training Project.] Secondly, there is the 'subordinate' union tendency of Johannesburg (these are more usually known as 'parallel' unions which operate in parallel with white registered unions); third come the 'mobilizing' unions (which as mobilizers deserve qualified approval) of the then Trades Union Advisory Coordinating Council (TUACC) which started in Natal and was later also organised in the Transvaal through the Industrial Aid Society. TUACC has subsequently grown into the Federation of South African Trade Unions (FOSATU), whose difficult birth has been well described by Phil Bonner (1979). Its difficulties arose from rivalries between groups of unions and from an inordinately complicated structure of committees at provincial and national level, with consequent lack of communication between committees. This subservience to provincial boundaries, perhaps in part imposed by the size of the country and great distances between centres, seems to characterize many South African bodies which can ill afford to waste their meagre resources.

The fourth tendency is '. . . The "nationalistic" Black Allied Workers' Union (BAWU) which is the workers' arm of the Black People's

Convention (now legally prohibited) and expresses black consciousness ideology *and an ambiguous attitude towards capital*, (Hemson 1978: 24, emphasis added).

Another Marxist author, David Davis, gives further details of the union groupings. When he wrote (1976) 21 African trade unions existed, of four of which little was known. The remainder were divided into three groups, those associated with TUACC (now FOSATU), the Urban Training Project and the Trade Union Congress of South Africa (TUCSA):

TUACC	6 unions	10,870 members	
UTP	7	7,900	
TUCSA	4	20,250 *	
Others	4	1,070	
21		40,090	(Davis 1976: 94–95)

* *Note*: This figure includes Miss Lucy Mvubelo's National Union of Clothing Workers, with 18,500 members, also stated by Davis on the preceding page as 23,000. The recent 'official' history of SACTU states that, despite the TUCSA affiliation, there is to this day a solid SACTU faction within this union (Luckhardt & Wall 1980: 222).

Davis' total membership figure agrees with that given by Du Toit two years earlier (quoted in D. Thomas 1980: 92). Since then there has been considerable growth, as may be seen from the various figures quoted below. It should be noted that, as Robin Smith says, 'There are wide variations in the estimates of Trade Union membership as the higher estimates are based on enrolled and the lower on paid up membership' (Smith 1980: 68, footnote 1). Wiehahn puts the proportion of the latter to the former at 70% (RSA 1979b: para. 3.35.1.).

Since these figures were produced, a number of developments have occurred. In September 1980 the Council of Unions of South Africa (CUSA—comprising nine Unions, according to the SAIRR) was formed from the old Consultative Committee of Black Unions (CCBU) and has nine member unions with an estimated membership of 30,000. Seven FOSATU unions had, by the end of 1980, received Governmental permission to open their constitutions to all races. TUCSA, with 60 unions and 286,555 membership, removed all reference to race from its constitution. In 1981 membership soared again (SAIRR 1981: 164–7 and 1982: 181–3).

Though Davis' figures remain out of date, his comments on the various groups are not. He has little time for the UTP, which is reformist and presses for purely black, rather than non-racial, unions. BAWU, its offshoot, is unable to distinguish between the ill-disposed whites within TUCSA and '. . . white activity elsewhere within the labour movement': in other words, it does not properly appreciate the contribution of any whites, however progressive their credentials, to the process of black liberation. As for Lucy Mvubelo, she is seen by Davis as 'white supremacy's willing dupe within the black labour movement.' He looks back as far as 1959, when she,

Number and Membership of Black Trade Unions in South Africa

Source and date of data	SAIRR: end 1979 Unions.	SAIRR: end 1979 Membership	SAIRR: end 1981 Unions	SAIRR: end 1981 Membership	Wiehahn: Unions.	May 1978 Membership	Smith: Unions.	Smith: Membership
Affiliation FOSATU (formerly TUACC)	9[1]	45,000[2]	10	94,617			10[3]	30,400
UTP	5							
CCBU	4							
CUSA							7	10,000
(formerly CCBU)			8	49,000				
TUCSA	7			63,000[4]	11[5]		11	32,000
Unregistered unaffiliated	5		14				2	12,000
Total	30				27	50,000–70,000[6]	30	84,400

Sources: South African Institute of Race Relations 1980: 264–5; 1982: 181–3
RSA 1979b: para. 3.35.1.
Smith 1980: 67–68.

Notes:
1. FOSATU also had four Coloured affiliates, of which three were registered.
2. For eight African and four Coloured Unions, at April 1980.
3. In addition, Smith notes two Coloured affiliates.
4. Sixty unions were affiliated to TUCSA, with 209,000 Coloured and Indian members, 97,000 white and 63,000 black.
5. Wiehahn identifies these unions as parallel, but does not explicitly state that they are affiliated to TUCSA.
6. Elsewhere Wiehahn estimates membership at 55–70,000 (RSA 1979b: para. 3.17.1 (iv)).

with help from the ICFTU, formed the Federation of Free African Trade Unions of South Africa (FOFATUSA) '. . . with the aim of weakening SACTU and breaking the link between the political organisation of the people, the ANC, and the African trade union movement'. More recently, in 1973, she successfully opposed a resolution at the AFL-CIO's annual conference in Miami, which would have called on the American labour movement to give SACTU full support as '. . . the only trade union movement that is recognised by the Black South Africans and the United Nations'. In the end all reference to SACTU was deleted from the resolution (Davis 1976: 101–102; see also Luckhardt and Wall 1980, especially 381 ff. where it becomes clear that SACTU's antipathy for ICFTU results partly from the latter's willingness, once it found it could not persuade SACTU to become a 'non-political' reformist organisation, to '. . . slander SACTU as a "communist front"', so that it is not surprising that SACTU affiliated to the World Federation of Trade Unions (WFTU) in 1955. Furthermore, the short-lived rival FOFATUSA had 'a Pan-Africanist Congress (PAC) leadership looking for a base amongst African workers').

There is certainly a case to be made against TUCSA, whose attitude towards black unions has vacillated over the years. However, in recent years, before black unions could be registered, TUCSA settled on a policy of 'adopting' parallel unions, so that they could, at least in theory, have the benefits of registration at one remove, and send delegates to the annual TUCSA conference. Furthermore, at TUCSA's 1979 conference its President spoke out against the government's initial refusal (later reversed) to allow migrant blacks to join trade unions and against the ban on racially mixed unions. (He may, of course, have done this with an eye to the growth in trade unionism which must follow Wiehahn.) At the same conference a motion supporting the strikers at Fatti's and Moni's and Eveready was only narrowly defeated, after a recount (SAIRR 1980: 265).

Clearly, TUCSA's style is reformist and non-confrontational and it is fairly generally acknowledged that the parallel system, which since Wiehahn has lost its *raison d'être*, was unsatisfactory. But Davis' case, which is as much a loyal defence of SACTU as an attack on TUCSA, is unlikely to make converts amongst those who do not already believe that SACTU is indeed the only legitimate representative of black South African unionism and that the political and economic struggles should in no circumstances be separated.

Davis is somewhat less antagonistic to TUACC, as it then was called. Even this body, however, failed to inculcate revolutionary working class theory and therefore fell into economism. Furthermore, its militancy attracted the attention of the then Bureau of State Security (BOSS); consequently, its leaders failed to deliver the goods, and were upstaged by their members' spontaneous action. Of TUACC's journal, the *South African Labour Bulletin*, Davis says '. . . a heavily academic journal, the Bulletin nevertheless feels compelled to reassure the regime by sinking to

anti-Soviet smears and fashionable references to "Soviet imperialism"'
(Davis 1976: 96–98).

The detachment of some outsiders from the practicalities of life in South
Africa is well illustrated by that quotation and by Davis' conclusion that
the way forward is for the UTP and other bodies 'to grab the opportunities
available and unite with the TUACC unions within a single black union
federation'. The final objective of such an alliance must be for SACTU to
provide an umbrella for them all. 'In no way can a genuine working class
organisation therefore attempt to isolate itself from the struggle for
political rights without betraying the interests of its members' (*Ibid*: 103).

It must not, however, be thought that all Marxists are equally convinced
of the importance of SACTU. 'A Reader' in *The African Communist* has
argued that it is entirely wrong to say that no substantial or lasting
concessions can be got without smashing the whole system. On the
contrary, 'the idea that every gain won by the working class is merely
absorbed by capital to its own advantage totally underestimates the gains
in many spheres made by the working class in different countries'. This
author rejects the view that the trade union movement should put forward
general demands which cannot possibly be met, instead of specific ones
which perhaps could be. In general he considers that 'This "over-
politicization" of the trade union sphere leads above all to the obliteration
of the specific role of the revolutionary trade union movement . . .' Finally,
he takes SACTU on on its own ground by declaring that, apart from
considerations of personal interest, the exaggeration of SACTU's
importance '. . . lies in the economistic conception of the political struggle
and a related underestimation of the importance of class alliances in the
struggle'. SACTU should recognize that although its own role lies in the
work place, it should nevertheless allow some place in the struggle for other
classes (*The African Communist* 1980: 81–89).

It is remarkable that such a criticism should appear in such a journal, for
there is little in the above which could not be translated into terms readily
acceptable to liberals. This again illustrates the large amount of common
ground that exists, at least in relation to short-term tactics.

Throughout the debate runs the theme, noticed in an earlier chapter, of
the precise role of the whites in the revolution. A recent Communist
formulation holds that:

> It is also in the long-term interests of the non-exploiting section of the white
> population to participate in the anti-racist, anti-fascist struggle. The main
> content of the struggle is the national liberation of the African people—a
> struggle led by a revolutionary alliance headed by the African National
> Congress and which includes the South African Communist Party.
>
> (*The African Communist* 1978: 17)

This carefully worded formulation does not, however, accord with
present reality. For one thing the removal of impediments to black
advancement must lead, as Robert Davies observes, to '. . . some
heightening of the struggle between capital and white wage earners'

(Davies 1979: 192). That struggle however is made less abrasive by the process of softening up (which Davies calls 'ideological class struggle') upon which Ministers insist before endorsing measures which damage white working class interests. This concern for the white working class exists because (and here we come back to the role of the state in capitalist society) '. . . the bourgeois state exists as the factor of cohesion and locus of class struggle of a capitalist social formation and not as the mere instrument of the dominant classes . . .' (*Ibid*: 193). It has still to be explained why the white working class tends to identify itself with the dominant whites, rather than the exploited blacks. However, instead of explaining, Davies here provides yet another example of the removal of problems by careful use of words, for in his view the white working class will give relatively little trouble to the South African Government when it reduces the white workers' privileges; this is because of '. . . the fundamental political polarization of the white wage-earning class towards the bourgeoisie' and '. . . the new petty bourgeois class determination of most white wage earners'. Davies adds that '. . . to imagine that the removal (from white workers) of specific economic concessions will automatically produce changes in political polarization, would be crude economism', but he does not say what causes the workers' present polarization towards the bourgeoisie, nor why they have a petty bourgeois determination (*Ibid*: 193–94). Presumably the missing link is race or ethnicity, but in that case Davies, despite his Marxist vocabulary, is himself showing an intellectual determination or polarization which comes perilously close to the liberal. Indeed, he seems to be expressing (capitalist) common sense.

Such quotations as the following, from the author of 'The Road from Soweto', may help to explain why white workers tend towards the bourgeoisie or petty bourgeoisie:

> The black working class must be on its guard against attempts by the white trade union movement to control the growth of black workers' organisations in industry. It is only when the white workers stop collaborating with our class enemy and act as part of a united working class that they will be welcomed as brothers.
>
> (*The African Communist* 1977: 42–3)

As so often, the source and wording of the message diminish its impact. There is little in the sentiments themselves which Miss Mvubelo (the reformist leader of the National Union of Clothing Workers) or Mr Grobelaar (Secretary-General of TUCSA) would reject. Indeed, TUCSA itself asserts the brotherhood of black and white workers, when it insists that it has no objection to blacks entering the closed shop, its purpose as a trades union body being simply to ensure that the closed shop policy is enforced. But a call to action by the Communist Party is hardly likely to make friends in South Africa.

Another author, Simon Clarke, writing during the South African recession, took a rather different view from that of Davies of white responses to black advancement. He rightly predicted increased white working class militancy, but wrongly thought that 'It is certainly to be expected that capital and the state will turn this militancy against the black working class' (Clarke 1978: 71). In fact, it would be truer to say that the white working class was unequivocally shown that the government (or 'state apparatus') intended to maintain the slow improvement of black labour conditions when it crushed the illegal strike by 6,500 mineworkers in March 1979, which started in sympathy with the strike at O'Kiep mine against the employment of skilled coloureds (Cooper 1980: 47). The mineworkers' strike is well recorded in a special issue of the *South African Labour Bulletin* (October 1979), though perhaps too little is made of its symbolic importance for the white working class as a whole. Furthermore, none of the contributors mentions the personal antagonism between the Minister of Labour, Mr S. P. Botha, and Mr Ari Paulus, the miners' leader. Their personal feelings were known and a confrontation was predicted well before the strike occurred—another example of the importance of the personal factor in great events.

Clarke draws attention (as does O'Dowd from a very different point of view and in rather different language) to the difficulty for the government of containing the political struggle generated by the intensification of class conflict in the economic sphere. Here he is surely correct, as he is in predicting that the government will respond with a mixture of concessions and heightened repression. Neither government nor O'Dowd, however, would welcome Clarke's conclusion that the task of the revolutionary must be to use the contradiction '. . . and to drive the struggle on to the point at which the proletariat can take its place as the ruling class' (Clarke 1978: 72).

It is not difficult for liberals and Marxists to agree on the reasons for such improvements in black labour conditions as have occurred. There is also a considerable measure of agreement that they are important, though they are interpreted in different ways. Government and business men use them as propaganda (much of it true) to support the view that 'real' change is under way in South Africa; Marxists see them as fighting back by the bourgeoisie against the march of history.

As Robert Davies puts it, the reforms which began before Professor Wiehahn's series of reports were '. . . important moves in the class struggle (which) will figure prominently in resurgent reformist ideologies directed both inside the country and abroad'. Almost certainly job reservation and similar practices were no longer in the interest of the bourgeoisie, because of the shortage of skilled labour which could only be met by opening skilled jobs to Africans. The removal of job reservation '. . . does represent a limited but real victory for the popular masses. But it is a victory which it is quite certain the bourgeoisie will attempt to turn to its advantage'. The task, therefore, is to devise new counter-strategies (Davies 1979: 181–2 & 197).

To the question of why the bourgeoisie had found it necessary to mount this 'offensive struggle' for change now, rather than in the sixties or

95

seventies, he replies that *ad hoc* measures to 'float' the colour bar upwards, combined with foreign investment, had previously been sufficient. But in the international climate of the late seventies, foreign investment was lacking, probably as a result of the Soweto riots: furthermore, the economy was in crisis, and at such times capitalism can no longer bear inefficiency.

This explanation is adequate as far as it goes, but it does not explain the continuing pressure for reform in industrial relations which went on through the subsequent boom years, a boom fuelled largely by the high price of gold and lively foreign investment interest. It seems more fruitful, therefore, to see the capitalists' unease as a motive for change sufficiently strong to survive fluctuations in the economy, strong enough, indeed, both to persuade the government to set up the Wiehahn Commission and to translate some of its proposals into reformist legislation. I turn now to a consideration of the Wiehahn and Riekert proposals.

CHAPTER 9

The Wiehahn and Riekert Commissions

The appointment of the Wiehahn and Riekert Commissions and their subsequent reports, with the report of the Schlebusch Commission on the constitution (which will be discussed in Chapter 14), represent the most important outward and visible signs so far of the new climate of thinking among the Afrikaner élite.

Professor Wiehahn (of the University of South Africa) was appointed by the State President on 21 June 1977 to lead a Commission of Enquiry into Labour Legislation and to report and make recommendations on the whole field of labour relations in South Africa. The Commissioners set themselves a gruelling programme of meetings until Christmas 1977 and at first were generally expected to report in January 1978, so that legislation could be passed through the 1978 session of Parliament. That timetable proved over optimistic and in the end the report was presented to the State President on 15 February 1979 and laid before Parliament in June (RSA 1979b). It then transpired that this was only the first of a series of reports to be prepared by the Commission.

It was apparently left to Wiehahn to choose his thirteen fellow Commissioners, no easy task, given the need to include at least token black, coloured and Asian representatives and the fact that some of the others, like the Presidents of the right wing Confederation of Labour (CFL) and of the Trades Union Council of South Africa (TUCSA) could hardly have been left out. With this very mixed membership, it seemed highly unlikely that the Commission would be able to produce a unanimous report, and as it turned out there were minority reports on almost all the important points.

Dr Riekert (Economic Adviser to the Prime Minister and Chairman of his Economic Advisory Council) faced no problem of unanimity, since he sat as sole Commissioner. He was appointed in August 1977 to look into a range of Acts (including such fundamental legislation as the Group Areas Act) not already covered by Wiehahn and throughout his enquiry maintained close liaison with the Wiehahn Commission. His task was enormously wide, since he had also to examine regulations and administrative practices related to the Acts listed in his Commission, as well as '. . . all other acts, excluding those administered by the Departments of Labour and Mines' and '. . . ordinances of provincial administrations and by-laws of local authorities' in order to produce a comprehensive report on all legislation relating to the utilization of manpower, with the exception of laws administered by the Departments of Labour and Mines. Riekert hoped to complete this huge Commission within a year, if only because he was in his last year of government service before retirement. His preoccupation was to improve human relations 'across the board' at almost any cost. He believed that great changes were inevitably coming to South Africa—his Commission and Wiehahn's would simply give an administrative push to forces which were already in operation. He hoped to scrap a great many laws and regulations and to assimilate to 'normal' legislation, many which only applied to blacks. He was in favour of black equality so far as jobs and wages were concerned, but did not underestimate the difficulties imposed by the recession and by white unemployment. His report was presented to the State President on 29 August 1978, and published on 8 May 1979 (RSA 1979a).

The Riekert report is an immense work, which future students of the utilization of labour in South Africa will no doubt regard as the most authoritative available of the position as it stood in 1978. The report was the subject of a subsequent White Paper and has also been widely commented upon by academics and others, notably in a valuable special issue of the *South African Labour Bulletin* (November 1979; see also Thomas 1981). It will be dealt with only in outline in this chapter, the bulk of which is devoted to the Wiehahn report.

Dr Riekert's recommendations, although they improve the opportunities of urban Africans, do so at the price of ensuring that unemployment remains in the homelands or is exported to them. (For a detailed study of unemployment in KwaZulu see Claassens 1979.) His overriding concern was to ensure that black workers who have permission to live permanently in the black townships on the peripheries of white towns and cities should not be wasted. Such workers, therefore, whose permission to reside derives from Section 10 of the Blacks (Urban Areas Act of 1945 (formerly known as the Natives (Urban Areas) Act and of course amended since 1945) should, under the new Black Labour Regulations made to put Riekert's proposals into effect, find their conditions of residence and work-seeking significantly eased, while those who have no such permission will find their access to the urban areas and to legal work considerably reduced. This tightening up is to be achieved in two ways; on the one hand the system of labour bureaux and influx control will be rendered more efficient, so that labour is only released from the homelands in response to demand in the white areas. On the other hand, employers who employ labour illegally (that is, workers who have not been recruited through a labour bureau, or who lack qualifications under section 10 of the Urban Areas Act) will be subject to heavy fines or even imprisonment. Draft bills, prepared for Dr Koornhof, the Minister of Co-operation and Development, late in 1980, suggested that the officials responsible for them were not in

98

sympathy with Riekert, since the bills would probably have destroyed section 10 rights. They were, however, allowed to fade away.

Future historians may well see Dr Riekert as the meeting point of two great strands in white South African thinking. On the one hand his belief in a grand design, whereby the movement of people and all the details of their housing and employment can be minutely controlled by governmental regulation, places him squarely in the Verwoerdian tradition. Such a belief in the potential mastery by man of his environment is open to the same kinds of objection as confront the more ambitious Marxists. It has been gently mocked by that humane Afrikaner W. A. de Klerk (De Klerk 1976), whose mockery has itself been sharply criticized by one of his Marxist reviewers (O'Meara 1977). One saving grace of the 'grand design' has been that it has not worked with complete efficiency, so that unqualified Africans have tended to slip through the net. One of Dr Riekert's main purposes was to put a stop to this.

On the other hand, Dr Riekert stands in the tradition of Senator Fagan, whose report in 1948 urged white South Africans to accept blacks as permanent residents in the towns, rather than visitors who were to be allowed to stay only as long as their services were required in the white economy. That line of thought was decisively interrupted by the National Party's victory of 1948, but has now been as decisively revived by Dr Riekert. The fact that the broad outline of his recommendations has been accepted by the South African Government is of the utmost importance, not only because 'suitably qualified' urban blacks will never again be seen as temporary sojourners. It also opens the way to the abandonment of the 'ideal' that eventually there should be no black citizens of white South Africa. Nothing can prevent that abandonment from being seen as a major shift in policy, but the prior acceptance of the principal of black permanence would give such a *volte face* additional plausibility and render it less unacceptable to the white electorate. Similarly, if blacks are to live permanently outside the homelands, it becomes easier to convince the electorate that arrangements for the urban blacks' political representation are not merely desirable, but imperative.

Where Dr Riekert straddles two traditions, Professor Wiehahn belongs firmly to the 'new thinkers', the *verligtes*, within Afrikanerdom. It is reasonable to assume that he, as well as liaising with Dr Riekert, will have discussed his findings in some detail with the government well before the report was presented. The result was that his first report accorded in most respects with the thinking of the more *verligte* members of the government and the subsequent white paper was laudatory in tone (RSA 1979c). Many of Wiehahn's recommendations were accepted in whole or in part; the main reservation, though moderately expressed, was that Wiehahn, in pursuit of the acceptable goal of minimal governmental intervention in industrial relations, had perhaps under-estimated the degree of state involvement which it would be necessary to retain.

The principles underlying Professor Wiehahn's approach were expounded by him in a speech at Palm Springs, California on 19 June 1979. The six principles, which he described as 'inherent in any modern system for the regulation of industrial relations' were: the right to work; freedom of association; the rights to bargain collectively and to withhold labour; the right to protection (e.g. workmen's compensation and unemployment benefits) and the right to be trained. The Commission was also strongly influenced by consideration of the pressures exerted by foreigners, so that South Africa needed to justify itself internationally and to ensure that South African methods of industrial relations did not develop in accordance with foreign models for lack of sufficient guidance at home. This preoccupation with the international dimension becomes clear from a number of passages in the report and in several contexts. For example, the report is suspicious of foreign money and training for unregistered African unions; furthermore, the Commissioners believed that such unions are seen by non-labour bodies abroad as vehicles for change in South Africa not strictly confined to the labour movement.

The government accepted a number of Wiehahn's recommendations in the White Paper and brought them into effect in the new Industrial Conciliation Amendment Act (No. 94 of 1979), which came into force on 1 October 1979. Only the more important points will be commented on here:

1. The government endorsed the recommendation that a National Manpower Commission should be created and it was, in fact, swiftly set up, with effect from 1 November 1979.

2. The government accepted Wiehahn's overall approach to industrial relations, as indicated in the Commission's report:

> . . . the fundamental principles underlying all adjustments to South Africa's industrial relations legislation should be: The preservation of industrial peace as a primary objective; the establishment and growth of a unitary and integrated industrial relations system incorporating both the industrial council and committee systems; the fullest possible expression of the principle of self-governance; and the simultaneous promotion of decentralised consultation and negotiation at regional and enterprise levels. (RSA 1979c: para. 6.1)

It is worth commenting here that by no means all industrial relations specialists accept that a primary purpose should be the preservation of peace. Douwes Decker, for example, sees the objectives more in terms of the regulation of conflict and the adjustment of power (see p. 119).

The dual system of industrial relations is, as we have seen, given legislative effect by the Industrial Relations Act of 1924 (for Industrial Councils) and the Blacks Labour Relations Regulation Act of 1953. The former provides that agreements reached between employers and trade unions in an Industrial Council should have the force of law. Therefore, the conditions which had to be satisfied before a strike could legally be called were extremely tough. Africans were excluded from registered trade unions (the only ones which could be represented on Industrial Councils) by the provision that only employees could be members of such unions. 'Employee' was defined to exclude Africans, though to include coloureds and Asians, but the 1924 Act was amended in 1956 to prevent the further registration of racially mixed unions, and to ensure that those that already existed had white executives and that their branches were racially segregated. In 1977, 41 mixed unions survived, of which 4 were in the process of cancellation (RSA 1979b: para. 3.17.1).

The Black Labour Relations Act provided an alternative system, initially of Works Committees and, by an amendment in 1973, Liaison Committees as well. Under this Act the conditions for a legal strike were even more stringent than those provided under the Industrial Conciliation Act. (For a detailed consideration of the conditions imposed by both Acts see Cooper 1980). Whereas the Industrial Conciliation Act provided for negotiations at an industry wide level in the Industrial Council, committees operated only at the level of the individual enterprise.

3. The government accepted with some reservation the recommendations that any individual should be allowed to join any union, subject to the proviso that unions should be free to prescribe in their constitutions whatever qualifications for membership they deemed suitable, including qualifications of race. Furthermore, according to the Wiehahn report, any union: 'which meets the requirements for registration in the restructured system should, irrespective of the colour, race or sex of its members, be eligible for registration and full participation in the bargaining and dispute prevention and settlement machinery provided for in a statute common to all' (RSA 1979b: para. 3.72). The government accepted the principle of freedom of association but at first confined membership to 'individuals in fixed employment', that is, non-migrants:

> . . . the most important need of the day is to give Black workers who are in permanent jobs, and who therefore constitute a permanent part of the labour force, access to machinery which was in the first instance developed for and is being utilised by South Africa's permanent labour force . . . the Government is not inclined to admit, without further reflection and advice on the probable impact of such a step, large numbers of temporary workers to the trade union movement at precisely a time when the industrial relations system is being subjected to heavy demands in terms of innovation and adjustment (RSA 1979c: para. 6.2.1).

Thus, for the time being, the right of trade union membership was restricted to permanent residents who were in fixed employment. However, the Minister intended to seek early guidance from the new National Manpower Commission on how the regulations should be administered and the criteria upon which he should grant exemptions.

The rejection of Wiehahn's recommendation that migrant workers should be eligible for union membership was very widely condemned.

However, some commentators also pointed out that Wiehahn's advocacy of migrants' inclusion could hardly be termed enthusiastic, since he had taken pains to emphasise the difficulties which would face unions if they decided to recruit migrants (see e.g. *SALB* August 1979: 60). It is not possible to estimate the extent to which the Minister took note of the protests, but he did quite quickly use the powers conferred on him to admit migrants after all (except those from states which are not, or were not, part of the Republic) so removing one of the main planks upon which dissatisfaction with the Wiehahn report had rested (White Paper on Part II of the Wiehahn Report, RSA 1980b: para. 3.3).

It was assumed in the White Paper that racially mixed unions would not be allowed to register, but at the Committee stage of the Industrial Conciliation Amendment Bill 'the Minister was empowered to register mixed unions where the number of employees of different population groups made it expedient to do so' (*SALB* 1979: 27).

4. The government accepted the recommendations that statutory provision should be made for provisional registration of trade unions and employers' organizations, but that existing bodies should not be required to re-register. Provisional registration would, the government thought:

> ... provide protection especially to employee organisations during the organising activities that precede full recognition, that it will help to ensure that representative organisations comply with stringent requirements and maintain high standards, and that the possibility of premature recognition of unstable organisations will in this way be obviated (RSA 1979c: para. 6.4).

Registration was to be a necessary condition of agreements enforceable under statute being made between employer and employee (*Ibid*: para. 6.10); Of course unregistered unions would still be able to make agreements enforceable at common law, though the point is not made in the White Paper.

5. Not surprisingly, the government accepted the retention of the existing prohibition of political activities by trade unions. The passage in which it did so nicely encapsulates much official South African thinking on the subject, in particular the division which is so strictly (and misguidedly) made between the economic and the political:

> The Government is well aware of the dangers of unbridled political activity by trade unions. Industrial relations solely concerns the relationship between the parties in the work context, and politics has no place there. In this regard South Africa has an enviable record which must be maintained at all costs.
> With this in mind, and especially in view of the onslaught at present being directed at South Africa and the efforts which will undoubtedly be made to exploit the industrial relations system for political gain, the Government accepts these recommendations (*Ibid*: para. 6.5).

6. The government also accepted that under the new dispensation it should appoint financial inspectors to examine minutely the affairs of Industrial Councils, employers' organizations, federations of employers'

organizations, and so on. Although all kinds of bodies connected with industrial relations are included in the list, it does, however, seem that the government was principally concerned to inspect the books of black trade unions.

7. The Government noted that the Wiehahn Commission sought to strengthen both industrial relations at the level of an industry as a whole, through the Industrial Council, and at the level of the enterprise, through the committee system. (Rather confusingly, Liaison Committees were henceforth to be called 'works councils'). The government endorsed the dual intention and the recommendation to bring the two sets of arrangements together into a unitary system, which Wiehahn made on the basis of the West German system. He did not think foreign models could simply be transplanted, but the Commission was interested to learn that in Germany 'centralized and decentralized consultation and negotiation are not conducted in isolation, but are co-ordinated through the system of interlinkage between the two levels' (RSA 1979b: para. 3.117). However, in the new system, minorities (for which read 'whites') must be protected and allowed to establish a separate organization if they so wish (RSA 1979c: para. 6.7.2).

The government accepted, further, that although works committees and works councils could not be allowed to arrogate to themselves the power of Industrial Councils to conclude legally binding agreements, nevertheless the former bodies should be encouraged and strengthened as much as possible. Where no Industrial Councils existed, the objective (within the foreseeable future) would be to give the bodies 'the same autonomy as industrial councils. It must be remembered that the principles of self-governance and decentralization, imply devolution of decision-making to the lowest possible level' (*Ibid*: para. 6.7.4).

8. The extension of trade union rights to Africans, who will now be represented by (registered) unions on Industrial Councils, meant that whites, though not mentioned as such, needed further protection. The Commission recommended, and the government accepted, that this should be done by:

a) introducing 'a statutory requirement of strict parity in the representation of the various employee parties to the council'; b) allowing existing members of an Industrial Council to veto the admission of new ones; c) inserting clauses in Industrial Councils' constitutions stating the procedure for handling the deadlock which might arise from the exercise of the veto; d) recourse to the Industrial Court (whose setting up was recommended by the Commission and accepted in the White Paper) (*Ibid*: para. 6.9.).

Although it accepted the right of veto, which has, understandably, been widely attacked, the government did qualify its acceptance, though in words of some obscurity. The government was confident:

... that the parties to industrial councils will apply these mechanisms judiciously. Any ill-considered or insensitive action in this connection could inflict grave harm on relations between the population groups ... The

103

Government will not hesitate to halt any undesirable trends which may emerge or to intervene to protect an injured party should the existing measures prove inadequate (*Ibid*).

In Parliament the Bill was amended to allow an appeal to the Industrial Court against a veto. Nevertheless, the at present unregistered African unions are likely to be gravely disadvantaged, because existing members of Industrial Councils will probably prefer to admit parallel unions, that is, black unions linked to white ones (*South African Labour Bulletin* August 1979: 63).

9. The Commission was divided on the question of the closed shop and the government (pending further advice from the National Manpower Commission) sided with the minority, which found against the practice. The government decided to suspend the right to reach closed shop agreements, but would allow those already in existence to continue. Again, the decision seems to have been influenced by the new rights of Africans:

> Untenable threats to labour peace within individual enterprises and in entire industries, with an undertone of racial conflict, are foreseen should it be possible to conclude agreements of this nature with one or more trade unions in a situation of racially-based trade union plurality (RSA 1979c: para. 6.11).

10. On the deduction by employers of trade union membership fees (known in the USA as the 'check-off' system) the government was unenthusiastic, but agreed that it could continue for registered unions only, and subject to safe-guards for the individual.

11. The government gives the impression of having ducked out from under some of the Commission's trickier recommendations. It did, however, accept that the principle of work reservation (i.e. reservation of certain categories of jobs for whites) should be abolished and that, subject to consultation with all the parties concerned, the few (at that time five) remaining work reservation determinations should be phased out (*Ibid*: 6.13.1 & 6.13.4). On the other hand, it reacted with caution to the Commission's view that work reservation should be eliminated in the mining industry, subject to the negotiation of suitable safeguards (for whites) between the parties concerned, and to the suggestion that the Industrial Council system should be extended to the mining industry, which had hitherto been excluded from it. Such questions, it thought, should be left to the parties concerned (*Ibid*: 6.14) and a similar line was taken over such principles as 'equal pay for work of equal value' (*Ibid*: 6.13.3).

12. The government accepted the establishment of an Industrial Court, which would interpret labour laws and regulations, hear cases of 'irregular and undesirable labour practices such as unjustified or unfair changes in the established labour pattern of an employer', (effectively, a change from white to black labour) and generally pronounce upon legal questions arising from the industrial relations system (*Ibid*: 7.3).

13. The Commission got to grips with the extremely important question of apprenticeship training for blacks outside the homelands, which was

already possible for artisans in the building trade but not otherwise. The government accepted that in future anyone might become an apprentice anywhere in the Republic, though, perhaps disingenuously, it based its agreement on the presumed benefits which would eventually accrue to the homelands if their citizens were trained outside (*Ibid*: 8.1.1). It was provided by the Commission and accepted by the government that any application for indentures must continue to be approved by the relevant Apprenticeship Committee, (which would, of course, be controlled by whites). The obvious difficulties are hinted at in part two of the Wiehahn report and in the White Paper on it, though once again the government approaches the matter with some circumspection. The Commission recommended that:

> The National Apprenticeship Board constantly keeps itself informed of those factors that militate against the indenturing of apprentices, and submits its views on appropriate actions in such instances also to the National Manpower Commission (RSA 1980a: para. 3.22.1).

The government replied in equally polite language that the Board had always kept itself informed, etc. The White Paper continues:

> In the light of the adaptation of official policy with regard to the indenturing of apprentices . . . namely that persons of all population groups should be permitted to be indentured as apprentices, the Government trusts that the Board in fulfilling its functions in this connection will be mindful of the changed line of policy (RSA 1980b: 4.1.1).

Thus the dialogue proceeds by nods and winks.

14. Finally, the Commission recommended that the provision of segregated facilities (lavatories, canteens, etc.) should no longer be subject to law, but should be regulated by the parties involved, either at industry level or in particular work places. The government accepted the recommendation, but once again is cautious. It:

> . . . wishes to record its firm intention of not permitting employers to exceed the prudent rate of development in this regard . . . By its very nature this is a delicate matter which must be approached circumspectly in order to avoid injury to intergroup relations (RSA 1979c: 9.1.1).

The second report of the Wiehahn Commission and its White Paper are largely concerned with fairly technical matters relating to apprenticeships and training, though the White Paper does also report on progress made towards putting into effect the provisions of the Industrial Conciliation Amendment Act of 1979, and the third and fourth reports deal with such matters as registration for employment and workmen's compensation. These documents will not be dealt with further here. Instead I turn to some of the criticisms which have been voiced of the Wiehahn Commission, but excluding consideration of the difficulties, such as whether or not to register, which face black trade unions. These are dealt with elsewhere (see Chapter 10). Similarly, a number of criticisms of the Commission's recommendations have already been noted in this chapter and will not be repeated.

First, the editors of the *South African Labour Bulletin* have drawn attention to the difficulties facing a union which is refused membership of an Industrial Council. Members of such a union will then have to choose between joining a registered or parallel union or giving up their jobs (*SALB* August 1979: 66).* [See note on p. 107].

Secondly, attention has been drawn to the misleading figures produced by Wiehahn of the shortage of apprentices and artisans. The Commission noted a shortage of 9,667 artisans and 597 apprentices in April 1977, mostly in metal, electrical, motor and building industries. These figures were taken from the Department of Labour's Manpower Survey, but the *SALB*'s editors point out that perusal of the Survey itself reveals that the shortage of artisans did not occur primarily in the sectors named, but in 'government and provincial administrations' (3,799 artisans) and 'South African Railways' (2,209) (*Ibid*: 70). At a more general level, many jobs which at one time were skilled have probably become 'de-skilled' with the development of South African manufacturing, so that Africans who are said to be moving into skilled or semi-skilled artisan work may in fact not be doing so.

Claassens makes a similar point:

> Here one enters the debate as to whether mechanisation leads to increased skill requirements as opposed to generalised deskilling. It can be argued that a process of generalised deskilling will create the need for new skills in the labour process. Deskilled work may still require a certain degree of familiarity with industrial processes which uninitiated migrants may lack. However, it does seem that the 'skills shortage' in South Africa may have been considerably over-emphasised (Claassens 1979: 52).

Another argument concerns the difficulties facing a racially united union which applies for registration. The Act provides that:

> . . . trade unions applying for final registration may also apply to the Minister for the registration of a union with membership drawn from more than one population group. However, this proviso is not available to unions applying for provisional registration (Cheadle 1979: 108).

Since provisional must precede final registration, it seemed that a mixed union wishing to register must 'de-mix'. This, however, is not as simple as it sounds because the unions are not mere arbitrary bodies, but voluntary associations operating according to rules. One such rule would govern the expulsion of members; for example, misconduct might provide good cause. However, as Cheadle drily comments: 'The fact that a member falls within the parameters of the "inadmissible membership" (i.e. is the wrong colour) will not constitute misconduct' (*Ibid*: 111). Quite apart from this special problem (on the face of it, overcome by the Amendment mentioned on p. 102 above), it appears that the Registrar's powers are extremely wide and that no appeal lies from his decision.

Further difficulties arise from the Wiehahn Report in connection with the Industrial Court. Of these the most striking is that there is no right of appeal. The Court may only, of its own accord or at the request of a party to a proceeding, refer a question of law to the Appellate Division of the Supreme Court. Cheadle comments that:

> Whereas matters before an administrative or arbitrative tribunal might only require decisions on questions of law, it is desirable that matters being adjudicated on before a court of law, are made subject to appeal (*Ibid*: 120).

The problem here is that the Industrial Court is both a court of law and (in its 'special division') an administrative tribunal.

Other criticisms could be cited, most of which proceed from an ideological predisposition radically opposed to that of the Commission. The Commissioners are clearly nurtured on capitalism and their recommendations have the effect of making South African capitalism work better, not of undermining it. Equally, they are convinced of the value of trade unions, but not of all trade unions; they must be responsible, well conducted and non-political and the room for difference about what these words mean is only too obvious. Many individuals and bodies, ranging from the Garment Workers' Union to the then British Ambassador to South Africa have given the report at least a cautious welcome, but these commentators have all been 'moderates', who see the Wiehahn reforms as indeed reforms, if as yet insubstantial.

The fundamental question is whether or not the Wiehahn and Riekert reports mark the beginning of an irreversible process of change, the end of which is not yet discernible to the outsider and perhaps not even clearly imagined by the South African powers that be. If the answer to that question is 'yes', then a degree of patience is justified. If it is 'no', and the so-called reforms are no more than a flash in the pan, then desperation or despair may be more apt responses.

---

* It appears from draft legislation published on 13 August 1982 that unregistered unions are to be permitted to join Industrial Councils. (*The Guardian*: 14 August 1982).

CHAPTER 10

Trade Unions After Wiehahn

Although it is reasonable to believe that the appointment of the Wiehahn Commission formally marked the beginning of an irreversible process of reform in industrial relations, it must be said that with the exception of such enlightened managements as Smith's, the Commission's liberalizing intentions have been slow to filter through into employers' attitudes. It may be added that they have been faced with exceptional labour unrest: in the words of *The Times*' headline on 4 August 1980, 'Protests about poverty-line pay are met with crude nineteenth century response'.

After the widespread strikes of 1973 (for an analysis of these see Ademiluye 1978), there was a lull in industrial relations. The number of strikes fell from 246 in 1973 to below 50 in 1978 (*The Guardian*: 4 August 1980). By the beginning of August 50,000 black workers were estimated to have gone on strike in 1980, probably more than in 1973, compared with 22,000 in 1979 (*The Times*: 4 August 1980). Not only were strikers more numerous than in previous years, but the strikes were on the whole more sophisticated, sustained and successful. Furthermore, they enjoyed a considerable support in the black community at large and there is little doubt in the minds of expert observers that the workers have become far more politicized than hitherto. For example, according to *The Times* (4 July 1980, quoting Marianne Roux) referring to the meat boycott in the Cape 'The arrest of union leaders does not seem to have affected the resolve either of the strikers or those applying the boycott'. [*See note on p. 121].

The strikes can be seen both as traditional disputes and as part of a general movement towards black militancy. This is not to say that the movement is co-ordinated, but the activities of coloured school and university students in the Cape and the strikes by African workers reflect a shared mood. The strikes relate to inflation, increased rents in Soweto and so on, but they also draw strength from black triumphs in Zimbabwe, Mozambique and Angola, from the ideology of black consciousness and from armed strikes (that is, attacks on such targets as a Bank in Silverton on 25 January 1980 and on Booysens police station in a suburb of Johannesburg on 4 April) by insurgents of the African National Congress (*The Guardian*: 4 August 1980).

A brief account of some of the strikes in 1979 and 1980 will illustrate the varying responses of employers. The meat boycott mentioned above arose from the sacking of about 800 workers in the meat industry who had gone on strike after the Table Bay Cold Storage Company had refused to recognize a committee elected by the workers. The employers then refused to negotiate with the men's spokesmen, from the Western Province General Workers' Union (WPGWU). This in turn caused the meat boycott, which gained such widespread community support that meat sales went down by 60%.

A few days later a strike by car workers (their number has been variously estimated between 8,000 and 10,000) in the Volkswagen plant at Uitenhage led the motor industry's Industrial Council in the Eastern Cape to offer a 20% rise in wages, which was widely regarded as a major victory for the two unions which represented the bulk of the strikers (*The Guardian*: 25 June 1980). *The Times* (4 July 1980), however, points to the role of the Port Elizabeth Black Civic Organisation (PEBCO) the same body as had been behind the strike at the Ford plant in 1979 (for a full account see Whisson *et al*. 1979). That strike had been by Ford informing a leading black activist in PEBCO, Mr Thomazile Botha, that he must either give less time to his civic activities or be dismissed. Thus, the strike was an act of political solidarity with Mr Botha, who was subsequently banned and fled to Lesotho. According to the *Financial Times* the unions were completely by-passed during the Ford dispute, whereas at Volkswagen the black activists had been less obviously prominent than at Ford's and had chosen to work through the unions. Since many of the Volkswagen workers belonged both to the Uitenhage Black Civic Association and the union, the successful conclusion of the strike made it possible for the union to emerge with some credit (*Financial Times*: 8 July 1980).

A further example of a company yielding to a combination of industrial and community pressure is the successful conclusion of the strike at Fatti's and Moni's (which is described in detail in McGregor 1980). This started on 25 April 1979, after workers in the Bellville South factory of the United Macaroni group had presented a petition signed by 45 African and coloured workers to management through the Food and Canning Workers Union, asking for higher wages. The union was registered, but had been obliged to start a separate union for its African members. The two unions, however, always operated as one. The coloured workers involved were told by management that they must choose between the factory's liaison committee and the union, and that there would be difficult times ahead if they chose the latter. They refused; dismissals followed, 68 African and 20 coloured workers then went on strike and stayed out for seven months. Despite repeated attempts by Fatti's and Moni's to break the strike, by for example seeking to deal directly with individuals rather than with the FCWU, the employers were eventually obliged to settle with the union.

The number of workers involved was small, but the strike is significant for a number of reasons. Two important features were the solidarity of African and coloured workers and the boycott of Fatti's and Moni's products, in which such diverse organisations joined as Chief Buthelezi's Inkatha movement, the Soweto Committee of Ten and students from the

University of the Western Cape. Although management claimed that the boycott did not affect sales, the company's profits for January to July 1979 were, at R 186,000, only about half those for the corresponding period of 1978.

The most important aspect of the settlement was, as McGregor says:

> . . . that an employer had signed a contract with an unregistered union (the AFCWU). Both the FCWU and the AFCWU were referred to jointly as 'the union' in the agreement. This is particularly remarkable in view of the fact that in this case management had insisted on dealing with the two unions separately. They will never be able to do this again.
>
> (McGregor 1980: 129)

The Fatti's and Moni's management had done its best to break the strike, with plenty of help from the state in the shape of the police and the Western Cape Administration Board, but it failed. A very different outcome ended the strike of municipal workers, again variously estimated, this time between 6,000 and 10,000, in Johannesburg at the end of July 1980. This strike was organised by the newly formed Black Municipal Workers Union (BMWU) and on the face of it was in support of a straightforward demand for higher wages, though as workers' awareness grows that labour power is in itself political power such a distinction between the economic and the political makes rapidly decreasing sense. The Municipality reacted with firmness of an extremely nineteenth century kind. First, it brought in replacements from the nominally independent Venda. Then it deported 1,100 or 1,200 strikers to Venda and the Transkei, after which the remainder went back to work without a rise. Throughout it refused to negotiate with the unregistered BMWU, and dealt only with the Union of Johannesburg Municipal Workers. This body was not only favoured by the Municipality, but also, during the strike, was granted provisional registration by the government in terms of the Wiehahn legislation (*The Times*: 4 August 1980).

This episode illustrates very well the difficulties of the Wiehahn dispensation. As we have seen, a union may only take part in the cumbersome negotiating procedures of the Industrial Council if it registers and is accepted by the existing members of the Industrial Council for the relevant industry. But once a union has decided to register (a by no means easy decision, as will be argued in the next section), it may take some months for registration to be granted. The BMWU was only formed about a month before the strike and could not expect to register before the end of September. But how, asked one official '. . . could we ask angry workers to wait another two months until we had been registered?' (*Ibid*).

Thus there are conflicting views among employers about how to deal with strikes. Probably none of them positively likes dealing with unregistered unions, but some are beginning to realise that these are the bodies which in many cases can genuinely claim to represent the workers: indeed, as we have seen, the Federated Chamber of Industry has gone as far as to urge employers to negotiate with every body which seems to have a plausible claim to representation. The wish among employers to rely on the Liaison Committee system, or to deal with unions of their own choice, is understandable enough, but probably a recipe for disaster.

TO REGISTER OR NOT TO REGISTER?

The post-Wiehahn legislation allows African unions to register (and mixed unions at ministerial discretion), which at first sight is a considerable step forward. It is, however, increasingly being seen as a means whereby the government can control the black unions, rather than promote their members' interests. It is true that the government already controls white, Asian and coloured unions in the same way, but some blacks fear that registration would expose them to an even greater degree of control than is suffered by the other racial groups.

A memorandum by the WPGWU puts forcefully the case against registration (WPGWU 1979). The memorandum notes '. . . it is not surprising that the TUCSA parallel unions should be following the line of least resistance and should therefore be happily seeking registration.' But surely, it goes on, the right question is 'registration on what terms?'

Part of the reason for the trade union movement's disarray, WPGWU points out, is that protest had at first been directed against the government's refusal to allow migrant workers to belong to registered black unions. Thus, a union which at present organized migrants as well as settled urban workers would necessarily have lost that proportion of its membership if it decided to register. When the government gave way and allowed migrant membership after all, the independent unions were taken unawares and had not thought out their next response.

In WPGWU's view, however, the concession is more apparent than real, if taken together with the recommendation by Wiehahn, which the government accepted, that registration would only be granted to unions which could show themselves to be 'sufficiently representative'. Clearly, as Wiehahn himself points out, it will be in the 'pure self interest' of unions aspiring to registration to exclude migrants, since the difficulties of organising these workers are relatively so much greater than with settled labour. A second argument is that, whilst racially united unions are not permitted 'In these heady days of so-called "movement away from apartheid" it would ill befit a workers' organisation to accept clear racial segregation of this sort to obtain official approval'. (*Ibid*: 119). Here, however, the WPGWU may be on unfirm ground, since a few pages earlier it had stated that there are good reasons to believe that the ban on mixed unions might be removed in the near future (*Ibid*: 116) as indeed it was.

The memorandum moves on to a more general attack on governmental control of trade unions. '. . . we hold the principle of worker control no less sacred than we do the principle of freedom of association', but the former principle is threatened in a number of ways. These include the lack of clarity about the powers and functions of the Industrial Court, the lack of criteria for registration, and the variety of other controls like possible

111

vetoing of the election or appointment of office bearers, financial controls, etc. (*Ibid*: 119–120).

Furthermore, since entry into the Industrial Council system involves pleasing '. . . the extreme right wing registered unions who are current members of many of the Industrial Councils, the progressive unions will have to give up their real strength, which lies in the organization of workers in the individual factory'. Of course, by failing to register, the unregistered unions will forgo the right to enter into legally binding agreements, they will cut themselves off from stop order facilities (the automatic deduction of union dues from wages by the employer) and may well find themselves in competition for membership with unions which have decided to register. But the WPGWU believes, perhaps over optimistically, that all these risks should be run and that progressive unions should refuse to register 'until such time as the state agrees to accept our principles of freedom of association and workers' control of the unions' (*Ibid*: 125). Foreign support for such a course can be expected (though again this may be over optimistic): '. . . the very notion of registration, the very notion of special laws and restrictions on the Trade Union Movement, is utterly foreign and unacceptable to the international trade union movement' (*Ibid*: 126).

The memorandum accepts that, if one leaves aside the complicated question of provisional registration, which is now the necessary preliminary to full registration, the controls implied by registration are no greater than those already suffered by registered unions; that, however, provides no guarantee against further controls being imposed in future. But the real heart of the case is that, even if there are no new controls, the unions will still be adversely affected, because the political intention of the Wiehahn report is to bring the black unions under central control through the Industrial Councils. It also, and this is a quite different point, makes the assumption that opposing class interests can in fact be harmonized. Both points are summed up in the following quotation:

> It (participation in the Industrial Councils) forces us into a prescribed round of bargaining at the level of the total industry—i.e., at a level at which the bosses are 100% organised and yet at which the black unions are very weak. Even more importantly, the Industrial Council system presupposes that the state can establish a neutral body comprising boss and worker representatives who could be happily reconciled at all times. Our experience makes this view difficult to accept (*Ibid*: 129).

The WPGWU view of the law is very similar to that of FOSATU, but with the significant difference that FOSATU has decided to register under certain conditions. In the words of the WPGWU memorandum, '. . . FOSATU will not accept a registration certificate which contains racial bars or requires acceptance of provisional registration. We will not apply for registration until these are removed from the law'. (*Ibid*: 133)

Hulton Cheadle takes the *SALB* to task for publishing the memorandum, on a number of grounds. He sees the WPGWU as a body which '. . . has until recently chosen to remain very isolated. It is now belatedly and somewhat frantically attempting to generate debate', but not in the right forum. The real debate should go on in labour organizations, not academic journals, and to choose a public forum is both imprudent and theoretically misguided. The WPGWU is theoretically at fault in holding '. . . a general position that reflects a concern to take strong stands against the state, but a more accommodationist stand toward capital' (Cheadle 1980: 9). As for prudence: 'When labour movements are weak and confronted by powerful state and managerial forces, then public debate as to the actions of the organizations concerned is misguided'.

The debate over registration is taken further than the WPGWU memorandum in an article by Martin Nicol, in which he sharply attacks the line taken by FOSATU (Nicol 1980). He believes FOSATU is quite wrong to state that 'There is no doubt that it is the years of struggle by the workers *and the representative organizations* (Nicol's emphasis) that have led to the changes in the legislation'. On the contrary, 'Is the state really concerned about the African union movement as it exists today—with less than 100,000 members, many of whom belong to tame parallel unions? . . . The most striking feature about the African trade union movement . . . is its weakness' (Nichol 1980: 50). The state, therefore, through the new Industrial Conciliation Act, is not trying to co-opt the working class, but to divide it by co-opting the black petty bourgeoisie and some strata of skilled workers.

A good example of the new attitude is shown by the white South African Boilermakers' Society's decision to form a black parallel union, MAWU, a decision that was not opposed by FOSATU, on condition only that the society confined itself to recruiting blacks in skilled jobs. This, however, as Nicol points out, directly contradicts FOSATU's aim to establish '. . . broadly based industrial unions . . . so as to escape the fragmented, craft based divisions that characterize the weak registered trade union movement. More important, a stance like this splits the African working class exactly on the lines envisaged by the state' (*Ibid*: 51).

Secondly, Nicol reproaches FOSATU for its cautious attitude towards PEBCO. The unregistered United Auto Workers' (UAW) had taken a weak line in the Ford dispute, which was why, as the press suggested, the workers turned to PEBCO for leadership. Ford agreed to negotiate over the reinstatement of workers with a committee organized by PEBCO, but insisted that the UAW be present. The Union then refused to ask Ford to re-employ any workers who did not belong to it. Its purpose was to keep politics out of the factory, '. . . exactly the stance which the state wishes to encourage in African trade unions' (*Ibid*: 52). It is also the stance, as has already been noticed, desired by employers.

Nichol acknowledged that:

There are good reasons why African workers organisations should exercise care in defining their relationship to bodies such as PEBCO. If a union is to represent the class interests of its members, it must be democratically controlled by the workers and not subordinated to the needs of other classes . . . But one suspects

113

that FOSATU's reason for being unwilling to associate itself with bodies like PEBCO is rather its fear that such alliances will meet with the disapproval of the state. In the first issue of *Isisebenzi*, FOSATU's newsletter, workers are pointedly reminded that SACTU (pictured as FOSATU's most immediate predecessor) 'was forced out of existence and into exile because of its close links with political organisations'. (*Ibid*: 52–3).

It is perhaps not altogether fair to reproach FOSATU for not wishing to follow SACTU into the impotence of exile. But Nicol goes even further and says that FOSATU's 'ban' on politics is not a neutral stance—in other words, it plays into the white hand:

> A willingness to compromise with the state and white workers, but not with black political movements which command the support of a majority of a union's membership still further follows the designs of the Wiehahn Commission (*Ibid*: 53).

The danger facing FOSATU, therefore, is that of 'legalism'. That is, it may involve itself in the mass of legal battles which the new Industrial Conciliation Act will engender. Furthermore, it may be seduced into 'clutching after paper members to spread before the Registrar of trade unions' in order to show him that one or another affiliate is sufficiently representative to be worthy of registration (*Ibid*: 55–6). The main point Nicol, in common with the WPGWU, is making here is that the secret of organization is to promote militant worker solidarity at factory level, and to avoid the bureaucratic entanglements which must follow involvement with the Industrial Council system. In the short term something may be achieved by gathering 'paper members', but in the long term workers will only follow those whom they believe genuinely to represent them and even a small degree of compromise may prejudice this long term aim.

Nicol certainly has a point, though it must be doubted whether FOSATU would achieve anything at all if it fully accepted his prescriptions. As it is, the organization, though clearly unpopular with the authorities, does achieve a good deal. This may readily be seen from the papers it submitted to the ICFTU conference in Brussels in February 1980.

The documents are in a sense raw material. Some of them are concerned with the European Community's Code of Conduct for firms with interests in South Africa (treated in detail in Akeroyd *et al.* 1981). Formerly FOSATU was inclined to dismiss the code as a capitalist smoke-screen, but the replies prepared by some of its affiliates in 1979 to companies' reports presented under the code suggest that by then FOSATU was ready to take the code seriously.

The replies are to the reports by Cadbury Schweppes (criticised by the Eastern Province Sweet, Food and Allied Workers' Union) and by Eveready and Tube Investments, to both of which 'counter-reports' were produced by the Engineering and Allied Workers' Union of South Africa. Even to get sight of the reports was not easy. In the case of Tube Investments no copy was forthcoming from the company (although the report is a public document); when the Union asked the Department of

Trade for a copy of one report it was told that it could be consulted at the British Consulate-General in Durban, but 'for reasons of copyright' no copy could be taken, though notes could be made. Such fantastic caution on the British Government's part can only reinforce the doubts that have been widely expressed about the seriousness with which the government took the code, even under the Labour Administration. (The copyright difficulty could have been simply dealt with by asking companies concerned to allow copies of their reports to be given to enquirers. They could hardly have refused.) The doubts have, of course, been greatly increased by the refusal of the Conservative Government's Secretary of State for Trade even to name in Parliament the companies which had produced unsatisfactory reports under the code. They were subsequently named in the newspapers.

Despite the difficulties the unions saw that the code was of at least potential value, and that they were in a position to provide a kind of report which would not be possible for the Department of Trade, nor indeed for most academic observers. Their 'counter-reports' consist of detailed critiques of the reports presented by companies to the Secretary of State for Trade, often alleging that certain statements are simply untrue, sometimes that they are merely misleading. The fact that the unions rebut so much of the companies' reports naturally does not in itself demonstrate that the latter are untrue, whether intentionally or otherwise, but the differences of perception of the facts between management and labour do at the very least point to severe misunderstandings, which in turn suggests that industrial relations in these undertakings must be less than satisfactory.

For example, the reply to Cadbury Schweppes highlights the company's unwillingness to deal with any union except its own in-company union. The reply to Eveready denies the company's assertion that the black employees have for some years been able to negotiate formally with management in a Liaison Committee; instead, it states, a Works Committee had been established as recently as May 1979, and was expected to meet for the first time on 18 September. In Tube Investments the accuracy of the company's report, so far as it concerns relations within the undertaking, is not denied, but the union states that:

> . . . a works committee was established in 1973 after a fierce struggle . . . The workers are not happy about the effectiveness of the committee but have no option since the company refused to recognise the Engineering and Allied Workers' Union, in 1975, which represented about 50 per cent of the total black workforce.

These three reports illustrate the practical work of FOSATU affiliates, and three different kinds of industrial relationship. In one a 'tame' union is favoured by the employer, in the second there is a new works committee and no mention of black unions, and in the third a works committee established some years ago, with which the union is dissatisfied.

A further FOSATU document quotes the section of the Code of Conduct which enjoins companies to accept African unions if their employees

115

decide that is the form of representation they wish to have. It goes on:

> This statement is quite clear but as the selection of documents attached indicates, the Code of Conduct has not in any way assisted unions in achieving recognition. This applies to both registered and unregistered unions . . . FOSATU believes that the real issue at stake is the development of a union movement that can represent the aspirations of workers in South Africa. Measured against this the Code has been a failure and no amount of monitoring or blustering by non-worker organisations can overcome this.
> If the EEC governments want their code to be taken seriously they themselves will have to take the Code more seriously and penalise companies who do not comply.

The fact, however, that FOSATU takes great trouble to prepare case studies and 'counter-reports' does suggest that it judges the code to be at least a potentially useful tactical weapon. Its indirect value should also not be ignored: one reason for the greater effectiveness of strikers in foreign than in South African-owned companies is that pressure may be brought to bear by trade unions on the parent company in, for example, Germany. Officials of such bodies as the Geneva-based International Metalworkers' Federation may also assist in negotiations in South Africa as well as providing training and other aid to affiliated unions there (Thönessen 1980).

On the whole employers welcome the extension of the definition of 'employee' to cover blacks, and the consequent possibility of black trade unions being registered. But the at present unregistered black trade unions, which although only covering 1% of the work force are attracting a surprisingly wide range of allies, are, as we have seen, faced with a difficult decision. One strong pressure towards registration comes from the fairly widespread view among employers that if unions refuse to register they should not be recognized. For example SEIFSA, the engineering employers' federation, issued guidelines to members stating that they should insist on membership of the Industrial Council as well as registration. They should then confine negotiations to the Industrial Council and not make any separate 'in-house' agreements on matters which could fall within the Industrial Council's remit (WPGWU 1980: 73). This is exactly what the black unions fear most; the employers' policy forces them away from their source of strength, the individual plant, to the level of the industry as a whole, where they are poorly organized. This, as we have already noted, provides one of the strongest arguments for refusing to register and instead concentrating on building up and maintaining support in the work place.

Another difficulty facing the independent unions is the strong appeal of the 'non-political' model of industrial relations to employers and many employees. For example, the Motor Industry Workers Union (MIWU) probably struck a chord in many potential members' minds when it said:

> Employers trust us because they know that we are only interested in making things better for our members, and are not a political organisation. So you are safe in our ranks. We will fight for your right as a worker, and protect you in

116

your jobs, but we will never place you on the wrong side of the law (Quoted in FOSATU 1980: 76).

According to FOSATU, currently registered (white) unions are rushing to organize blacks, and an unprecedented number of companies have been introducing unions to their African workers. The decision facing the independent unions, therefore, is whether to compete for members, perhaps only 'paper members', with companies' tame unions, or to rely on superior organization and understanding of the workers' true interests to gain them the workers' loyalty. As has been suggested above, the important fact about the Fatti's and Moni's strike was that it showed that an employer could be forced, by a combination of industrial and community action, to deal with an unregistered union.

The solution favoured by management amounts to an extension of the parallel union system, combined with Liaison Committees dominated by management at works level. Thus the committee will deal with purely local issues, leaving a role for the union only at national or provincial level and this limitation appears to be accepted with equanimity by parallel unions. Multinational companies have, again according to FOSATU, taken the lead in giving access to these recently-formed parallel unions (Leyland and MIWU provide a good example) because:

> These firms have been under pressure from their home countries. By granting recognition and facilities to parallel unions for African workers, a great deal of credibility accrues to them overseas and pressures are thus substantially reduced (*Ibid*: 83).

Tame unions, however, are not always successful. According to the Cadbury Schweppes' 'counter-report':

> if you ask any worker about the so called agreement between the company and its Multiracial Union (In Company Union) the reply would be negative. The workers had no part in drawing up any proposals to the company as no consultation had taken place between the union and workers.

Similarly, in-house committees often meet strong opposition. For example, the independent Metal and Allied Workers Union, reporting on its relations with Glacier Metals, says that it believes the company to have set up its Industrial Relations Committee in order to avoid dealing with the union. The company's conditions for recognizing the union were 'so formulated as to subordinate the union to their newly established IRC, leaving even the responsibility to recognize the union to this body'. Later, Glacier refused to recognize the union because it was unregistered (*Financial Mail*: 31 August 1979).

The employers' enthusiasm for parallel unions is mirrored by TUCSA's decision at its 1979 conference to encourage its affiliates to organize African workers in this way and if necessary to compete with pre-existing independent unions. Cooper and Ensor argue that:

> TUCSA's main concern is to prevent the emergence within the registered trade union movement of a more militant trade unionism and one which will challenge, rightly so, the privileged position of white workers in the labour

117

structure . . . TUCSA is also afraid that an emerging militancy, if left unchecked, could lead to the involvement of the union movement in political activities even though this is outlawed by the state (Cooper and Ensor 1980: 116–117).

Thus the TUCSA conference turned down a resolution to give full moral and financial support to the Fatti's and Moni's and Eveready strikers because i) TUCSA opposed boycotts and at the time both companies' products were being boycotted; ii) the unions were not affiliated to TUCSA and iii) the Eveready strike was financed from abroad, with 75,000 Swiss francs from the International Metalworkers' Federation (*Ibid*: 119). (These authors do not, however, record that, as has been mentioned on p. 92, the resolution was only narrowly defeated.)

In the competition with the independent unions TUCSA naturally presents the former as irresponsible, not really independent because they receive money from abroad (under the Fundraising Act this may be prohibited) and geared for confrontation rather than collaboration. The government, however, seems to have become aware of the depth of feeling in unregistered unions, so much so that the Minister of Labour, Mr S. P. Botha, has urged employers to deal with them if necessary, rather than running the risk of unnecessary strikes.

It must be added that even their critics do not present all parallel unions as dominated by their white partners. In most cases the relationship is 'parental' but in some it is supportive (Hendler 1980: 106). The latter are however the exceptions: most parallel unions are remote from their constituencies, have produced a low level of consciousness in the workers and 'in the absence of real struggle' place great emphasis on the need for benefit funds (*Ibid*: 107). Most of them have their education programmes conducted for them by TUCSA and the Institute for Industrial Relations (IIR). The IIR courses, according to the secretary-general of three of the TUCSA unions:

> . . . do not teach workers the art of organising, but the technicalities of running a union, negotiating, settling disputes and discipline procedure in the factory. There are also joint courses for union members and management with the emphasis on the partnership between employers and employees (*Ibid*: 105).

Hendler adds that the courses appear to offer no places to the rank and file and merely foster élitism and bureaucracy—a trend which is reinforced by the major role played by management in setting the courses up (*Ibid*: 106).

Clearly, employers and TUCSA on the one hand, and the independent unions on the other, have very different notions of industrial relations. TUCSA and the employers evidently favour a model in which the interests of workers and employers need not necessarily be opposed, though they often will be. The independents, however, believe that opposing interests are a necessary fact of the nature of industrial man. They may at times co-exist in fragile harmony, but any interruption in the class struggle can only be artificial and temporary.

Douwes Decker, in an important paper presented to the 1980 conference of the South African Institute of Race Relations, acknowledges the remarkable courage of the government in extending trade union rights to all South Africans. This, combined with 'the general acceptance by the black unions of the nature of the rights offered to them, indicates that South Africa is facing a new era in its industrial relations system'. The question now is 'will industrial peace in the sense of maintaining as much as possible of the status quo, or industrial justice, become the objective of the new decade?' (Douwes Decker 1980: 2). Douwes Decker holds that the industrial relationship is primarily a power phenomenon:

> The relationship between managers, employers and their organisations and companies on the one hand, and workers and their trade unions on the other hand, is one based on conflict . . . the conflict cannot be resolved. Reconciliation for a specific period of time is possible if the two groups form parties which recognise and respect each other's legitimate existence and are prepared jointly to formulate rules to govern their interaction . . . rather than attempting to control the power of the trade unions it is essential that a situation is created where industrial conflict can be institutionalised (*Ibid*: 4).

The pursuit of industrial justice entails the admission of trade union rights, including the right to strike. If industrial justice is achieved, then industrial peace will follow, but to aim directly at industrial peace is likely to carry with it the temptation to play down trade union rights, and so to lead to industrial disorder.

Douwes Decker goes on to examine employers' responses to the post-Wiehahn trend in industrial relations. He regards the SEIFSA guidelines, referred to above, as a crucial document and misguided in a number of ways. First, it was worked out without consultation with the unions. It insists on registration and participation in the Industrial Council as the price of recognition, thus confusing registration, which is in the gift of government, with recognition, which is the business of individual companies. (We have seen an example of this at Glacier Metals). Thirdly, since registration depends partly on the representative quality of the union (that is, the percentage of workers in the undertaking who are already members) it denies the principle established in the UK and USA that recognition 'is dependent on potential membership and not only the actual percentage of workers who have joined the union'. Fourthly, the guidelines recommend against allowing black unions facilities or access for the purposes of organization and recruitment. Fifthly, they fail to clarify the relation between committees and unions, though their implication is that unions should be confined to activity at the Industrial Council level, with negotiations on matters specific to a particular factory being left to a committee. (An example of such a lack of clarity is described in the Chemical Workers' Industrial Union's report on its struggle for recognition at the Henkel works.) Finally, on legalistic grounds they deny stop-order facilities to registered unions.

SEIFSA has taken a step forward by being prepared to negotiate at Industrial Council level, but its lack of detailed guidance at plant level will,

Douwes Decker believes, lead employers to grant unions a kind of limited and unofficial recognition in the work place. This will lead to disastrous industrial relations, precisely because it will be unofficial, so that proper rules to govern the interaction between management and union will be lacking. The lack of guidance may stem from a misunderstanding by SEIFSA of the supportive role which is played by German unions in the committee system. This misunderstanding can in turn be traced back to an influential article by the University of South Africa's Institute of Labour Relations, which was 'a crucial input to the Wiehahn Commission' (*Ibid*: 17–20).[1]

Douwes Decker continues that employers in general expect the end of the closed shop in the '80s. If, at the same time, unions are not allowed to recruit in the work place they will inevitably have problems in maintaining membership, and he suggests that awareness of this dilemma may underlie 'the sentiment of "we can manage without trade unions" which is increasingly becoming prevalent in the South African situation' (*Ibid*: 21). Douwes Decker also attacks employers for their preoccupation with racially mixed trade unions and, in a passage which illustrates this central difference between his own thinking and that of FOSATU, defends the desire of blacks for exclusively black unions:

> Surely some thought about the different standards of living between the white and black communities suggests that it is unrealistic to require black and white workers to be able to find enough common ground in one organisation. (*Ibid*: 21 and 22).

They are unlikely to reach leadership positions in mixed unions. It is questionable whether white workers want them. His solution sounds not unlike a more equitable version of the present parallel unions:

> ... a federation of unions of different races ... would recognise the gap between the interests to which the black and white workers through their trade unions want to give voice but at the same time facilitate finding enough common ground through a federative structure to ensure that one set of demands is placed before an employer or an employers' association. (*Ibid*).

Douwes Decker goes further and suggests that one of the advantages of allowing trade unions to function effectively in the work place is that their activity does not then spill over from the economic into the political sphere. In support of this view he says that in the Fatti's and Moni's dispute, one important outcome had been that a boundary line between the activities of the trade union and of PEBCO was identified, though not allowed to develop.

It is a pity that Douwes Decker does not elaborate this point, since the other accounts of that dispute emphasize the interrelated character of the industrial action and community back-up, rather than their separation. His belief, too, that political and economic action can be clearly separated directly contradicts those who would see them as being necessarily related. But, leaving theoretical considerations on one side, it does seem at least to accord with common sense to say that trade union action in South Africa must have political effects both within and outside South Africa. The struggle for better wages is not precisely the same thing as the struggle for the vote, but they run on parallel lines, and unlike parallel lines may be expected to meet before infinity.

1 (Quite apart from its academic competence, one would expect this institute to be influential, since its staff are Afrikaans speakers and it is part of a university dominated by Afrikaners. Since completing his reports, Professor Wiehahn has joined UNISA's business school, where he will be closely associated with the Institute. Its two leading members, Professors Bendix and Swart, have, however, moved to the University of Stellenbosch, where they are reputed to find the Cape academic air freer to breathe. (See *Financial Mail*: December 12, 1980.)

* According to the report of the National Manpower Commission, tabled in Parliament on 25 May 1982, there were 342 strikes in 1981, nearly all of them illegal, involving nearly 93,000 workers, 93 per cent of them black. The figure for strikes in 1973 was now given as 370, involving 98,000 workers.

(The Guardian: 26 May 1982)

CHAPTER 11

Afrikaner Academics

In this chapter I examine academic influences in South African politics. To do this more than superficially would demand a book or a doctoral thesis. Fortunately one of the latter is in progress and some work on the subject has also been done by Dr Pierre Hugo of the University of South Africa, commonly known as UNISA (Hugo: 1977). Here I do little more than touch upon some of the many questions which merit further investigation. In giving the enquiry some structure in my own mind I have relied greatly on the guidance of Ben Vosloo, formerly Professor of Political Science in the University of Stellenbosch, who is himself one of the more influential academics in South Africa. I have not considered those engaged in such disciplines as the natural sciences or engineering, but only those who are prominent in the political, social and economic fields.

One noticeable characteristic of the Republic's academic community is that its members are frequently in the public eye. They may acquire influence, as in any society, in a number of ways. Some may become notable simply because of academic excellence, which means that their books are read and their thoughts passed on to their students. But many others become prominent because they are recruited from the academic world to become decision-makers, like Professor Neil Barnard, a young professor of political science in the University of Potchefstroom who became head of the Department of National Security (DONS, now renamed National Intelligence Services, formally BOSS, the Bureau of State Security). Other academics have a foot in both worlds, so that they may sit on commissions of enquiry, be co-opted to advise Ministers and civil servants and exercise a more widespread influence through the media, without giving up their academic bases.

On the whole, English speaking academics are virtually ignored by the governing élite. This has obvious undesirable consequences; on the one hand some of the leading Afrikaner academics are over-worked; on the other, some of their English-speaking counterparts become frustrated or disaffected. In that case they merely confirm the Afrikaner prejudice, that criticism from English speakers tends not to be constructive, but rather to undermine white society. Thus Afrikaners are frequently allowed a latitude to say things, which if said by English speakers would be seen as destructive, or even subversive. It follows that English speaking academics are likely to be more highly regarded than Afrikaners by Africans, coloureds and Asians, precisely because they are outside the magic circle of Afrikaner power.

There are, of course, some exceptions. For example, Dr Denis Worrall, lately MP for the Gardens division of Cape Town, could serve as the ideal type of the trusted English speaking academic, who has made a second career in politics. Dr Worrall is widely travelled, has a doctorate from Cornell University in the USA (where he has also taught) and was a member of the Progressive Party before he joined the Nationalists and became a major figure in the *verligte* ascendancy. The process of his acceptance by Afrikanerdom was long, but the seal seems to have been set upon it by his appointment as chairman of the constitutional committee of the recently established President's Council. As an English speaker he is not eligible for membership of the Broederbond. (Nor is an Afrikaner eligible if he is married to an English-speaking woman.)

A very different ideal type is represented by Dr Willem de Klerk, who occupies a unique position at the heart of Afrikanerdom, buttressed by family connections and (it is generally believed) membership of the innermost circle of the Broederbond. Dr de Klerk's father was a Cabinet Minister, as is his brother now; he is a nephew of Strydom, and has a regular platform in his column in the Sunday newspaper, *Rapport*. It was he who first coined the terms *verlig* and *verkramp*, to describe individuals who were, respectively, open-minded or hidebound in their political views. Though not strictly speaking an academic, since he holds no university position at present, he is a noted intellectual, as well as being the 'ultimate insider'.

It is important before proceeding further with the classification of the academics, to be clear about what a *verligte* is and is not: the discussion here will be short, and is expanded in Chapter 15. *Verligtes* most certainly are not liberals; indeed they distrust and despise them as representatives of an alien tradition. On the contrary, they are nationalists, committed to working from within the party. It is possible to leave the party and remain a nationalist, in the sense of retaining one's attachment to Afrikanerdom, but anyone who does so forfeits all influence, except that which can be exerted through teaching and writing.

From within the party, the *verligte* may engage in lively controversy and genuinely innovative thinking, though for an Afrikaner to explain this to an outsider is often as difficult as it can be for a British Conservative to explain to a left wing member of the Labour Party that there are real and constructive differences of opinion between Conservatives. For the *verligte* much remains sacred, but a mixture of moral sensitivity and political acumen forces him to accept that if Afrikanerdom is to survive it must change, and in ways which to the *verkrampte* will seem radical, revolutionary and wrong. Thus, the *verligte* will discuss new constitutions, be prepared to amend the Immorality Act and Mixed Marriages Act, perhaps even abandon Group Areas and Population Registration. For the *verkramptes*, led by the able and charming Dr Treurnicht, any of these is

123

the thin end of a wedge which, once inserted, will never be removed.

In the universities there are, naturally enough, academics who remain unashamedly *verkramp* and some who think it prudent to seem so, but a significant minority are energetically *verlig*. These are the men (with virtually no women) who have the ear of government in the academic world.

Universities differ in character and atmosphere and in the type of influence their senior members seek to obtain. Stellenbosch is widely thought to have a special place in Afrikanerdom, indeed one Professor called it 'Afrikanerdom's holy place', though it must be added that another thought of it as something akin to a holiday camp after the excitements of Pretoria. Certainly, Stellenbosch, being near to Cape Town, is well placed to influence Parliament during its sessions and the fact that the Prime Minister is himself a Cape man and a *verligte* tends to bring Stellenbosch into the centre of things. It is widely believed on the Stellenbosch campus that, because the university has a special place in the government's heart, campus politics tend to be noticed at national level. Some students have highly placed fathers and uncles who follow student politics closely, which in turn means that senior academics will think it proper to involve themselves quite closely with student politics. Similarly, PFP supporters at Stellenbosch are close to the PFP in Parliament, whose leader, Dr Van Zyl Slabbert, is an old Stellenbosch man.

Those Stellenbosch academics who are interested in politics tend to be preoccupied with the notion of 'the Establishment' (a term which appears to have passed into the Afrikaans language) and with influence in it. In their definition, the Establishment is small; it excludes most Members of Parliament and most members of the civil service and centres on Cabinet Ministers and Deputy Ministers. Senior academics belong to it, provided they satisfy the essential conditions of faithfulness to Afrikanerdom, as do prominent clergy of the Dutch Reformed Churches and senior members of other professions.

It is fairly easy to understand why Stellenbosch does not see most civil servants and Members of Parliament as targets of influence. On the whole, most MP's are considered to be very poorly informed, partly because they fail to cultivate close links with civil servants. Secondly, only the most senior civil servants accompany their Ministers to Cape Town for the parliamentary session, leaving the great mass of the bureaucracy in Pretoria. Thus, even if the Stellenbosch academics considered the civil servants suitable targets, there would be few at whom to aim. To all this must be added that some Ministers very firmly hold the view that civil servants are for carrying out policy, not making it. The distinction is naïve, but in so far as it is valid it provides a further, though limited, justification for influence seekers concentrating their attention on Ministers.

It is also generally believed that P. W. Botha is by nature a listener, who admires qualifications, and that he reads more than his predecessors. He has clearly been anxious, since the beginning of his period as Prime

Minister, to draw academics into the policy-making process, in marked contrast to the antipathy shown by Verwoerd and Vorster, though it must, in fairness, be added that when Vorster made his famous attack on academics who had too much time on their hands and spent it meddling in politics, he was thinking primarily of one particular professor at UNISA who supported the Progressive Party. Later, he was annoyed by the *verligte* recommendations made by the Theron Commission (RSA 1976), thanks to its academic members—and this annoyance was, of course, fuelled by their opponents. However, he was certainly not opposed to academic qualifications as such, for at one time eleven of his cabinet had been at Stellenbosch in their student days, compared with five of P. W. Botha's in early 1980.

The view from the north is quite different from that gained from the University of Stellenbosch. Academics at the University of Pretoria have no use for the concept of 'the Establishment'; they regard the concentration on Ministers as misguided and, naturally enough, reject the notion that Stellenbosch has a specially influential position in Afrikanerdom—though they admit that it may once have had it. The University of Pretoria concentrates on the bureaucracy rather than Ministers and is the home of the most influential economist in South Africa, Professor Jan Lombard, whose views on regional policy have already been noted, and whose report on Natal and KwaZulu will be discussed in Chapter 14. (His free market school of economists is at loggerheads with that of Professor Terreblanche at Stellenbosch, who is preoccupied with the redistribution of wealth and the vision of South Africa as partly a third world country, with the economic problems endemic to the third world.) Furthermore, numerous civil servants have studied at the University of Pretoria, where many have read Political Science and Public Administration. These subjects have been taught at Pretoria since 1908, and the Department's links with the bureaucracy are strengthened by the fact that every year seventy or so promising civil servants are chosen to take a diploma in Political Science and Public Administration. Pretoria, therefore, in the words of a senior economist, 'is geared to the main shaft' of public affairs.

Pretoria of course is not the only northern university. The lively Randse Afrikaanse Universiteit (RAU) at Johannesburg (founded to counterbalance the English-speaking University of the Witwatersrand) contains a number of 'influentials' in Politics and Economics and some innovations, like the Department of National Strategy, presided over by Professor H. de V. du Toit, who was formerly Director of Military Intelligence. The relatively easy going atmosphere of RAU (which does not, however, conceal the disquiet of some senior members at the emergence of a group of PFP students, pathetically small though it is) is thought to owe something to the fact that its former Vice-Chancellor, Dr Gerrit Viljoen, once studied at Cambridge.

UNISA too, though overwhelmingly Afrikaans speaking, is relatively free and easy. Since it is a correspondence university (one of the forebears of England's Open University) contact with students is limited, but they belong to all races and live in all parts of the world. Here, as elsewhere, the most senior positions will probably be held by nationalists who are also members of the Broederbond, but there are some PFP academics, and among the political scientists may be found the constitutional advisers of the New Republic Party.

Afrikanerdom is a small society and the active members of its élite are few in number. The links between them tend to be made at university rather than school, and surprisingly often the élite member turns out to come from an often poor, rural background, from which he was released by a university scholarship. Once they have acquired membership of what at Stellenbosch is called 'the Establishment' most members are determined to retain it, though there are some lone wolves who have never wished to join the Establishment, or who bear ejection from it with equanimity. Hermann Giliomee has spoken of 'the decomposition of the élite' and 'the fatigue of the bourgeoisie' and it is certainly true that within the élite there is growing room for disagreement and increasingly fierce debate. But this debate takes place within the élite, not between it and fellow-Afrikaners who are outcasts from it. In other words, though nearly all the glittering prizes South Africa can offer have fallen to Afrikaners, Afrikanerdom's obsession with unity continues. However, the minimum conditions are changing which an individual must satisfy, if he is to remain a 'true Afrikaner' and so participate in the preservation of that unity.

The obsession with unity is nicely illustrated by the, to non-Afrikaners, seemingly trivial matter of Dr Van Zyl Slabbert's candidature for the Council of the University of Stellenbosch. Dr Slabbert is in most senses a true Afrikaner, but unlike the many young intellectuals who flirt with the Opposition, but then decide it is speaking an alien language, he joined it and has now become its leader, and in so doing he has added to the seriousness with which the PFP is taken by the government. The threat of a PFP onslaught on the Council of Stellenbosch mobilized the NP Establishment. The voting figures remain secret, but the threat was taken seriously enough for current honours year (that is, fourth year) students to be urged to vote as well as senior members of the university. The students' participation, though allowed under the rules, had largely fallen into disuse; its revival helped to ensure that Dr Slabbert was duly defeated.

In assessing the links that bind Afrikanerdom traditional distrust of English speakers must never be forgotten. One very senior Afrikaner academic saw a certain internationally respected English speaking colleague as 'one of the handymen of the old imperialism'. Since the PFP is perceived as anti-Afrikaner (and nothing will persuade many Afrikaners that this is not so) any idea floated by the Opposition can only be implemented by nationalists, and then only when its tainted origins have been forgotten. In the minds of some traditionalists all political decisions are ultimately moral and religious; but the Opposition is associated with politics as practised in Europe, where it is thought by some Afrikaners to be about power and riches.

That is an extreme, but still influential view, and in some minds the hatred bred of the Anglo-Boer war (and particularly the concentration camps) will never die. It is reinforced in some parts of the country by such rituals as matches between the English and the Afrikaans speaking schools, which may face each other across the street, and annually re-enact the war on the rugby pitch.

Within Afrikanerdom a man, once branded as not quite a true Afrikaner, is likely to stay so for life, just as the true 'insider' will probably have been 'spotted' young and brought on slowly through such organisations as the Ruiterwag, before gaining admission to the Broederbond. The dissident will very rarely be tarred and feathered and the grosser firms of ostracism are less often practised than in the past. There are, however, still some exceptions; for example, Dr Tötemeyer lost his membership of the NP after bringing SWAPO's Daniel Tjongerero to speak to the students of Stellenbosch, having already been gravely rebuked by Mr Vorster (the Chancellor of Stellenbosch University) for saying publicly that SWAPO must be involved in the constitutional discussions in Namibia.

But for a man who lives in the world of ideas other sanctions are effective, like loss of access to the SABC or (for a cleric) to the pulpit; the drying up of invitations to speak to, for example, National Party Youth branches or to write for the newspapers; reluctance of editors to print his letters, and so on. The unorthodox nationalist may also simply be ignored: one of the most striking examples of freezing out in recent years was the extraordinary failure of the government to appoint Professor S. P. Cilliers, Head of the Department of Sociology at Stellenbosch, to the Theron Commission, which investigated the position of the coloured people. His unrivalled knowledge of the 'coloureds' counted for nothing against his history of unorthodoxy, notably his departure from SABRA (the Bureau of Racial Affairs, Afrikaans counterpart of the Institute of Race Relations) in 1962.

For the 'respectable' dissenter, that is the *verligte* who manages to maintain access to Ministers and civil servants, both personally and through institutional links, there are certain simple rules, which may be summed up in a general injunction to use the proper channels. Thus, a man who speaks out publicly against the government when he could have spoken privately to Ministers (and very possibly have had his views seriously discussed) will be as publicly rebuked. A famous example is the one quoted elsewhere (p. 71) of Dr Wassenaar, the chairman of Sanlam, who wrote a book attacking the extent of state ownership of the South African economy and was in return attacked in Parliament by the Prime Minister. At a less exalted level, the man who wishes to float ideas will be ill-advised to write articles in the English language press. To do so may merely be counter-productive, which is why some of the more statesmanlike English speaking editors sometimes deliberately play down stories about dissent within Afrikanerdom, in order not to frustrate ideas with which they sympathize. The Minister who likes a proposal, but needs independent

127

voices to help him, will not welcome a whole page of support from the *Rand Daily Mail*, but will have his hand strengthened by a single column in *Beeld*.

There is much discussion among academics, indeed it is one of the dominant themes in private conversations, about the morality of staying in the NP fold in order to exert influence from within, bearing in mind that all Afrikaner academics have the special reason for political orthodoxy that there is nowhere else that they can teach. Since the penalties, in terms of lost influence, are so obvious and so effective, most men decide to stay, though often with misgivings. There have, however, been some famous cases of defection from the Broederbond, notably by clerics, of whom the most famous was The Rev. Beyers Naudé, who became Director of the short-lived Christian Institute. That body, now banned, attracted enormous attention, because it provided a focus for Christian opposition to apartheid which included both English speakers and Afrikaners, but despite his complete rejection of the Broederbond and all its works, Dr Naudé never revealed the secrets which had been entrusted to him while he was a member. In a more recent case, a member resigned because his students believed membership to be immoral. However, since his resignation was not motivated by that belief (which he did not share) but by a desire to develop a better pastoral relationship with his students, the latter declared that his resignation was meaningless because the motive behind it was wrong. Thus he achieved the worst of both worlds.

A problem related to that of staying or leaving the fold is part moral, part political and concerns academic independence. The question is whether a teacher who seeks influence in other ways than through teaching and writing (such as through personal or institutional links with government) can remain independent, if, indeed, he wishes to do so. The Prime Minister, who is certainly understood to value expert advice, is believed to think that it is often best given by individuals who retain an independent base outside the governmental system, and he tends to favour the creation of a 'think-tank' on the British model to the secondment of academics to Departments of State. On the other hand, there have been plans for political and social advisers to be appointed with the same rank as the Chief Economic Adviser to the government and the political scientist and sociologists who may be appointed to these positions and join the advisers' staffs may lose the intangible benefits of academic detachment, but will undubitably gain influence in terms of access and institutional links.

It is possible to construct a typology of academics, in terms of Establishment membership, ranging from those who are at the Establishment's core, through candidate members, to whose who are outside, but indispensable on intellectual grounds, to those who are right out, though in some cases respected for their teaching and writing. The typology can, of course, be refined and extended and it must be borne in mind that an individual's membership of a particular category may become more or less secure over time. None of the groups contains more than a very few English speakers, since most of them are simply irrelevant to the Establishment.

In group one, those who are fully accepted, might be included such Stellenbosch Professors as Mike de Vries (a chemist, who is now Rektor of the University), Christoph Hanakom, an anthropologist, who has joined the President's Council, Piet Cillie, for many years editor of *Die Burger* and now Professor of Journalism, A. J. Van Wyk, Dean of the Faculty of Law, who was a candidate for the Rektorship, and Julius Jeppie, a political scientist who served on the Consolidation Commission.

Other Stellenbosch Professors, whose membership of the central core of the Establishment is in doubt, for an interesting variety of reasons, include Ben Vosloo, S. J. Terreblanche and Willie Esterhuyse. The first of these has been highly regarded for his evidence to the Schlebusch Commission on the Constitution, but his standing may have suffered a little following a BBC interview in which he said South Africa might have a black Prime Minister in twenty years. Terreblanche, the economist, is a Broederbond member, member of the SABC board of governors, member of the Economic Advisory Council and was on the much smaller Panel which advised on Economic Strategy and Priorities, yet he enjoys something of a reputation as a maverick—who is, of course, totally opposed to the free market economics of Professor Lombard and his school. Esterhuyse, the philosopher, may have been damaged in two ways by his book *Afkeid van Apartheid (Farewell to Apartheid* 1979), first for having written it at all (though the title was not of his choosing), and secondly, for having failed, having demolished the moral base of the ideology of apartheid, to point the way to a replacement. Any slight damage which may have been done to Esterhuyse's reputation for reliability is, however, probably counter-balanced by his reputation for being extremely 'well-connected' by ties of friendship within the Establishment.

The category of 'candidate members' is difficult to typify because it is affected by so many unquantifiable subjective factors, but there is less doubt about Category 3, the academics who are outside the Establishment, yet indispensable to it. Professors Sadie, the noted economist, and S. P. Cilliers, the sociologist, are obvious examples. In a somewhat different sense, Professors Dirk Kotzé and Daan Kriek of UNISA might be held to belong to category 3, since the only reason for their exclusion from the 'core' Establishment is that they advise the opposition NRP. On the other hand, the NRP is often considered a 'think-tank' for the NP, which has indeed already taken over some of its ideas (such as the conviction that the urban blacks must be regarded as a separate political entity) and could ultimately amalgamate with the NP.

In category 4, those who are right outside the establishment, yet have influence and respect through their work, obvious members are the Stellenbosch philosophers Johannes Degenaar and André du Toit and the historian Hermann Giliomee. All three have personal followings of exceptional students (one of whom was unsuccessfully urged by his tutors at his former university not to sit at Degenaar's feet on the completely untrue ground that he was an atheist); all lack influence, except what they have gained through teaching and writing; all are widely travelled and well known in the academic and other worlds outside South Africa, and it may be that their short-term influence is overestimated by foreigners; all are, perhaps ironically, good ambassadors for South Africa's rulers, because they are living examples of the diversity which exists, and is allowed to survive, among the élite. Though their worldly influence in their own country is low at present, it may eventually be very great. For if any more or less peaceful future is to be achieved for South Africa, it will have to be negotiated at something rather like a Lancaster House Conference, and in that case the Degenaars, or their pupils in the next generation, may be among those who speak for Afrikanerdom.

In the past there have been famous clashes between academics and government, but now the watchword is co-operation in the Prime Minister's effort to modernize, and to consolidate *verligte* dominance within the NP. The clashes included frequent disagreements between SABRA and Verwoerd. (SABRA was then an *avant garde* body which has since become *verkramp* and under the chairmanship of Professor Carel Boshoff, who also succeeded Dr Gerrit Viljoen as chairman of the Broederbond, has become preoccupied with the question of a white homeland). One major disagreement, which led to the removal of Professor S. P. Cilliers and others from the executive Committee of SABRA, was over the possibility of establishing a coloured homeland. The ousted Committee members considered this an impracticable and immoral aim; furthermore, it was inconsistent, since the homelands policy was defended by the National Party on the ground that it entitled distinct cultures to survive; yet on cultural grounds there was no distinction to be made between 'coloureds' and Afrikaners. Nor did Verwoerd relish being told by academics that, if the homelands were ever to grow into plausible advertisements for his policy of 'separate freedoms' a positive and extensive effort must be made to develop them: they could not just be left to turn into rural slums.

A further cause of friction was given, as we have seen, by the *verligte* recommendations of the Theron Commission. Naturally, Stellenbosch academics are concerned with coloured questions, given the large coloured population of the Western Cape, and they were well represented on the Commission. The *verligte* recommendations were less influential than they might have been, since they were supported only by eleven of the eighteen members. These eleven consisted of six coloured and five white members of the Commission, and three of the five were academics. The academic alliance with the coloured members had not been expected, and Vorster was particularly angry with the academics, who had perpetrated what he saw as a bad case of the tail wagging the dog. They were, however, 'saved' by the Cape Establishment of the NP, though Professor Theron herself could thereafter no longer be considered a member of the Establishment.

Though, for a number of reasons, many of the Theron Commission's recommendations were not implemented, it can be argued that they were indirectly influential, in that they altered both official and public assumptions about poverty. The case made by the Commission as long ago as 1976 for the alleviation of coloured poverty was by 1979, in the view of at least one member, being made for the blacks some years earlier than might otherwise have been expected, because opinion had been prepared for it by Theron. One visible manifestation of this change in attitudes was that the regional committees set up in 1979 by Dr Koornhof, the Minister of Co-operation and Development, to consider the conditions of urban blacks, were given very similar terms of reference to those of the Theron Commission itself.

Though it is clear that many academics have influence on the thinking of fellow members of the élite, their influence cannot be measured. Nor can it always even be identified, for politicians are no more likely than anyone else to acknowledge the origins of their ideas, even if they are aware of those origins. It would, however, be possible to undertake a much fuller study of the academic role in politics than the sketch I have drawn here. Such a study would proceed in a number of ways. First, it would not be out of place to examine in detail the pervasive influence of certain university Faculties generally acknowledged to be of outstanding quality, such as Law at Stellenbosch, by establishing the number of their pupils who later reached positions of power in the political and other fields.

Secondly, the academic treatment of certain policies would be examined; de Klerk, for example, has already written about the intellectual roots of apartheid (de Klerk 1976); a similar and more extended treatment could be given to the academic contribution in such other areas as the ever-changing line on the homelands, or the political position of the urban blacks, or to thinking about South Africa's constitutional future (I shall examine the last of these in Chapter 14).

Studies of a different kind would focus on the role of friendship in the exercise of influence, and the part played by luck. It would also be of interest to carry forward the work done by Dr Pierre Hugo, and mentioned at the beginning of this chapter, on a small group of academics who joined together to press for specific political changes in 1971, and of the much larger group which organised to oppose them. (For the former see Hugo 1977.)

Since the army is one of the organisations which can promote change in a *verligte* direction, or even enforce it after a coup d'état, it would be of value to know how far academic influences permeate the army. Unfortunately, however, although the officers' school at Saldanha is a Faculty of the University of Stellenbosch, it is unlike most university faculties in that foreigners may not visit it without permission from Pretoria, which is not readily given. Thus, it is not easy to check assertions about the high academic quality of the officer corps, though these assertions are certainly consistent with the view accepted in the South African army that seventy per cent of success in guerrilla warfare depends upon non-military measures of welfare and persuasion.

Finally, there is much movement within the Dutch Reformed Churches and hot debate on questions of race relations. The debate surfaces at the level of the Synod, but is perhaps more significant at the level of the individual congregation. These may vary enormously in political and racial attitudes; for example, Malmesbury, in the western Cape, is said to be very conservative, whilst its neighbour, Somerset West, is very open.

A study of the academic role in change in the Churches would be of great value. It would cover the way in which members of departments of theology in universities recruit their staff and would survey the attitudes of individuals and particular departments, for they have immense influence through their students, most of whom become clergymen in due course. Such a study would also examine the influence of academics who take part outside their teaching in the institutional life of the Churches, as Elders in the local congregations, or at the higher levels of the Ring (representatives of a group of congregations, who alone have the power to dismiss Ministers) and of the Synod.

Even in the absence of these further studies, however, it is possible to reach some conclusions about the academics' contribution to the current debate about South Africa's future.

First, the academics have 'never had it so good' in the sense that the Prime Minister respects and values them and is anxious to bring them into the process of policy making. Secondly, they are much in the public eye and on the whole enjoy high prestige. Finally, however, though many are in unrivalled positions of influence or potential influence, they do not, as a group, appear to be able to accelerate the changes which are so generally agreed to be desirable, and even essential if Afrikanerdom is to survive. The direction of change is becoming clear, but its speed remains a maddening crawl, partly because the electorate at large has no clear idea of where the changes are going and where they will end.

The academics play their part in determining the direction and specifying interim goals, and so in preparing the minds of the electorate for a process of change. The greatest contribution they could make now would lie in clarifying what end result is being pursued, or ought to be pursued, and in speeding up its attainment. The risks are great, but the academics are the group best placed within the élite to take the risks.

CHAPTER 12

Student Politics

The trouble in Stellenbosch University early in 1980 provides an excellent case study of the seriousness with which senior Afrikaners in the National Party take student politics. As was suggested in the previous Chapter, they are taken particularly seriously at Stellenbosch, because it is seen by many as the heart of the establishment. A threat to Stellenbosch is a threat to the Party in the Cape, and ultimately to the Party in the whole of South Africa.

The trouble started when Hilgard Bell, then Chairman of the Stellenbosch Students' Representative Council (SRC), gave an interview in the *Weekend Argus* (16 February 1980) in which he shared his thoughts on current politics. Bell, aged 24, believed himself to be typical of young Afrikaners: 'I think a lot of young people on this campus feel we should move away from apartheid as we have grown up with it'. In fact his views are probably far more typical of *verligtes*, of whatever age, than of the majority of his own contemporaries, as some of his remarks illustrate. For example, he saw Black Consciousness as divisive, because, like extreme Afrikaner or Jewish groups, it precluded voluntary movement between ethnic groups. Of apartheid he said 'The moral justification for it is just not there' and of Christianity 'I think it means not believing in discrimination'. He admired the leader of the Opposition, Dr Van Zyl Slabbert, was disillusioned with the record of the National Party and even doubted that it could guarantee peace if it stayed in power over the next ten or fifteen years.

None of these *verligte* views is particularly unacceptable in the present climate within Afrikanerdom, to which Bell yields to none in his passionate commitment. His real offence was twofold: he gave the interview in an English language newspaper, and he described the constitutional proposals (which at that time were still on the table, though generally expected to be superseded by the proposals of the Schlebusch Commission) as '. . . a lot of bull. They're riddled with problems, they're immoral and they are wide open to corruption. And they don't really change anything. They don't take blacks into consideration at all.'

In private it was widely agreed that Bell's remarks went no further in their spirit than would many of those constantly made by his elders and that the phrase 'a lot of bull', though perhaps robust, could hardly be found offensive. On the other hand, even his sympathizers also thought, again in private, that he had been insufficiently circumspect and, above all, that he

133

should not have been interviewed by an 'English' paper. Nor was he helped by the headline 'Inside the Mind of an Elite Afrikaner'.

In public he was berated for the disrespect shown to the leaders of Afrikanerdom in so forthrightly condemning the constitutional proposals. The concern expressed itself in various ways; the Rector of the University discussed Bell's remarks with him and five fellow-members of the SRC issued a press statement dissociating themselves from what he had said. To these, Bell replied: 'I stand by my statement absolutely . . . What I am sorry about is that the language in which I expressed myself may have offended some people because it was so harsh'. (*Cape Times*: 22 February 1980)

That did not end the matter. A few days later a petition was launched among the students calling for a mass meeting to be held to repudiate that section of the SRC (still a majority) which continued to support Bell. The students who launched the petition were mainly head students of men's residences. They needed two hundred signatures on their petition, which drew attention to the 'incalculable harm' done to the image of the university, and within hours had collected five hundred. By now it was clear, and a spokesman for the drafters of the petition confirmed, that the issue was political and the grievance was against the *verligtheid* of the student chairman and some of his colleagues. (*Cape Times*: 28 February 1980)

The scope of the debate was dramatically (if in some eyes excessively) broadened by the Prime Minister himself. Mr Botha, it was announced on the front page of *Die Burger*, had caused his private secretary to write to the SRC to withdraw his promise to speak to a meeting (the date of which had not yet been fixed) to be organized by the SRC; he would, however, address a meeting if it were organized by the local youth branch of the National Party (*Die Burger*: 29 February 1980).

On 5 March the majority of the SRC rejected a motion that the Prime Minister should be offered an apology, and this in turn precipitated the resignation of three SRC members, who thought it disgraceful that the work of the committee which had devised the constitutional proposals and had been chaired by the Prime Minister (before he succeeded Mr Vorster) should have been described as immoral and wide open to corruption (*Die Burger*: 7 March 1980).

There followed a proposal by two of the ten surviving members that the SRC should resign *en bloc*, because they doubted whether it was any longer truly a representative body. Seventeen (which later rose to twenty) of the thirty-two hostels had distanced themselves from it and others had expressed disappointment at its actions. The majority, however, believed that they should remain in office and explain themselves at a mass meeting of all the university's students, since in some of the hostels they had been refused an opportunity to address the residents (*Cape Times*: 14 March 1980). The two proposers resigned nevertheless (*Die Burger*: 17 March 1980).

At the same time as Bell was having a difficult time on his home campus, he did receive guarded support from leaders of other Afrikaans universities. Only the chairman of the Free State University's SRC refused to comment (though he agreed that Bell had supporters there), but other leaders were less reserved. Broadly speaking they agreed that it was no longer necessary to be a good nationalist to be a good Afrikaner, that the present political dispensation could not last and that any new constitutional deal must give blacks a political say (*Weekend Argus*: 15 March 1980).

The SRC had thought it inappropriate to apologise as a body to the Prime Minister, since Bell's original interview had been given strictly in his personal capacity. Bell did, however, write a personal letter to Mr Botha, assuring him that it had never been the SRC's intention to insult anybody and saying that, if the Prime Minister regarded himself as having been insulted, he apologized.

There followed, on 20 March, a mass meeting of 3,000 students, which voted overwhelmingly to disband the SRC, leaving its business to be carried on by an executive committee, on which, ironically, Bell continued to sit with his arch-rivals. Unfortunately, Bell was given no opportunity to speak to the motion, through some peculiarity of procedure. It was possible, though rather unlikely, that he would have been able to swing the meeting behind him, but as things stood the vote against the SRC was decisive.

The SRC, divided though it had been, had shown itself in some ways a remarkably *verligte* body; for example, some of its members had participated in an unprecedented visit to Soweto, in which they had held long discussions with young blacks and with such older leaders as Dr Motlana. They had also invited the leaders of the Inkatha Youth Wing for a three day visit, (which has resulted in the setting up of permanent links) and their visitors had been highly impressed that such an invitation should come from Stellenbosch. By contrast, they noted, their leader, Chief Buthelezi, had met hostile demonstrations when he received a doctorate at the nearby University of Cape Town. However, as the reporter who had started the whole trouble at Stellenbosch later commented, it seemed likely that any future student leaders would be far more cautious. (Shauna Westcott in *Weekend Argus*: 22 March 1980). Not long afterwards a motion came before the student parliament that candidates for office must state their political allegiance, and thereafter a committee was appointed to devise new procedures for the parliament itself (*Die Matie*, the Stellenbosch students' newspaper: 22 May & 25 July 1980).

It may well be that in a few years the removal of the *verligte* Bell will be seen as a turning point in student politics in South Africa. Some such feeling may have influenced the University's Rector when he addressed a meeting of the lively current affairs society, SAAK, in July 1980 on the twin themes of the need to restructure Stellenbosch's political institutions so that polarization would in future be avoided, and the role of Stellenbosch as the architect of change in South Africa. The purpose, he said, must be to work, under the motto 'South Africa first' towards a community in which equality and equality of opportunity could be achieved. (*Die Matie*: 8 August 1980) The speech was also reported in the national press.

The unprecedented heckling of the Prime Minister, which occurred when he duly addressed a meeting organised by the National Party Youth branch at Stellenbosch on 10 April 1980, was another indication that the wind of change was beginning to blow through young Afrikanerdom. The incident was naturally very differently reported in the Afrikaans and English newspapers, the former concentrating on the content of the Prime Minister's speech, the latter on the hissing and booing he encountered in question time. To treat any elderly person disrespectfully, even if he does not occupy a position of great responsibility, is almost unthinkable for young Afrikaners, yet students not only dared to walk up to the rostrum and ask searching questions about (to take the most dramatic example) the government's refusal to release Nelson Mandela, but also to show dissatisfaction with the answers. As the distinguished political correspondent Fleur de Villiers reported:

> There was laughter when Mr Botha described the South African Press as one of the most free in the world and there was anger when he turned on his student tormentors to tell them to get back to their books and to treat their Prime Minister with more respect. . . . The change reflects more than a shift in the thinking of the young Afrikaner elite who no longer regard the state as a cultural father and economic patron, and who instead are beginning to question the legitimacy of the entire South African political system (*Sunday Times*, Johannesburg: 13 April 1980).

It is not, unfortunately, known how many of the audience showed open hostility to the Prime Minister, but one can certainly agree with the 'seasoned Stellenbosch observer' whom Miss De Villiers reported as saying that students would not have dared to show open dissent five years ago. Nor would Chris Heyman, the student who asked the question about Mandela, (he was also a part time lecturer in political science) have dared then to expatiate to a journalist on his dissatisfaction with the answer (Helen Zille in *Rand Daily Mail*: 12 April 1980).

Yet another example of innovation at Stellenbosch was the 'mini national convention' organized by SAAK later in April. This consisted of four evenings of speeches by a wide variety of well known figures from all racial groups, ending with a panel discussion. Participants in the week's events included Dr Slabbert, the Leader of the Opposition, Dr Nthatho Motlana, chairman of Soweto's Committee of Ten, another *verligte* nationalist, Dr Denis Worrall (who, as has already been noted, later became Chairman of the constitutional committee of the new President's Council), Mr Fanyana Mazibuko of the Soweto Teachers' Association, Dr Oscar Dhlomo, Secretary of Inkatha, Mr David Curry, leader of the Coloured Labour Party, Professor Marinus Wiechers (the extremely *verligte* Professor of Law at the University of South Africa) and a number of others. The notably *verligte* nationalist MP, Mr Wynand Malan, refused to attend, precisely because the conference had the air of a national convention in miniature, and therefore smacked of the policy of the opposition Progressive Federal Party. (For Stellenbosch students' political views see also Gagiano *et al.* 1982.)

It might be said that this initiative was hardly earth-shaking, but that would be entirely to misunderstand the atmosphere of Stellenbosch and the temper of Afrikanerdom at large. It may be, as *Die Matie* has claimed, that Stellenbosch is the most *verlig* of all Afrikaner institutions of tertiary education, but, as the same editorial went on to claim, the *verligte* minority rests on a large majority who are politically apathetic (*Die Matie*: 8 August 1980). Against those odds, to invite a group of eminent speakers of all races (though all were, necessarily, rather 'establishment' figures) showed a constructive nonconformity which must give some hope for the future.

It can, of course, be said that to arrange such a 'mini national convention' is in a sense small beer, but the Stellenbosch students could reasonably answer that students could hardly be expected to do more, and that at least their eminent guests accepted the invitations (see *Die Matie*: 1 May 1980). It may also be said, with some truth, that at an English language university none of the participants would be regarded as exciting and some, like Dr Dhlomo, might get a poor reception. The answer to this, I believe, is that Afrikaner students, unlike the vast majority of their English-speaking contemporaries, have some chance—as candidate members of the Establishment—of being taken seriously in their contributions to the debate about the future of Afrikanerdom. Thus the 'moderation' for which they might be berated in more radical circles reflects both sound political sense on their part about what lies within the limits of the possible now, and a prudent awareness that an Afrikaner man or woman who gets a reputation for 'wildness' when young is likely to jeopardize any prospect of future influence.

For the English speaker (there are, of course, exceptions to the generalization) gaining such a reputation does not matter to the same extent, since he is unlikely to achieve a position of influence, save in certain limited fields—notably business. There is, furthermore, greater tolerance extended by Afrikaners to Afrikaner 'dissidents', provided always that they do not dissent in the wrong forum, nor to an extent which calls in question their fundamental commitment to the Afrikaner people. We have seen that the Stellenbosch SRC chairman was dismissed by the student body largely because he spoke out in an English language newspaper, a choice of medium which, in turn, threw doubt upon his credentials as a 'true Afrikaner'.

After a lull of some months there occurred a further event which is of great significance in Afrikaner student politics, and therefore of more than trivial interest in Afrikaner politics at large. This was the split in the Afrikaanse Studente Bond (ASB), which came to public notice in July 1980, just before the ASB's congress. For the first time two observers from Inkatha were present at the congress, but none came from the English speaking National Union of South African Students (NUSAS), partly because NUSAS had received no formal invitation, and partly because it disapproved of Inkatha being invited, whilst other more radical black bodies were not. Inkatha had had a meeting with the ASB early in July at ASB's request. They were reported to have got on well (*Beeld*: 8 July 1980) and Gatsha Buthelezi, the leader of Inkatha, said afterwards that he was once more hopeful about the future after talking to these young Afrikaners (*Beeld*: 9 July 1980).

The congress, particularly Inkatha's attendance, had been extensively reported in the Afrikaans press. One public figure who addressed it was W. de Klerk, editor of *Die Transvaler*, and member of the innermost circle of the Broederbond. The *Transvaler* approved his statement at the congress that the Afrikaner could only improve his very bad image by communication, and endorsed his praise of Buthelezi and Inkatha for their willingness to talk.

At the congress there appeared (according to *Die Matie*) to be a general movement to the right, balanced to some extent by a splinter group on the left. The motions passed showed a strong National Party influence, though the motion proposing the establishment of a white homeland was rejected because it was excessively close to an extreme of Party thinking, whilst failing to recognize the wrongs in the situation of the Republic as a whole. There was criticism of the government's performance and doubts were voiced about the centralization of power round the Prime Minister, but the watered down character of most of the motions passed indicated that the ASB as a whole was not ready to engage in active criticism. It did, on the other hand, pass motions asking for better education for 'non-white' population groups, and deploring the use of power as a so-called 'solution' to racial problems.

The splinter group saw the ASB as impotent and stagnant. Its leaders were Theuns Eloff (who two years earlier had been widely noticed as the *verlig* and charismatic leader of the ASB, but of whom little had been heard in the interim) and Absie de Swardt. In all, eighteen delegates supported the view of these two leaders that time had run out and that it was time to talk to other ethnic groups. Fourteen of the eighteen were from Potchefstroom, including the chairman of the Potchefstroom SRC and his deputy, two from the University of the Orange Free State and two from the Rand Afrikaanse Universiteit. The strongest opponent was the 1979/80 Chairman of the ASB, perhaps piqued that his role during his year of office had been overshadowed by De Swardt's.

The speakers envisaged a new student organization in which there would be no ethnic or other qualification for membership, though ethnicity and (group) identity were recognized as realities, which must be protected by free association, not laws. The only qualification would be a commitment to the Christian religion. *Die Matie* welcomed the creation of the new body, in an editorial headlined 'Cloud on the Horizon' (*Die Matie*: 25 July 1980).

There followed a series of visits by Theuns Eloff to Afrikaans campuses. At Stellenbosch he said that, looking to the future, the time was ripe for a multi-racial students' organization. The fact that the ASB had nearly passed a motion calling for a white homeland could only increase uncertainty about its competence to deal with the problems lying ahead; nevertheless, members of the new organization could also be members of the ASB. The only qualifications were Christianity and loyalty to South Africa (*Die Matie*: 8 August 1980). The same issue of the students' newspaper carried a more orthodox article by an ASB supporter, emphasizing the 'left' group's lack of success at the recent congress. He reminded his readers that both its motions, the one calling for an Act entrenching human rights and the other for the inclusion of blacks in the new President's Council, had been voted down. The far right HNP youth had also tried to break up the congress, but without success.

Die Matie also carried an interview with Tony Weaver, Chairman of the SRC in the University of Cape Town, in which he welcomed the possibility of a multi-racial students' movement. But he considered the Christian qualification a handicap. Furthermore, so long as leaders of black, brown and Indian universities felt they had no part in the initiative, it would be written off as a purely Afrikaner movement and blacks who participated would be in danger of being seen by their own constituencies as sell-outs (*Ibid*). (It was decided at the founding congress on 12 & 13 September that Christianity would not after all be a necessary qualification for membership, although the Congress itself subscribed to Christian principles, including belief in the sovereignty of God and his word. See *Die Matie*: 18 September 1980.)

The split was naturally given extensive coverage in the English language press, which as usual did nothing to help the new body (by now named Polstu, Stupol having been considered and abandoned for obvious reasons) in Afrikaner eyes. However, it was also reasonably well reported in some Afrikaans newspapers. Jan Louis du Plooy, chairman of the Potchefstroom SRC (who had earlier given Bell some support at Stellenbosch) became chairman of Polstu and one of the new body's first acts was to arrange a meeting with NUSAS, which was reported to have been successful, though without any immediate result (*Beeld*: 30 July 1980).

Shortly afterwards, Du Plooy called for the removal of section 16 of the Immorality Act (which forbids cross-racial sexual relations) and the complete scrapping of the Mixed Marriages Act (*Beeld*: 13 August 1980). This followed a speech by Alwyn Schlebusch (then leader of the Party in the Orange Free State and Minister of the Interior, subsequently Vice-President of the Republic) to Pretoria students, in which he said the government was still considering proposals for the 'improvement' of the Immorality Act (*Beeld*: 8 August 1980). The number of students who aligned themselves with Polstu was not at first great; the branch formed at Stellenbosch had 32 founder members, though they were hoping to send 50 delegates to the next ASB congress (*Die Transvaler*: 13 August 1980); at RAU 38 joined, despite jeers and rotten eggs (*Die Transvaler*: 14 August 1980). At its headquarters, Potchefstroom, Polstu suffered a set-back when the majority of a mass meeting of 1,500 students voted to dissociate

139

themselves from it without allowing it first to state its case: nevertheless, 45 joined (*Rapport*: 18 August 1980). At about the same time the results of a questionnaire administered by the sociology department of the University of Pretoria suggested that the majority of students there were *verlig* (*Beeld*: 15 August 1980). Very surprisingly, du Plooy, despite much opposition, was re-elected Chairman of the Potchefstroom SRC (*Transvaler*: 28 August 1980).

Thanks to support from business, Polstu now has sufficient funds to bring out its own periodical *Crux*. The April 1981 issue gives details of the organization's activities, notably political and economic study projects and tours to Namibia, Zimbabwe and the USA. Contact had already been made with individual black student leaders, and Polstu was ready to establish relations with any other student organizations, including the black ones. The paper emphasizes that there is no conflict between membership of Polstu and of the ASB, since the former is a political body and the latter a broader based cultural organization. (However, some spokesmen have said that Polstu should aim to fill the political vacuum between the ASB and NUSAS.) Polstu's main guiding principles are that change in South Africa is essential, that force must be rejected, and that peaceful change can only be brought about through increased contact between the racial groups. To this end, a number of positive actions had already been taken, for example, a campaign had been waged at Bloemfontein against those who wished to prevent Bishop Desmond Tutu addressing a meeting on the campus and at Potchefstroom the branch had shown a film on the life of the founder of the ANC Youth League.

It is worth recording Polstu's statement of principle adopted at its founding congress in September 1980 (printed in English translation in *Crux*, April 1981):

Full citizenship for, and equal political participation by all people born or naturalized in the territory of South Africa constituted as on 31 May 1961. This does not mean that Polstu prescribes any particular constitutional model.

A just economic system providing equal and universal access to the benefits created by the South African economy, closing the prosperity gap through economic progress.

The undelayed abolition of statutory discrimination on the grounds of race, colour or creed. Also the realisation of a society which, while protecting separate identities, guarantees certain fundamental freedoms and rights, maintaining a spirit of mutual goodwill and co-operation.

An educational system with equal access to opportunities and facilities characterized by high standards, incorporating the academic freedom of independent scientific enquiry.

The Rule of Law as guaranteed by a Bill of Rights enshrined in the National Constitution with recourse to an independent judiciary.

The same issue of *Crux* contained a letter from Chief Buthelezi beginning 'We were all fascinated by the enterprise of Polstu' and going on to remind readers of Inkatha's adherence to the same and similar principles; full citizenship rights for all; no fragmentation of South Africa on ethnic lines;

economic rights; freedom of association; full educational opportunities and a Bill of Rights.

There is, of course, nothing revolutionary about Polstu's principles, which espouse no particular constitutional solution and are consistent with continuing differentiation between the races, provided only that it is not enshrined in law. Yet the body's determination to concern itself with the future of the black majority of South Africa's population and to work towards the acceptance of blacks as equal citizens is of the greatest significance in the context of young Afrikanerdom. That the movement is taken seriously by those in authority is proved by the warning delivered to Polstu by Mr Louis Le Grange, the Minister of Police, against its planned contact with the black Congress of South African students and Azanian Students' Organization, bodies which he described as ANC inspired (*The Guardian*: 3 July 1981). Whether it will, in fact, be able to establish close links is open to question. Similarly, it must be doubted whether Polstu will be able to do much to bridge the great gulf that is fixed between Afrikaans and English-speaking youth. Links with the black groups are, of course, more urgent than with NUSAS, since the immediate future lies in black and Afrikaner hands.

I have gone into some aspects of student politics at length because they illustrate some general propositions about white politics in South Africa. First, although it is far too soon to evaluate the effectiveness or durability of Polstu, it is a lively example of the cracking of Afrikaner unity. Anyone inclined to jubilation or despair by this observation should, however, note that, beneath the cracks, that unity may even be being reinforced at a deeper level by such movements. For Polstu says nothing which would undermine the essentials of Afrikaner culture, language, religion or 'sense of identity'; what it does forcefully put across is that if Afrikanerdom is to survive as a cultural entity it must prepare itself to share power, not merely wield it.

It can be argued that Polstu is an expression of disillusion with the progress made by *verligtes* in the *verligte/verkrampte* debate. A more fruitful analysis, however, sees it as a body promoting the natural and evolutionary extension of that debate. The limits of permissible thinking among the Afrikaner élite have expanded at a great rate in recent years: ideas and solutions may be discussed, at least in private or semi-private (the release of Nelson Mandela is a good example) among Afrikaners, which a few years ago would have put their proponents beyond the pale. Polstu appears to be seeking to create an organization in which Afrikaner nationalists can, without losing their Afrikaner credentials, sit down with renegade Afrikaners, members of the white opposition parties, and the great majority of the South African population who have never aspired to membership in Afrikanerdom, because they are English-speaking or black. This is, of course, a tight-rope, though it is one on which many more senior members of the élite are also balancing. On the one hand, if young orthodox Afrikaners cannot be persuaded that Polstu will not ruin their social acceptability and career prospects, they will not join. On the other, fear of being seen as participants in just another exercise in Afrikaner introspection may force Polstu's leaders to escape from the *verligte* tradition into more radical initiatives, which will soon inhibit their effectiveness on the Afrikaans campuses.

The wider political world in South Africa pays great, to European eyes surprisingly great, attention to political movements among students; one could ask for no better example than the Prime Minister's decision to involve himself in the discord at Stellenbosch. Senior Professors and university administrators follow the ups and downs of student politics with the keenest attention and there are persistent reports that the Broederbond does its best to get members of its junior wing, the Ruiterwag, into representative posts in all Afrikaans universities. For example, according to a newspaper report (which relied on an informant who had to remain anonymous) in 1974 sixteen of the eighteen available seats on the Pretoria SRC were won by Ruiters (*Sunday Times* Johannesburg: 9 March 1980). The hostel system also provides an admirable mechanism for acquiring and maintaining control and it is interesting that at Stellenbosch during 1980 a seminar was, for the first time, arranged to bring together 55 potential leaders from the various hostels, still in their first year as students, to develop their leadership qualities. A glowing account of this innovation was given by one of the SRC leaders most opposed to Bell (*Die Matie*: 8 August 1980).

The obsession of most Afrikaners with unity goes a long way to explain the extraordinary interest in student politics, and in youth generally, displayed by senior Afrikaners. To oppose from within, preferably in private organizations which are not open to publicity, is acceptable, while to oppose openly attracts the risk of ostracism. The obsession with unity is linked in the orthodox Afrikaner mind with the nightmare of defections to the opposition, though any rational assessment must conclude that the PFP poses no threat to the continuance of National Party power. Nevertheless, the NP hierarchy in the Cape has been genuinely worried by the 'movement to the left' at Stellenbosch, and in the Transvaal there have been voices delivering the same message. In June 1980, on three successive days, *Die Vaderland* drew attention to the fervour of the left at Stellenbosch, warned that the PFP was gaining ground in the university and urged the NP to look to its laurels (*Die Vaderland*: 25, 26, 27 June 1980).

Membership of the PFP demands courage and may close some career avenues which would otherwise be open to young Afrikaners, but it does not necessarily bring exclusion from the communion of Afrikanerdom. This may come with the rejection of religion, and certainly follows the expression of serious doubt about the overwhelming value of Afrikaner culture or the self-evident importance of ethnicity. To deny these is to deny the folk memory of struggle out of poverty and oppression by the English, which Moodie (as we have seen) calls the 'foundation myth' of Afrikanerdom. In fact, few Afrikaners, whether students in Polstu, or academics like Degenaar, Du Toit or Giliomee, would make these renunciations. To do so would be foolish, because it would entail the loss of influence; nor can it be expected. Progressives and *verligte* nationalists agree, as we shall see in the chapter on Constitutional thinking, that there is no reason why Afrikaners should abandon their cultural identity, provided only that they do not expect to maintain dominance over all other cultural groups. The constitutional debate is about how this is to be done, given the range of thinking in the party and, in particular, the *verkramptes'* strength in the Transvaal, and much of the debate is mirrored at the level of student politics.

CHAPTER 13

Parliament and the 1981 Elections

Since Mr Botha himself has been intellectually convinced (at least partly by officers of the Defence Force) of the need for reform, however much his emotions may rebel, he must be classed as a *verligte*. For him the politics of domination have given way to the politics of survival, but this is by no means true of the whole of Afrikanerdom. Even before the 1981 elections showed the strength of the Herstigte Nasionale Party's support the Prime Minister was held back by fear of a split in the party, which would be led by the redoubtable Dr Andries Treurnicht, the National Party leader in the Transvaal. The Prime Minister's fears of something approaching a UDI in the Transvaal may seem exaggerated for a man who has a life-time's experience of operating the party machine and great skill in imposing his will on the party. He has, after all, been an organization man ever since he gave up his university studies to take a job as a junior party functionary and is now undisputed leader of the Cape. Furthermore, Dr Treurnicht is said to be as obsessed with the desire to maintain the unity of Afrikanerdom as is Mr Botha. Nevertheless, for whatever reasons, Mr Botha was not confident in 1980, and that lack of confidence reduced such progress as there was to a dispiriting crawl. Early in 1982, however, the long-awaited split occurred (many commentators believe Mr Botha provoked it) and Dr Treurnicht was expelled from the party. (See Chapter 18, postscript, for further discussion of the split).

Not only does Mr Botha hold a position of great power in the party but in recent years the power of the Prime Minister has also greatly increased. Mr Botha has streamlined the civil service and put his own men in many of the command posts and has greatly strengthened the Prime Minister's office, so that Parliament, which in any case is an irrelevance for most of the population, is becoming of decreasing significance to the white group as well. Nevertheless, it retains some relevance as a forum for debate between government and opposition and between varying tendencies within the ruling National Party, and in view of that continuing, if diminished, relevance it seemed worthwhile, in the context of the examination of change in South Africa, to try to assess the strength of the *verligte* movement and the depth of *verkramptheid* in the National Party caucus, if only because the brave talk of change could obviously not be translated into legislative action if the majority of the dominant party's Members of Parliament were very *verkramp*. Mr Botha has no House of Lords to which to kick *verkrampte* MPs upstairs, and if he had he could not always influence the selection of their successors. Guesses varied wildly about how many MPs would follow Dr Treurnicht into the wilderness and the research was designed to find an answer. The research, (of which a preliminary account appeared in *The Times* of 4 July 1980 over the names of Steven Georgala and the present author) was undertaken in 1980; at the elections of April 29, 1981, some members retired and made way for newcomers, others had gone to the new President's Council and a few lost their seats, but there is no reason to suppose that the new caucus was greatly more *verlig* or *verkramp* than it has been in 1980. In the event, 16 members left the party, including Dr Treurnicht; 12 of the 16 were in our most *verkrampte* group.

Using what is often called the Delphi Technique (after the oracle) we asked 12 academics, politicians and journalists, all experts in their different ways, and with a wide acquaintance in Parliament, to rank each of the 133 Nationalist MPs at the time (a seat in the Orange Free State was vacant) on a *verlig/verkramp* scale, where a score of one indicated the most *verlig* and five the most *verkramp*. The panel was unavoidably skewed in two respects: its members were drawn largely from the Cape and those members who were Nationalists themselves tended towards *verligte* views. Most members of the panel would have been reluctant to have their individual opinions of Members of Parliament made public and we therefore agreed to publish only aggregate results, but were permitted to make known the names of the members of the panel. They were the professors of economics, politics and sociology at the University of Stellenbosch (Professors Terreblanche, Vosloo and Cilliers) the leader of the Parliamentary Opposition, Dr F. Van Zyl Slabbert of the Progressive Federal Party, another opposition MP, Mr W. M. Sutton of the New Republic Party, and a leading nationalist backbencher, the *verligte* Dr Denis Worrall, who has since become Chairman of the Constitutional Committee of the President's Council and so is in a position to play a leading part in the process of constitutional change. The political journalists, chosen from English and Afrikaans newspapers in the Transvaal and the Cape, were Mr Michael Acott and Mr Gerald Shaw of *The Cape Times*; Mr Paul Greyling of *Die Burger* (published in Cape Town), Miss Fleur de Villiers of *The Sunday Times* (Johannesburg) and Mr Van Heerden and Mr Kleinhans of *Die Transvaler*. The two last acted as a team and were counted as one respondent, so that the final panel consisted of eleven members.

Some characteristics of the Nationalist caucus in 1980 may be briefly noticed. All but one were male; most went to school at or near their birthplace and often to the nearest university to their homes; the majority had one or more university degrees, so that there appears to be no significant correlation between education and degree of *verligtheid*; the great majority were married and had children; the more *verkrampte* groups tended to be older; nearly all the surnames were Afrikaans; the church and the law were strongly represented.

The scores given to an MP by each respondent were aggregated and

145

divided by the number of panel members who had felt able to express an opinion of that MP. As can be seen from Table 1, the results yielded four groups, scoring averages of 1.0—1.9, 2.0—2.9 and so on. The first, the most *verligte* contained only 14 members, whereas there were 35 in the most *verkrampte* group (4.0—5.0) and the remainder were evenly divided, with 42 scoring 2.0—2.9 and 42 with 3.0—3.9. Of course some MPs were much better known than others, though only 11 were commented on by fewer than five panel members (see Table 2). It was noticeable that all the 14 members of Group 1 were well enough known for 8 or more of the 11 respondents to have an opinion about them, whereas only 55 per cent of Group 2, 26 per cent of Group 3 and 49 per cent of Group 4 were known to so many.

Of the 14 in Group 1 nine came from the Transvaal, including three ministers (Dr Koornhof, Co-operation and Development; Mr R. F. Botha, Foreign Affairs; and Mr Janson, National Education, Sport and Recreation) and a deputy minister: four came from the Cape, including one minister (Mr Heunis, Transport) and one from Natal. However the Cape dominated Group 2, with 25 out of the 42 in that Group. They included the Prime Minister and three other ministers: Dr Van der Merwe, Industry, Commerce and Consumer Affairs; Mr Smit, Posts and Telecommunications and Dr Munnik, Health, Social Welfare and Pensions. The Speaker, Deputy Speaker and three of the six deputy ministers were also Cape members of Group 2. The Transvaal's 10 representatives in Group 2 included four ministers: Mr S. P. Botha, Manpower Utilization; Mr Schoemann, Agriculture; Mr Steyn (who later became South African ambassador in London) Community Development, Coloured Relations and Indian Affairs; and Mr de Klerk, Mines, Environmental Planning and Energy. Of the remaining seven in the group, four came from Natal and three from the Orange Free State. The last included Mr Schlebusch, Minister of Justice and the Interior (subsequently the first Vice-President of the Republic) and one deputy minister.

It is striking that no less than 13 of the 17 full ministers covered in the study (the eighteenth, Mr Horwood, was a member of the Senate) and five of the six deputy ministers belonged to the two most *verligte* groups. In other words, in this respect the Prime Minister made good use of his power of patronage; if Cabinet alliances are made in line with political sympathy, Mr Botha had a clear majority behind him. If, however, they are made also in line with provincial loyalties, which would not be surprising, given the long years of distrust between Transvaal and Cape, then he was at a disadvantage, since eleven ministers were Transvaal men, including one from Group 3 (Mr Le Grange, Police) and three from Group 4. These three, however, held relatively junior portfolios: they were Mr Raubenheimer, Water Affairs and Forestry; Dr Treurnicht, Public Works, Statistics and Tourism; and Dr Hartzenburg, Education and Training. The Deputy Chairman of Committees was also a Transvaal member of this group. (For a summary see Table 3).

146

Indeed the Transvaal dominated Groups 3 and 4, with exactly half (21) of Group 4 and no less than 26 of the 35 members of Group 4. Thus 47 of the Transvaal's 66 members were moderately or extremely *verkramp*, which means that, given the federal nature of the party and the control each province has over the selection of candidates, there is rather little scope for the Prime Minister to advance *verligte* members from the Transvaal, simply because there are relatively few of them. In other respects however, Mr Botha has cause for satisfaction. Only 35 MPs belong to the most *verkrampte* group and it must be obvious to all MPs that, in general, political advancement is more likely to come the way of *verligtes* than *verkramptes*. (Dr Treurnicht may seem an exception at first sight, but in reality what is remarkable about him is not that he was a member of Cabinet, but that so powerful a party leader should have held such comparatively unimportant office.) Furthermore, the Prime Minister has consolidated these advantages by 'freezing' the number of seats in each province, although population movements should entitle the Transvaal to additional seats. Remarkably, however, he did not fully take the opportunity offered by the introduction of nominated MPs early in 1981 to strengthen the ranks of the verligtes for, according to Helen Zille (*Rand Daily Mail*: 22 January 1981) the most optimistic analysis by the disappointed *verligtes* was that five of the twelve would support them, whilst six could be classified in the Treurnicht Faction and one was an unknown quantity. Meanwhile the *verligtes* lost members to the President's Council, which naturally needed *verligte* members if it was to produce reformist recommendations. Of the ten nationalist MPs who joined it, 3 belonged to Group 1, 4 to Group 2 and 3 to Group 4.

South Africa's parliament runs for five years, so that the Prime Minister was not obliged to call an election until 1982. There was, however, much speculation early in 1981 that elections would be held during that year and in fact they were called for 29 April.

There were a number of reasons for the speculation. First, no fewer than 22 by-elections were pending, thanks to the cabinet reshuffle of August 1980 and the appointment to the new President's Council of a number of MPs. Several Ministers were without parliamentary seats, a position permitted under the Constitution, but for a maximum of one year.

Furthermore, Mr Botha (who had been elected leader of the party in succession to Mr Vorster) was believed to be anxious to have his own mandate for a cautious programme of reform and in that connection he needed to unite behind him the *verligte* and *verkrampte* wings of the party. He needed also to guard against defections to the right wing HNP and probably calculated that, whereas that party might win some by-elections, in a general election the faithful would unite behind him. Further advantages of an April election would be that the HNP would not yet have succeeded in raising its election fund (by January only R70,000 of the R250,000 target had been raised: see *Financial Mail* 23 January 1981) and that Mr Botha would be able to gain popular support for his Namibia policy during the lull in the negotiations with the western 'contact group'.

Since there was little prospect that the Nationalist representation in parliament would be significantly reduced from its then level of 133 of the 165 elected seats, much turned on the 'battle for the nominations' which preceded nomination day on 28 March. In many constituencies it was a foregone conclusion that whoever was nominated in the National Party interest would win the election, so that the battle was between *verligtes* and *verkramptes* seeking nomination (which is settled at provincial, not national, level) often in safe seats. As it turned out, however, only 32 nationalists, or 25 per cent of the parliamentary caucus were elected for the first time in 1981, 6 of them in newly delimited seats: a number of the newcomers replaced members who had joined the President's Council and others who had retired in the normal course of events, so that the contest for the nominations was not as important as had been expected. However, it is true that in some constituencies *verligte* candidates were beaten off and in a few the sitting member was replaced by a more *verkrampte* successor. A good example is King William's Town, whose white inhabitants feared cession to the Ciskei homeland.

The London *Times* truly remarked of the election that:

> To the mass of the unenfranchised non-white population it will appear a mere ritual of the boss tribe that has scant relevance to their aspirations. Although Mr Botha's reforms were indeed the key to the campaign, those reforms did not yet amount to much, though they irritated the *verkramptes*. There is little in his actual record at this stage to upset any but the most *verkramp* of voters.
>
> (*The Times*: 29 January 1981)

That may have been true, but the *verkramptes* were concerned more about what might happen than about what had already occurred and the Prime Minister was correspondingly preoccupied with the need to reassure them. Reassurance was no doubt given by the banning of two African newspapers and, on the international front, by the uncompromising line taken by the government on Namibia since the abortive Geneva conference of January 1981.

In February the government made a strong bid for the crucially important votes of pensioners and the public service by announcing increased pensions and average salary increases of 12 per cent in a mini-budget, increases justified by the staff shortages experienced in the public sector. Teachers, whose dissatisfaction with their pay had led to thousands of resignations, gained a 20 per cent increase.

During the campaign it became clear that Afrikanerdom was indeed divided against itself. Even Mr Botha, one of whose ambitions is not to be regarded in the history books as the Prime Minister who split Afrikanerdom asked in Parliament in February: 'Why must we hear every day that nationalist Afrikanerdom, must be divided as a pre-condition for change in South Africa? The Afrikaner is already divided' and in the same month *Rapport* summarized the divisions by listing seven organizations to the right of the NP, of which six were led predominantly or exclusively by Afrikaners. (*The Guardian*: 24 February 1981.)

According to one pre-election poll, the HNP's potential share of the vote had increased from 4.1 per cent in 1979 to 8.5 per cent in 1981. Apart from the HNP the NP was opposed on the right by the National Conservative Party, led by the discredited former Minister of Information, Dr Connie Mulder, who accused the NP of becoming 'left and liberal'. According to Stanley Uys the campaign accelerated the polarization between *verligtes* and *verkramptes* which had been growing since Mr Botha's election in 1978. Uys believed that a fluidity had been created in Afrikaner politics, which could never be controlled again by the old apartheid methods. Nevertheless, there were strict limits on the reforms Mr Botha had in mind: there was no intention to surrender white rule; though coloureds and Indians were on the Constitutional agenda, blacks were not; no desegregation was planned in, for example, white suburbs or government schools; and Mr Botha was not going to allow anyone to set the timetable of reform for him. (*Ibid*: 21 March 1981.)

Another opinion poll showed that NP support had dropped from 65 per cent at the November 1977 general election to 44 per cent, with a corresponding movement to the HNP and the 'don't knows', who accounted for nearly 20 per cent of the Afrikaner vote. Another poll put the uncommitted vote at over 28 per cent, but forecast that two thirds of these would go to the NP on election day. (*Ibid*: 23 March 1981.)

The government's reformist intentions were watered down in statements made for potential defectors to the HNP. For example, early in April the HNP's claims that treason was being committed against the white workers were countered by giving assurances that no worker would be forced to accept changes in work practices against his will and that white trade unions would be permitted to remain uniracial if they wished. However the Minister of Manpower Utilization avoided denying the claim made by the white Mine Workers' Union (several of whose senior officials stood for the HNP) that the Government intended allowing blacks to obtain blasting certificates (*Ibid*: 11 April 1981.)

The HNP leader, the charismatic Mr Jaap Marais, who opposed Dr Andries Treurnicht in his Waterberg constituency, accused the Prime Minister of having a 'secret plan', to be unveiled only after the election, to bring the coloured people back into Parliament, an issue on which Dr Treurnicht himself was by no means happy and on which Mr Botha took pains to be vague (*Ibid*: 15 April 1981.) The HNP view was that apartheid must be all or nothing. As one spokesman put it: 'Apartheid is like a spider's web. When the government tries to take away one of its strands, it endangers the whole structure'. The HNP believed that the NP were appeasers who had lost their will to rule. As one candidate said: 'We are a nation of granite, but we have leaders with feet of clay', the kind of remark that led NP spokesmen defensively to remind audiences of the benefits they derived from apartheid. For example, twelve times as much was spent on a white school child as on a black; there were only eight blacks (the children of diplomats) in white government schools; white pensions were triple those of blacks; the programme of proclaiming racially segregated residential areas continued apace and vast numbers of blacks had been removed to homelands. In short, as one minister retorted to HNP hecklers: 'If you really think blacks are so well off, why don't you change places with them?' (*Ibid*: 21 April 1981.) (Not until a fortnight before the elections did Mr Botha make a speech wooing potential PFP voters.) Indeed, two different NP pamphlets were in circulation, one stressing the reformist character of the NP, and urging white unity as defence against the communist 'total onslaught', the other asking such questions as 'Did you know that a married black man with one or more children pays more tax on the same income than a white person in a similar position?' (*The Observer*: 26 April 1981.)

The HNP leader went so far as to say 'This is the biggest kaffir-loving Government in the world.' The party believed that it was itself the guardian of true nationalist principles and that the government's 'integrationist' policies would lead inexorably to black rule. Mr Marais attacked on three main issues: continuing deliveries of food and other supplies to black neighbouring states which gave sanctuary to anti-South African guerrillas; he believed their supply lines should be cut and that if necessary they should be bombed into submission. Secondly, he was against such changes in petty apartheid as opening hotels, restaurants to blacks and to multi-racial sport, as well as more substantial measures like the removal of job reservation and permission for blacks to join registered trade unions and the establishment of the tri-racial President's Council. Thirdly, he attacked the government's economic policies:

'Money is being taken from ordinary whites, transferred to blacks and then turned into profits for his concerns. In this way the government is achieving its aim of economic equality between blacks and whites. This will be followed by social equality and ultimately by political equality.'

Dr Mulder, too, believed in separation of the races. The urban black problem could be dealt with by bringing blacks to work by high speed trains and returning them to the homelands at night (*The Times*: 17 March 1981.).

In the event the NP of course won the election, but the PFP raised its percentage of the vote from 17 in 1977 to 24 and its representation in parliament to 26 seats, and the HNP rose from 3 per cent to 11 per cent. The NP's share fell from 65 per cent to 56 per cent. Thus the HNP vote increased from 34,000 to 190,000, a considerable portent of disaffection, though the party did not win any seats. They did, however, greatly reduce the NP majority almost everywhere they stood, particularly in the Transvaal, though talk of some formerly safe NP seats having been turned into marginals has been somewhat exaggerated, Mr Marais, who was defeated at Waterberg by Dr Treurnicht, may also have been exaggerating somewhat when he said: 'Afrikanerdom is on the rise throughout the land. Do not underestimate the panic that will break out in government circles over the results', but if panic was too strong a word, the results certainly gave the government furiously to think (*The Times*: 1 May 1981.)

Dr Mulder came within 1000 votes of winning his old seat of Randfontein from the NP. The PFP's biggest success was to win Cape Town (Gardens) from the sitting Cabinet Minister, Dr Dawie De Villiers (who had come home rather unwillingly from his post as ambassador in London)—the first time a Cabinet Minister had lost his seat since 1948. The PFP also made gains from the NRP in Natal, though the NRP made gains elsewhere, notably King William's Town, and with eight seats, were only two worse off than previously. Surprisingly, they retained Provincial Council seats, whilst losing the same parliamentary constituencies, and so retained their control of the Natal Provincial Council (*The Guardian*: 1 May 1981). (The election results are summarized in Table 4).

The lesson of the election is that a substantial minority of Afrikaners are appalled by the Prime Minister's *verligte* policies, which now, with the clear vision of hindsight, begin to look more like rhetoric. The situation is serious for South Africa and the outside world (even more so since the split in the NP), because for so long as Mr Botha's loss of nerve persists, the one avenue of peaceful progress in the Republic is closed off.

TABLE 1

National Party Members of the South African Parliament ranked on 1 – 5 *verlig/verkramp* scale. Provincial Distribution.

	Transvaal	Cape	OFS	Natal	Total
1.0 – 1.9	9	4		1	14
2.0 – 2.9	10	25	3	4	42
3.0 – 3.9	21	10	8	3	42
4.0 – 5.0	26	5	2	2	35
Total	66	44	13	10	133

TABLE 2

National Party Members of the South African Parliament ranked on 1 – 5 *verlig/verkramp* scale. Number of panel who commented (full panel = 11).

	1	2	3	4	5	6	7	8	9	10	11	Total
1.0 –1.9								3	1	2	8	14
2.0 –2.9	1			1	6	6	5	2	5	5	11	42
3.0 – 3.9	1	1	2	3	10	5	9	6	2		3	42
4.0 –4.9	1			1	5	6	5	3	9	3	2	35
Total	3	1	2	5	21	17	19	14	17	10	24	133

TABLE 3

South African ministers, deputy ministers and parliamentary officers ranked on 1–5 *verlig/verkramp* scale.

	Transvaal	Cape	Orange Free State	Natal	Total
1.0 – 1.9	3 ministers 1 deputy	1 minister	—	—	4 ministers 1 deputy
2.0 – 2.9	4 ministers	4 ministers 3 deputies Speaker Deputy Speaker*	1 minister 1 deputy	—	9 ministers 4 deputies Speaker Deputy Speaker
3.0 – 3.9	1 minister 1 deputy	Chief Whip	—	—	1 minister 1 deputy Chief Whip
4.0 – 5.0	3 ministers deputy chairman of committees	—	—	—	3 ministers deputy chairman of committees
Total	11 ministers 2 deputies deputy chairman of committees	5 ministers 3 deputies Speaker Deputy Speaker Chief Whip	1 minister 1 deputy	—	17 ministers 6 deputies 4 officers

* The Deputy Speaker is also chairman of committees

TABLE 4
Summary of Final Results of General Election 29 April, 1981

POSITION IN HOUSE OF ASSEMBLY

	N.P.	P.F.P.	N.R.P.	TOTAL
Cape :	43	11	1	55
Transvaal :	67	9	0	76
O.F.S. :	14	0	0	14
Natal :	7	6	7	20
Total :	131	26	8	165

POSITION IN PROVINCIAL COUNCILS

	N.P.	P.F.P.	N.R.P.	TOTAL
Cape :	44	10	1	55
Transvaal :	67	9	0	76
O.F.S. :	28	0	0	28
Natal :	5	1	14	20
Total :	144	20	15	179

CHAPTER 14

Constitutional Change

It is remarkable that all South African political commentators and activists, except some on the far right, agree that constitutional change is essential if peace is to be preserved. Not all whites are convinced that even accelerated change can in fact preserve the peace and many blacks, not to mention numerous outside observers, believe that solutions can be reached only through violence. The difference between the optimists and the pessimists can be ascribed to their different conceptions of what would constitute a solution.

The range of proposals is wide, from varieties of federation and confederation to a universal franchise on a common roll in a unitary state. Blacks and outsiders tend, with varying degrees of passion, to believe that only the last solution can be enduring: only when that has been achieved will it be possible for the leaders of the new state to turn their attention to the cultivation and preservation of sub-cultures and local languages and to worry about the rights of minorities, which perhaps could be protected in a Bill of Rights. (For an interesting discussion of the debate about the balance between a *lingua franca* and local languages see Hirson 1981.)

Talk about change in South Africa has been going on for a very long time, so that the observer may be forgiven a feeling of despair at the desperately slow pace of actual change. Over twenty years ago Mrs Margaret Ballinger said: 'The starting point for such change must be the recognition of the process of African urbanization as inevitable and essential to our general economic advance.' (Ballinger 1960: 21.) She went on to call for the removal of industrial colour bars, the extension of trade union rights to Africans, property rights for urban Africans and representation of African townships on city and town councils and in Provincial Councils. She would not commit herself on the exact form African political rights should take, but considered that:

> . . . a system which would make Members of Parliament responsible to an electorate representing all sections of the population is most likely to produce the atmosphere and achieve the objectives to which the aim of national unity commits us.

> (*Ibid*: 26)

In more recent years we may trace many prominent ideas to the report of the Political Commission of Sprocas (study project on Christianity in apartheid society) which appeared in 1973 (Sprocas 1973.) This important

154

document concluded with a two stage 'model for transition', though the Commission emphasized that the model was a means of isolating issues and posing questions, and should not be taken to propose a strict chronology. Stage one covered the extension of economic opportunities and fundamental freedoms, the 'creation of viable sub-systems of representative government on a regional but not on a strict ethnic basis' and of similar communal authorities for 'population groups of the common area who are at present excluded from the parliamentary system, such authorities to have powers in local government and cultural affairs as well as to serve as the political representatives of the unenfranchised groups in negotiations with the central government'. Regional planning and co-ordinating committees were to 'co-ordinate the decision-making and planning process in all inter-dependent issues transcending the competence of the existing and newly created local and communal authorities, and to facilitate the reconciliation of different regional, functional and group interests in the common areas'.

There follows a process of devolution of powers, to the maximum possible extent, to the regional and communal authorities and, once this has been done, negotiations between these authorities and the central government, 'to prepare the way for a basic constitutional transition and determine the political structure of a new political system'.

One set of arrangements to which these negotiations might lead is described under stage 2. First comes the creation of federal institutions to manage a wide range of activities, including foreign affairs, defence, justice, finance, transport, commerce and planning. Communal authorities are to be created for whites, perhaps by adapting the existing Provincial Councils. Finally, South Africa would make the transition to an open society, with some degree of optional segregation. At this point race classification as now known would have been abandoned and replaced by a system of qualifications 'determined by the relevant authority in association with the federal government and judiciary, and to confer voting and, in certain cases, residential and property rights'. Some residential areas and all commercial areas would be open to all races, but there would continue to be proclaimed group residential areas for people who wished to have them, in which they would be free to provide services reserved for their own racial group. On the other hand, services provided by the federal government would be open to all.

It will be seen that, although Mrs Ballinger assumed the continuance of, for example, separate education and representation based upon separate groups, her concern was really with the individual, whereas the Sprocas commission's plan was based on the pluralist assumption that people should be seen first and foremost as members of groups. It was against this demolition of liberalism that Senator Edgar Brookes protested in his minority report. He was quite sure that the objective must be universal suffrage on a common roll (though he conceded that it could not be achieved overnight) and thought the report might well be seen as:

... Yet one more example of South Africans evading the real issue of human equality, and going along flowery garden paths (more flowery, more erudite and more attractive than Dr Verwoerd's homelands but still garden paths) that lead to no real end.

(*Ibid*: 244)

The Commission's thinking is very apparent in the current policy of the Progressive Federal Party, not surprisingly, since Professor David Welsh played a distinguished part in the formulation of both. What is perhaps more surprising is that, although Sprocas was sponsored by the South African Council of Churches and the Christian Institute of Southern Africa, both bodies deeply distrusted by the government, much of the Commission's thinking has been taken over by *verligte* nationalists, including some members of the government. Indeed, the convergence of thinking between nationalists and opposition, all focussing on some federal or confederal future, is one of the most striking aspects of current constitutional thinking in the Republic.

The Constitutional proposals of 1977 were the first fruits of the frenzy of constitutional thinking that has occupied many educated white South Africans in recent years. They were inadequate and criticized, as we have briefly seen, in many quarters. A useful first article on the proposals was written by Dr Denis Worrall (and gains additional authority from his subsequent appointment to the President's Council) in a set of conference papers (Worrall 1978) and criticisms may be found in the statement by Dr F. Van Zyl Slabbert (leader of the PFP) and Professor David Welsh of the PFP's policy (Slabbert and Welsh 1979) and by Professor Ben Vosloo of the University of Stellenbosch (Vosloo 1979).

Professor Vosloo's comments are perhaps of most interest, because he is a *verligte* nationalist. He thinks the proposals will be seen as historic, because they 'signalled the need for a new constitutional dispensation for South Africa'. They contained 'several consociational (a term to be explained below) elements, such as segmental autonomy, institutionalized coalition government and proportionality, but they deviated from consociational principles in a number of ways. These included the exclusion of blacks; the white majority in the electoral college; the lack of a veto for Indians and coloureds; the strong executive Presidency; the lack of planned adjustment in group representation to take account of changes in the proportion of the total population belonging to each racial group; and the lack of consultation with Indian and coloured leaders. Furthermore, there were difficulties in defining the various groups in view of the black, coloured and Indian dislike of statutory racial classification. Professor Vosloo was on the whole not optimistic, yet the plan represented 'one of the most significant developments in the constitutional history of South Africa' because it showed that the government realized that the current constitutional position could not continue; regardless of their political merit, the proposals involved profound constitutional and political reform and they

156

provided a mechanism for incremental constitutional change.

Although those proposals faded away, traces of them lingered in the interim report of the 1980 Commission of Inquiry on the Constitution (commonly known as the Schlebusch Commission), whose recommendations have substantially passed into law. The Commission believed:

(a) that the Westminster system of government, in unadapted form, does not provide a solution for the constitutional problems of the Republic and that under the present constitutional dispensation the so-called one-man-one-vote system will probably lead to minorities being dominated by majorities and to serious conflict among population groups in the Republic . . .

(b) that in the process of designing future constitutional structures there should be the widest possible consultation and deliberation with and among all population groups . . .

The Commission recommended:

i) The abolition of the Senate;
ii) The institution of the office of Vice-State President;
iii) The establishment of a President's Council with the Vice-State President as Chairman, to consist of sixty 'nationally acknowledged experts in their respective disciplines and persons recognized by their respective communities as leaders' and to be drawn from the white, coloured, Indian and Chinese population groups. The Council was to 'advise the State President on any matter' and any of its committees might 'consult a council consisting of Black South African citizens and established under an Act of Parliament, or with any Committee of such a council',
iv) The enlargement of Parliament by the nomination of an additional twenty members on the recommendation of the various party leaders, in proportion to the parties' representation in Parliament.

An addendum was entered by three Commissioners (from the New Republic Party) recording their preference for a single council to the proposed two bodies, and the PFP members went further and entered a minority report. They believed that constitutional reform should be the result of negotiation between leaders of all population groups and therefore that any statutory body set up meanwhile should be only of an interim nature. They were opposed to the institution of a State-Vice President, and to the establishment of a President's Council, principally because the latter excluded blacks, which in turn would necessitate the setting up of a separate Black Council. Finally, they opposed the addition to Parliament of nominated members.

In due course the Commission's recommendations were embodied in law, though no black council was established, since black leaders would have nothing to do with it, and the nominated members were reduced from twenty to twelve. The PFP was much blamed in *verligte* nationalist circles for its opposition to the black council, since it had been hoped by some *verligtes* that the constitutional committee of such a council would institute joint sittings with the constitutional committee of the President's Council, thus creating *de facto* the constitutional forum of all racial groups which the Schlebusch Commission was too timid to recommend in so many words.

Before we briefly recall some of the evidence presented to Schlebusch it may be worth while to elucidate the concepts of pluralism, to which almost all constitutional reformers are attached, and of consociationalism. The PFP has made the latter peculiarly its own, but it is also spoken of with approval, as we have seen, by Professor Ben Vosloo.

Some of the massive literature on pluralism is surveyed in Hanf's major study of political opinion in South Africa, now available in English translation from the original German (Hanf and others 1981). Pluralists, who descend in modern times from Furnival, who wrote of the plural societies of Burma and Indonesia (Furnival 1948), see societies in terms of groups or 'segments' rather than of individuals, and believe that stability, peace and individual satisfaction are most likely to be achieved in such societies if representative institutions exist at the level of the group, with indirect representation in the broader institutions of the total society. Segments may be defined in terms of culture, race or ethnicity, language, religion, caste, and so on. In South Africa the primary grouping, much reinforced in the consciousness of South Africans by legislation and custom, is race. Thus, Afrikaans and English speaking whites jointly belong to the white segment. Within the white group there are however cultural sub-segments; the English speakers and Afrikaners practise a degree of self-segregation, marked by different languages, churches, often separate schools, and a myriad of separate institutions, including even chambers of commerce (though no doubt firms owned by Afrikaners will belong both to their own and to a more broadly based chamber). There is also considerable cultural overlap between the Afrikaners and the coloureds, to the point where many of the latter are virtually indistinguishable from Afrikaners. Similarly, language and sometimes religion provide an overlap between white English speakers and some members of black groups. Although for political purposes all whites are envisaged by the Afrikaners' government as belonging to a single group, their purpose in dealing with the black population has been to ensure that they should think and behave not as one group, but as many: hence the homelands policy.

Thus the pluralist vision sees society as consisting of groups standing, as it were, side by side in horizontal separation. These groups will govern themselves to as great an extent as possible (this is the great difference from the centralized 'Westminster model') live and educate their children separately and perhaps (depending in many states on geography and custom but in South Africa also on legislation) intermarry seldom, and in general have little contact with members of other groups. For matters which concern members of more than one group there will be common institutions or, as in South Africa at present, institutions governing all groups but dominated by only one.

At the same time there will, in most plural societies, be at least some 'cross-cutting ties' between members of these different groups, like political party membership (forbidden for members of different racial groups) church membership (not forbidden, but there is often racial segregation within churches) a shared profession or a shared class position. Class provides the most obvious line of vertical division, cutting across the various segments, but even this is bedevilled in South Africa by the refusal of many white workers to acknowledge that they have an objective class alignment with blacks or, if they have, to accept that it is as significant as the racial division.

The most important statement, for practical South African purposes, of the consociational variant of pluralism, comes in Slabbert and Welsh's exposition of PFP thinking (Slabbert and Welsh 1979). The book owes much to the report of the PFP's Constitutional Commission (of which Dr Slabbert was Chairman) which was adopted as party policy in 1978. There is, too, useful comparative material about other plural societies, including Malaysia, Cyprus and the Lebanon, and an excellent critique of the constitutional proposals which were then before a select committee of the South African parliament. The writing suffers from jargon—notably 'consociationalism'; but perhaps this term is now so much in vogue in the literature of pluralism that it could not be excluded.

The authors' concern is not to write another 'five minutes to midnight scenario' but to propose means for a peaceful and negotiated settlement in South Africa. At present, as they rightly point out, the costs of maintaining white domination are not unbearable; but they can only increase, and the hope must be that there will be a white government of sufficient vision to identify the crucial moment, and call a National Convention to negotiate a new constitution before the whites' backs are to the wall. The authors believe that whites have as much right as blacks to call themselves Africans, but that if they are to survive in South Africa they must forswear domination before it is too late.

The constitution they recommend would be federal, though they recognize the difficulties of federations; it would allow one man one vote on common rolls, but not in a unitary state, and peace between ethnic and other groups would be maintained by limiting contact between them. In other words, group differences would be acknowledged as in, for example, Nigeria and the Sudan, not ignored. In the words of Lijphart (a leader of the consociational school quoted by Slabbert and Welsh 1979: 63), 'Because good social fences may make good political neighbours, a kind of voluntary apartheid policy may be the most appropriate solution for a divided society'.

Slabbert and Welsh do not sufficiently define 'consociational' techniques, though they illustrate them from the European examples of Austria, Belgium, The Netherlands and Switzerland. They are not confident that such techniques (of which the most important is negotiation between élites who all recognize that they stand to gain more from compromise than from obduracy) can be exported to South Africa—for the European exemplars are rich and the cleavages in society cut across one another, whereas in South Africa divisions of race, class and status all coincide. Apart from economic interdependence there are in South Africa few nodal points or 'generators of social tissue' to counterbalance the only too obvious divisions in society.

There is much plain speaking in this book. The authors believe that '. . . we are in the early stages of a war which, if not checked, will show an unbounded ferocity comparable with the Algerian war of 1954–62' (here, perhaps unconsciously, they echo Patrick Duncan, who wrote something similar in 1965): the crucial necessity is that the ruling group should issue invitations to a National Convention while there is still some chance that they will be accepted. How, exactly, the 'politically salient' groups are to be identified is not easy to determine; the authors suggest that they might best be identified by a judicial commission (on the Pearce model in Rhodesia— 1972) after all restrictions and bannings on individuals and organizations had been lifted.

Only a commitment to non-violence would be insisted upon from any participant in the Convention, because the authors consider (in my view wrongly, in the light of the Rhodesia conference of 1979) that it would be inconsistent to expect leaders to negotiate while their followers were engaged in guerrilla warfare.

Slabbert and Welsh insist (and surely they are right) that, whatever the Marxists say, race antagonism cannot be reduced to differences of class interest, though the two may coincide. They will not, at this stage, even guess how the groups represented at the Convention will define themselves, for that must be left to the operation of a free political process, but it seems reasonable to assume that they will be largely based on race. To guard against the obvious danger of domination by any single group, legislation in the Federal Parliament would be subject to veto by a 10 or 15 per cent minority. The decentralization of party organization and the lack of any single locus of power (since it would be divided between federal and state levels) would provide further safeguards.

Understandably, Slabbert and Welsh do not attempt to delineate the future states in the South African federation, though they point out that some states are bound to be richer than others, and attempts to redistribute wealth between states would, as always in federations, lead to conflict.

Therefore, a governmental commitment (well before the National Convention has negotiated the new constitution) to significant reduction in personal inequalities and access to 'life chances' will be essential if a federal constitution is to be negotiated. On the other hand, the commitment to greater equality will not lead to socialism: '. . . no society describing itself as "socialist" is at the same time a democracy, as we have employed the concept in this book . . .' This is a surprising statement, particularly as the authors have not defined democracy.

Despite the weaknesses which could be corrected, like the failure to define key terms, and the very tentative nature of the proposals (apart from broad statements of principle), this is an important book, which deserves to be read by anyone involved with South Africa. One cannot cavil at the lack of detail in the proposals because it is perfectly reasonable, at this early stage, for the PFP not to seek to particularize; as the authors rightly say, the first step is for the South African government to recognize the necessity of negotiation.

The convergence of white South African thinking on federal and confederal models is illustrated by much of the evidence presented to the Schlebusch Commission. (This attracted much press comment at the time: a useful summary of some of the more important evidence is in *Rapport*: 20 January 1980.) The evidence was presented not only by political parties, but also by academics and other individuals, including the Chairman of Sanlam, Dr Wassenaar, well known for his uninhibited attacks on the 'socialist' tone of the South African economy (Wassenaar 1977). He attacked the 1977 proposals on the correct ground that they would lead to enormous bureaucratic proliferation and advocated the establishment of three voters' rolls, open on a colour-blind basis to whites, coloureds and Indians. The main roll would elect 85 of every 100 members of Parliament and would require matriculation, a taxable annual income of R5000 (or a doctorate) and a minimum age of 25. An unqualified roll would vote for a further seven members and eight would be elected by a group interest roll representing agriculture, commerce, etc. Such a system would, Dr Wassenaar believed, lead to an Indian or coloured central government within ten years. (*Cape Times*: 15 January 1980.)

Professor Ben Vosloo's evidence was reported at length. He called for a constitutional committee of inquiry, with members drawn from all racial groups. The exclusion of blacks from the 1977 proposals made him liken the plan to Hamlet without the Prince, and in any case it was too complicated for the man in the street to understand. The new constitutional structure, which must be negotiated step by step, would include a Declaration of Human Rights; it would have to give acceptable and fair opportunities to all, in the economic field, and to develop their full potential more generally; job reservation, the Prohibition of Mixed Marriages Act, section 16 of the Immorality Act, and some aspects of the Group Areas Act should be abolished (*Cape Times*: 18 January, *Rapport*: 20 January and *Argus*: 22 January 1980). Later Professor Vosloo told the BBC that South Africa might well have a black prime minister in 20 years (*Argus*: 29 February 1980).

Professor S. J. Terreblanche, also of Stellenbosch University, put proposals for a Parliament of all races, represented in proportion to the percentage of national income generated by their racial group. In a 100 member Parliament this would give 70 white, 17 black, 10 coloured and 3 Indian members (*Rapport*: 20 January 1981.)

Further confederal proposals were put by Professor Roelf Botha, based on his recent book (Botha: 1978) in which he proposed consolidation of the homelands and the creation of two new provinces, with representatives of the homelands and the six provinces sitting in a confederal assembly. Professor Robert Tusenius also saw confederation as the only answer to South Africa's problems, combined with maximum devolution of function to subordinate units, which might be ethnic rather than geographical. Professor Anthony de Crespigny (then of the University of Cape Town, subsequently a member of the President's Council) with his colleague Mr Peter Collins, made the case for partition and the New Republic Party presented another version of the Federal/Confederal plan (*Ibid*).

The NRP's case deserves further exposition, if only because the party has the reputation of a 'think tank' for the National Party. The NRP evidence (drafted by Professor Kriek of the University of South Africa and translated into English by Mr W. Sutton MP) starts from the assumption that all population groups should be involved in drafting the new constitution, which is essential because the present dispensation, being based on the unitary principle, allows domination by a single group, in this case the whites. The latter:

> are only too conscious that the extension of the franchise on a one-man-one-vote basis to other cultural or race groups within the present system would land themselves in a minority position. . . it is completely unrealistic to expect whites to follow such a course.

The principles of a new Constitution will be: the plurality of South African society will be recognized and accommodated; all groups will be given the opportunity to govern themselves to the maximum extent possible, especially as far as determining their own continued existence; all groups will have a say in matters of common interest; no group will be afforded the opportunity because of numerical strength to dominate other groups; no forced destruction of group identity can take place.

Blacks in the homelands, whether 'independent' or merely self-governing, would be accommodated in a confederal structure, the other constituent of which would be a federation based on the black, white, Indian and coloured groups in the remainder of South Africa. In other words, the important principle is admitted that representation for non-homeland blacks is essential, and that this cannot adequately be provided through homeland authorities, as the pure theory of Verwoerdian apartheid had it.

The NRP believed that statutory race classification should be abandoned. At the same time it recognized that the group membership of any individual would have to be known and recorded, since so many of his political and other rights and duties would be bound up with that membership. The party believed that the pressure against classification flowed from its discriminatory results, but that there would be none of these in a society where pluralism was recognized and constitutionally accommodated; there would therefore be no pressure against a system of 'natural registration'. This would be done at birth and/or by acceptance in the community.

Though the NRP may here be thought somewhat optimistic, it is expressing the important principle that successful pluralism must rest on voluntary group membership. In the NRP system each racial group would presumably make its own rules of membership and exclusion, so that the whites could retain very much the same system as at present. Rules would have to be made for the, probably rare, cases of individuals unsuccessfully seeking to 'pass for white' who were rejected by the coloured group as well as the white, and for those members of the Indian and coloured groups who identified themselves as black for reasons of political solidarity.

The hierarchy of authorities would consist of five levels: local/ metropolitan, provincial or regional, community or group, federal, confederal. Once they had been set up (which would be after a long process of negotiation and evolutionary change):

> the allocation of functions must take place subject to the principle of subsidiarity, which means that no function will be accorded to a higher authority if it can in any way efficiently be carried out by a lower authority.

A further principle is that 'self-government is in principle preferable to good government by another group' but there would necessarily be matters, at all levels of authority, of interest to more than one group, and for these inter-group negotiating machinery would be set up. (It is interesting to note that the Cape Town City Council, in evidence to the Commission, called for the creation of a joint white and coloured organ of local government (*Argus*: 31 January 1980.)

The federal authority would be bicameral, with the lower house representing the public and the upper the constituent parts of the federation. The lower house would consist of members appointed by each group Parliament in proportion to the percentage of votes cast at the last general election for the parties represented in that Parliament. The upper house would consist of an equal number of members from each group, nominated by the executives (cabinets or otherwise) of each group Parliament. Such arrangements have the advantages of eliminating elections at the federal level, limiting co-operation between groups to their respective representatives and to an extent integrating the Parliaments at federal and group levels.

The federal executive would be chosen by both Houses at a joint sitting and the Chairmanship would rotate annually, as in Switzerland. The executive's Chairman would also be Head of State. Thus it appears that the NRP envisages the Head of State, who would have only nominal powers (though in his other capacity, as executive Chairman, he would presumably have substantial powers) rotating between the various racial groups.

Though the purpose is maximum effective decentralization, there would be numerous functions in which no single group or regional authority could operate alone, and where guidance would be needed from the federal authority. Further functions would be divided between federal and group levels. For example, the present Department of the Interior's responsibility for passports and visas would be federal, whilst registration of voters would be handled at group level. The federal authority would have exclusive control of foreign affairs, defence and security, industrial development and trade, strategic planning and energy, national transport, posts and telecommunications, though as many as possible of its functions would be depoliticized by being handed over to public corporations. Each group authority would be primarily dependent on its own tax base, though the NRP does seem to recognize that redistribution between groups would be necessary.

Finally, the new Federal Republic and the homelands would be linked in a confederation, to which other states in southern Africa might later accede, and whose authority would be the place for joint decision making in such matters as water, communications, health, monetary matters, defence, and many more. In the early stages some, but not all, members of the confederation would be independent. These would 'have to delegate certain of their powers to the Confederal organization while the non-independent members will have to assume additional powers and duties'.

It is easy to say, by way of comment, that the NRP plan is impossibly complicated, vague in parts, improbable of achievement and unlikely to secure any material improvement in the conditions of life of the great mass of the population. The party's evidence is, however, important because it contains many strands of what has gradually become governmental thinking and may therefore contain a number of pointers to the eventual shape of a federal or confederal South Africa.

Enough has been said of evidence presented by whites to the Schlebusch Commission to show that there has been a ferment of constitutional thinking among whites, and that many of the various plans presented share common features. These include the acceptance of pluralism and rejection of the Westminster model, the continuance of racial separation, whether geographically based or otherwise, and the purchase of continuing white autonomy by the extension of autonomy, similar at least in name, to other racial groups. (The 'Turnhalle' constitution of Namibia, which one might have expected to provide a ready model, is surprisingly little cited.) There is a fairly wide acceptance of the obvious proposition that the non-homeland blacks (often and confusingly called 'urban blacks', though many of them live in white country districts) who were ignored in the 1977 proposals, can be ignored no longer. There seems also to be fairly wide agreement that eventually South Africa will be a federal state, which will be confederal in so far as it rests on an agreement between independent states (in some variants the European Economic Community is, rather confusingly, cited as a confederal model) and it is generally agreed that the future state will continue to embrace the 'free enterprise' system, with curiously little being said about the great extent to which South Africa's economy is already under state control. Perhaps the most striking difference between the PFP's federal policy and that of other white groups is the former's emphasis on a national convention as the negotiating forum, and the latter's insistence that progress must come step by step. But this is little more than a difference of emphasis, for even the negotiations between groups envisaged by the NRP could easily take on the character of a national convention. Naturally this point is not made by the NRP, which would not wish to seem to adopt PFP policy or terminology, nor, indeed, that of the banned

ANC, which has called for a national convention since its foundation.

Perusal of the evidence presented by the Black Alliance (Inkatha, the (Coloured) Labour Party and two minor allies) makes salutary reading. The Alliance believed that the only way forward was by means of a national convention, which must include members of the exile groups. The Schlebusch Commission was itself deplorably unrepresentative, consisting as it did of whites only. The alliance was prepared to discuss consolidation of the homelands and provincial status for them (provincial status was, until questioning the Transkei's independent status became illegal in the Transkei, also the demand of the opposition Democratic Party in the Transkei) but not the unilateral excision of parts of South Africa, which must remain a single state. Ethnicity was a reality but constitutional rights should not be based on it. The future constitution must include a bill of rights, the redistribution of wealth, the protection of minority rights and 'regionality without ethnicity'—the last of these is, as we shall see, taken up in the 'Lombard plan' for Natal. The Alliance affirmed its faith in negotiation as the route to peaceful change, and called for the immediate release of the detained PEBCO leaders in Port Elizabeth. (*Cape Times*: 17 January, *Rapport*: 20 January and *Argus*: 21 January 1980.)

In a separate speech to a rally Chief Gatsha Buthelezi, Chairman of the Alliance and leader of Inkatha, said he believed the South African Government would have to negotiate with Inkatha and the ANC:

> I want to state sincerely that I think the time is not far off before history brings the South African Government, Inkatha and all of us in this alliance, together with the African National Congress, no matter how far apart we may seem at present.
>
> (*Argus*: 21 January 1980.)

Without governmental leadership there can be no peaceful change and it seems that, at least until the 1981 elections, the Government was firmly convinced of the necessity of change, and was set on a confederal solution, with economic devolution to regions in which political boundaries would be relatively unimportant, and the development of 'joint venture areas'. In conducting the Pretoria equivalent of kremlinology the views of the Prime Minister are of especial importance, particularly as in the last two or three years Mr P. W. Botha has been gathering unprecedented power into his own hands. It may therefore be valuable to reproduce in full (though not all the points directly affect the constitutional debate) Mr Botha's 12 point plan for national strategy, which he announced to the Natal Congress of the National Party in August 1979.

1. The acknowledgement and acceptance of multinationalism and of the existence of minority groups in the Republic of South Africa.
2. An acceptance of 'vertical differentiation'* linked with the principle of self-determination as far as possible.
3. The creation of constitutional structures by the black peoples that

---

* In parliament the Prime Minister explained that it was possible to differentiate between people while simultaneously applying the principle of equal treatment.

would enable the attainment of self-government in national states (homelands) whose territories should be consolidated as far as possible.

4. A division of power between whites, coloureds and Indians with consultation and joint responsibility on matters of common concern.

5. An acceptance of the principle that as a fundamental tenet of harmonious social conditions each community would have its own schools. This is not discrimination but the acknowledgement of mutual rights.

6. The scrapping of 'hurtful unnecessary discrimination'. The Prime Minister said he did not favour a system of enforced integration and was not prepared to bring the self-determination of his own people into question.

7. Acknowledgement of economic interdependence and properly planned utilization of manpower.

8. The striving towards a peaceful constellation of Southern African states with mutual respect for cultures, traditions, and ideals. All the states are to be equal through independence and the choice of whether the constellation should be a federation or confederation would be theirs.

9. The determination to defend South Africa in every practical way from foreign intervention. South Africa did not practise its politics from a position of weakness, but from a position of strength and decency.

10. To opt for a policy of neutrality in the conflict between the superpowers in which South Africa's interests would be of paramount importance.

11. Effective decision-making on the basis of a strong defence force and a clean administration.

12. The maintenance of the free enterprise system and the effective training and utilization of manpower.

The 12 point plan has confederal, federal and consociational aspects and is of course consistent with a wide range of possible outcomes; the interim report of the Schlebusch Commission and the subsequent legislation may be taken as one interpretation of it.

Though Mr Botha continues to see the urban blacks' political future as in some way linked with the homelands, he is also aware that some answer must be found to the citizenship question; it appears from, for example, the following answer to a London *Times* interviewer that he envisages an eventual common citizenship of the South African Confederation, with separate nationality remaining to various states in the confederation.

I think the solution can be found when we eventually come to the forming of a constellation of states in the shape of a confederation, in which provisions can be made for these problems.

(*The Times, Europa* supplement: 1 July 1980.)

In 1980, far more than in 1981, Mr Botha's readiness for change was forthrightly expressed and taken seriously both within and outside the

166

Republic. He brought leading *verligtes* into the government (Dr Gerrit Viljoen, General Magnus Malan, Dr Dawie de Villiers) and was plainly encouraged by the rather unexpected nationalist victory in the Simonstown by-election at the beginning of September, which he took as endorsement of *verligte* policies both by habitual nationalists and by some voters who might have been expected to vote for the PFP. The day before the by-election he vigorously attacked diehards in the party and said, in relation to the Immorality and Mixed Marriages Acts:

> I don't believe any nation depends on these laws for its survival. Therefore I reject with contempt the suggestion that I or any members of my cabinet are not true to the principles of this party.
>
> (*Times*: 3 September 1980.)

(Here we see, as so often, the need for defenders of widely diverging policies to claim that they are the true custodians of party principles.) A month later Mr Botha said of the same laws, at the Transvaal Party Congress: 'No law is a holy cow. If circumstances make changes necessary, I will change laws', a reply which, as *The Times* commented, would have been unthinkable under his predecessors. (*Ibid*: 3 October 1980.)

Perhaps the most comprehensive statement of governmental hopes and intentions, not officially disseminated, but clearly authoritative, is to be found in *Beeld* of 19 September 1980: an editorial described the article as 'probably the most important single report we have ever published'. The paper had learned 'on the highest authority' that the final result of the government's thinking might be a confederation of some fully independent and some self-governing states, with common citizenship, but different nationalities. It was, according to the paper's informant, 'very important to bear in mind that what is envisaged is not an over-arching confederal parliament, but a loose confederal consultative body'. Such a confederation would, it was hoped, gain international recognition. Separate residential areas and schools would be retained, but:

> attention will be paid to existing policy which no longer protects, but has become a danger to survival. This includes statutory discrimination on the grounds of skin colour alone.

Within the Republic itself:

> Whites, Coloureds, Indians and Chinese must get political equality and full civil rights. One trend of thought is that this could probably take place within one parliament, but on separate voters' rolls. The President's Council could play a very important part in the ordering of this dispensation.

The urban blacks would be represented through an organ of their own, at a level higher than the municipal or provincial, in the over-arching Confederal Chamber of Consultation. Such a Chamber could accommodate 'self-governing national states' (non-independent homelands) but the Cabinet considered it particularly desirable, in the interest of confederal consultation, that these states should accept full independence. It was expected 'in high Nationalist circles' that initially the President's Council would be mainly concerned with reconciling the aspirations of non-blacks. But the Cabinet was still completely opposed to black representation on the council since they 'were on a further level and a different path'. In the economic field there would be important developments concerning:

> the desirable consolidation of the territories of the national states and the stated policy of decentralized economic development on a regional basis in economic, not political, joint venture areas.

Thus, if *Beeld* was accurately informed, the direction of change contemplated by the government was clear enough in broad outline, though not yet in any detail. There were however areas of ambiguity. The article concluded that:

> Beeld was told that should laws such as the Immorality Act, the Mixed Marriages Act, the Population Registration Act, the laws governing separate pursuit of Sport, the Group Areas Act and others be changed and improved, situations could arise for which provision would have to be made after mature deliberation.

This probably means that the government was ready to receive from the President's Council suggestions as to how these laws could be improved, but realized that in the absence of legislation, custom might not be sufficient to maintain racial separation and in that case other measures would have to be discussed.

There is little in this programme to please Africans, though Hanf may be right in suggesting that a significant number of them might accept some form of federation or confederation as a second best (Hanf 1981.) Nevertheless, *Beeld's* editorial was surely right to see the revelations as important, if only because they set a broad outline, within which the government's policy might be expected to move forward, if, that is, the unity of Afrikanerdom could be preserved meanwhile. At the time the paper evaluated the mood of the government as being that the Prime Minister was prepared to lead the way, but that was before the elections of April 1981. It also believed that the programme might 'lure the Ciskei into the acceptance of independence'. The Ciskei was indeed so lured, but when the Ciskei Independence Bill was published it contained no provision for a common South African citizenship, one of the principal objectives on which Chief Sebe had set his heart.

Beeld concluded:

> In view of what we have announced today, we feel that the country is being well equipped politically to neutralize the pressing demands of the eighties and to overcome the obstacles. After all, we are wanting to live in South Africa and not merely survive. Courage of the highest order is required if that living is to be possible.

It may be that confederation would indeed enable South Africa to get through the eighties and even the nineties, but it seems that the election results (which of course also reflect some whites' reaction to Mr Mugabe's victory in Rhodesia) have at least temporarily dampened the government's courage and even further reduced the momentum towards change.

It is interesting to see that this programme not only reflects the thinking of many who gave evidence to the Schlebush Commission, but also of Mr Harry Oppenheimer, the Chairman of Anglo-American Corporation. Indeed his closeness to the government was symbolized by his being invited to open its exhibit on the 'constellation of states' at the Rand Show—an invitation which he thought symptomatic of the new relationship between government and private sector. On that occasion he called for the acceleration of internal reform, which was essential if South Africa was to improve relations with its neighbours, as was a freely elected and internationally recognized government in Namibia. Internally there must be:

> Education for blacks that is not inferior to that available for whites; the end of the pass laws in their present unacceptable form; decent housing and security for all blacks in the urban areas; equal opportunities for blacks with whites in the business of the country and in the professions; a proper share—not on a one man one vote basis—in political power for all our black population.
>
> (*Pretoria News*: 3 April 1980.)

There is nothing in that statement antagonistic to the general tenor of government policy, so that, if Mr Oppenheimer can indeed be taken to represent business opinion, there may be more to the *rapprochement* between government and business (whose inauguration was symbolized by the Carlton Centre Conference of November 1979) than has sometimes been thought.

There is, Bishop Huddleston might say, 'Naught for your comfort' in anything contemplated by government at present. The Centre for African Studies at the University of Maputo, in a valuable analysis of Mr Botha's policies, saw them not as a programme of change but as

> . . . a means of bolstering up and preserving the political and economic power of the ruling white power bloc . . . the process of restructuring going on in South Africa at present can in no way be regarded as a process of dismantling of the machinery of apartheid. Rather it is an attempt by the rulers of the apartheid state to fine tune that machinery so that it can act more efficiently on their behalf.
>
> (Centro de Estudos Africanos 1980)

Inside the Republic Mr Sam Motsuenyane, President of the National African Federated Chamber of Commerce, shows that the African middle class, on whom whites have pinned so many hopes in so many countries, are black first and middle class second. In a newspaper interview he said the confederal scheme was 'irrelevant to black aspirations'. He went on:

> We want a common society in a unitary state. This is what our African National Congress has been calling for and is still fighting for . . . ever since its birth the ANC has stood for equality of opportunity for black and white . . . Nor will the pitting of moderate black against proletarian or radical black end the clamour for fundamental rights in this country. They do not want to see people divided into separate nations, which the government is trying to do. They want a unified nation in South Africa.
>
> (*South Africa Foundation News*: June 1980)

169

Those are firm and unequivocal words from a man who is often portrayed as a sell-out to capitalism.

From the ANC itself, in the person of Mr Y. Zungu, the party's Chief Representative, came no less forthright words in a letter to the London *Times*. 'The reforms of Mr Botha lie in shambles precisely because they were designed to adapt but retain apartheid, not remove it . . .' The time for schemes of power sharing was long past, the only way forward was for '. . . all reasonable people to support the struggle of the people of South Africa led by the ANC for a just and non-racial democratic society as envisaged in the Freedom Charter . . .' Majority rule would not mean the end of whites in South Africa, for the Charter itself declares that South Africa belongs to *all* who live in it, but:

> . . . whereas our people, through their tried and tested organisation the ANC are prepared for reason, that should not be taken as a sign of weakness. For our will to resist and determination to fight until liberation is achieved surpasses the capacity of Botha and his henchmen to repress us.
> Sasolburg is only the beginning.
>
> (*The Times*: 22 October 1980).

It is of course difficult to assess the force behind the ANC, though the many incidents for which it is given credit by the government suggest that Sasolburg is indeed only the beginning, and that the ANC has at least a hit and run capability and perhaps also some established cells inside the Republic.

Meanwhile domestic political initiatives continue, two of the most important being the so-called 'Lombard Plan' and the Buthelezi Commission.

Professor Jan Lombard of the Department of Economics and the Bureau for Economic Policy and Analysis in the University of Pretoria, was commissioned by Natal sugar interests to prepare a plan for the constitutional and economic future of Natal and Zululand, but in fact included recommendations for the future of South Africa as a whole. The report was released on 1 August 1980, but had earlier been 'leaked' in time for the Natal Congress of the National Party, at which it created a considerable furore. Also in July 1980 a number of the report's main points were published in a popular format by Mercabank (Lombard *et al.* 1980).

The main report argued that land consolidation (that is enlargement of the homelands and removal of 'white spots') could no longer be the starting point; instead the accent should be on '. . . association, co-ordination and co-operation over the entire area of Natal, and indeed further afield . . .' (Bureau of Economic Policy and Analysis 1980: subsequent quotations in this section are all taken from this report. There also exists a much longer unpublished version.) The realities of which any plan had to take account were the high degree of human heterogeneity in South Africa; the high degree of economic interdependence; the white-dominated power structure; growing aspirations among blacks, coloureds and Indians and the growing onslaught from abroad on the legitimacy of the Republic '. . . now verging on a willingness to employ punitive sanctions'.

Certain solutions lay outside the range of possible futures, namely 'the present world of colour discrimination' and 'majority rule in the present unitary system':

> The first must go, whereas the second cannot be established . . . as in all other 'deeply divided societies', majoritarianism has no chance of a democratic outcome.

Instead, approaches to the problem should start at the regional level:

> Perhaps South Africa could reconstitute itself on the basis of a manageable number of domestically fairly integral (less divided) and largely autonomous regional authorities.

The final outcome must be the result of popular discussion, persuasion and agreement and in that connection the report drew particular attention to the appointment of the Buthelezi Commission (to which further reference will be made below) by the KwaZulu Government in April 1980. Nor should present boundaries be regarded as final. The advantage of using the present boundaries of Natal/KwaZulu, was that they already existed, but under a future constitutional dispensation some border districts might wish to opt in or out 'and take their chances on the other side of the regional border'.

Natal was peculiarly apt for constitutional experiment because its population was dominated by three groups, Zulus, whites (especially English speakers) and Indians:

> . . . the other groups' preferences would carry much more weight elsewhere in South Africa, which means that their extreme minority status in Natal could be protected only within an overall confederal system. In any case, it seems clear that political consensus among the three major groups in Natal/KwaZulu, with regard to the political style in that region, will be easier to attain than will consensus among all groups in South Africa about everything in the entire sub-continent.

A strong and irreversible trend towards urbanization was taking place, particularly among the Zulus; the dominant area of income production was the Durban Metropolitan Area, which in 1972 produced 59.8 per cent of the total product; the citizens of KwaZulu were highly dependent economically on Natal, since between 1972 and 1976 74 per cent to almost 80 per cent of KwaZulu's national income was earned outside its own borders; because land in KwaZulu was held communally:

> . . . future transfer of land to KwaZulu will not make much of a contribution to the economic development of the country, except perhaps if the land is made available for individual freehold tenure . . . the existing policies, including the homeland policy in its orthodox form, can no longer be regarded as a sufficient basis for the development of a stable political and economic order . . . a serious lag in the development of legitimate political institutions behind social and economic change has set in.

171

The report goes on that, with the exception of political groupings necessarily operating outside the Republic, all major political actors formally accept the plural nature of South African society and agree in desiring evolutionary rather than revolutionary change. (The authors drily comment that the latter preference is hardly surprising, given that revolutionary parties are banned). Furthermore, there is fairly wide support for some forms of federalism.

Any new dispensation must protect the integrity, or 'constitutional personality' of the Republic. Nevertheless, regional peculiarities strongly suggest a regional approach to the new order:

> The real question, therefore, is not that of the dissolution of this state, but of the restoration within it of the freedom of the smallest social units, the devolution of responsibility, authority and power down to the grass-roots of South African society, and the retention, at higher levels of collectivity, of only those powers pertaining to truly common functions.

The basic principle of association between groups is that it should be voluntary. Different groups may choose to share facilities, which one group might not be able to afford alone, but the removal of statutory discrimination would not entail outlawing voluntary group cohesiveness and conformity:

> While statutory discrimination between people on the basis of their colour is morally insupportable and practically unworkable, it would be equally wrong and impractical to introduce statutory integration.

The authors are clear that a new constitution for the whole of South Africa is sorely needed, but that people will not be willing to embark on a new path unless the destination is clear. What is required therefore is a declaration of intent to establish 'a confederation of otherwise independent states' (including the independent homelands) a constitutional arrangement which would also strengthen the process of decentralization of economic activity. The functional content of the federation would initially be economic (the authors make the comparison, to be found increasingly frequently in the literature, with the European economic community) but the intention is political:

> It may, indeed, be said that if the people of South Africa do not succeed now in creating a confederal political superstructure for the South African economy, the unitary superstructure will so entrench itself over the next few years, under the pressure of claims for political participation by urban Blacks, that soon very little opportunity for change towards confederal principles will be left.

The people of each region, the states in the eventual confederation, will be left to reach consensus on 'the nature and the principles of the domestic order' though the authors do hint that reaching consensus may not be easy. However, cultural and ethnic minorities can be reassured by their states' acceptance of basic confederal principles, and even more reassured if members of their own group form the majority in another state of the confederation.

172

The report concludes with proposals for Natal and KwaZulu, and here the authors at least state, though they do not really discuss, the obvious problem of how the group right to self-definition can be reconciled with the need to produce 'a free and open society that protects the civic, social and economic rights and liberties of individuals.' As for the KwaZulu homeland, they believe that the existence of a system of public administration there may be of some value in future, but that an independent KwaZulu will not fulfil black aspirations. Instead they see Natal as consisting of three 'building blocks' or 'sub-provincial geopolitical areas'. These are KwaZulu, the white-owned rural area along the main transport corridors and the Durban Metropolitan Area. In an important passage the report states:

> In view of the fact that people have become extremely sensitive about any exercise in population classification, it must be noted that the above classification does not in any way refer to individuals, but to the social systems in the three areas. No statutory barriers should be imposed upon *individuals* that wish to and are able to migrate from one social system to another. It is also possible that in time the present distinction in social systems may decline and eventually disappear. But at present they are real and ought to be accommodated in a new dispensation.

There would be three tiers of government: a regional authority composed of members elected by the three-provincial authorities; the sub-provincial authorities themselves and local government, including municipal and rural authorities, with maximum devolution of power to the lowest possible level. As we have seen, all laws discriminating on the basis of religion, colour and language would be abolished but:

> . . . the right of groups of whatever kind to legally establish, if they so wish, their group identity (to the exclusion of others) in terms of the normal rights and obligations provided for in civil law (rather than constitutional law), should be recognised in the constitution as a basic element of freedom.

Thus, although at the national and regional level such Acts as Group Areas and Population Registration will be abolished, at local or community level it will be possible for legally sanctioned segregation to continue, and any observer of the South African scene must expect that it would indeed continue for a considerable time.

The problems of negotiating the new dispensation, for Lombard and his collaborators see clearly that it must be a matter of negotiation and not imposition, are legion. Perhaps the most difficult task for the whites would be to find leaders of the other population groups with whom to negotiate, who would hold a genuine mandate from their constituents. Even if such leaders were found, the very long process of negotiation would go on against a background of violent incidents engineered by the ANC and perhaps of civil war, though it is not necessarily the case that these would by themselves interrupt the process or make its continuance impossible. Perhaps the best to be hoped for under the Lombard plan would be a set of unrepresentative leaders, similar to those who have accepted membership of the President's Council. It is probable that Chief Buthelezi could also be involved, but he must be well aware of the dangers of passing into history as another Bishop Muzorewa, and so might at the same time be expected to maintain and intensify his attempts to keep contact with the ANC in exile.

The appointment of the Buthelezi Commission in 1980 is therefore very much in point and it is worth bearing in mind that Buthelezi invited both the ANC and the government to nominate representatives on the Commission and that the government made the invitation to the ANC its pretext for refusal. The purpose of the Commission, as Buthelezi explained in a speech to the KwaZulu Legislative Assembly was to get away from white politics 'dominated by white constructions of what black political participation could mean' and make a formal black contribution to the political process.

Natal was the appropriate choice of region, not only because it was the headquarters of Inkatha, but for a number of other reasons. White political interests and party preferences were most evenly balanced there; it was the province in which whites were the smallest minority and depended most on black labour; the division of areas between black and white was so complex that neither could be administered without taking the other administration into account; and (perhaps most important in Buthelezi's mind):

> ... Natal is the province in which adult black workers in the 1973 labour protests demonstrated a capacity for spontaneous yet disciplined coherent action which, more than the brave but despairing rebellious Soweto youth, showed that our present stability is very shallow.

This black initiative was being taken 'on behalf of all the people of Natal as an example for the rest of our country'. The Commission's initial task would be:

> ... to consider the collective destiny of all people in Natal, with a view to making proposals which will add a new dimension to the political evolution of South Africa.

Its purpose would be to produce proposals so compelling that no government in Pretoria could deny Natal and KwaZulu the right and the facilities to begin implementing them and in order that the proposals should be representative, membership of the Commission was drawn from a wide range of political parties, the professions, commerce and industry and the academic world. The terms of reference were also widely drawn, notably to make recommendations on the constitutional future of Natal and KwaZulu within the South and southern African context; to consider the economic, social and administrative interdependence between the two areas; to report on their economic development needs and, more generally still:

> To identify any negative consequences of the present social, political and economic situation in Natal and KwaZulu which might indicate the desirability of changes in the system; such problems might include manifestations of marginality, alienation and apathy ...

It is clear that Professor Lombard's plan owes much to the evidence submitted to the Schlebusch Commission, and that, however much Buthelezi's own preference may be for a unitary state, the terms of reference of his Commission do not exclude an eventual constitutional framework which might share many of the characteristics envisaged by Lombard.*

It remains to consider the likelihood of any such plan coming to fruition. It must first be borne in mind that, although Mr P. W. Botha appears committed to a confederal future, he seems also to have lost momentum since the 1981 elections. In other words, the advantage of having opposition from the right concentrated in the HNP may be outweighed in his mind by the extent of that opposition, as indicated in the election results and the subsequent split in the National Party. No doubt the strength of HNP support owes something to Mr Mugabe's victory in Zimbabwe and will increase further if conditions there deteriorate, so that it is in Mr Botha's interest to try to ensure that they do not. But quite apart from international factors the elements of fear and prejudice in the opposition to *verligtheid* must not be underestimated.

On the black side it is clear, as we have seen already, that any federal or confederal future would be very much a second best. What must remain in doubt is the extent to which blacks of all population groups would support leaders who were prepared to negotiate towards such a solution. Furthermore, even if such leaders emerged, there is no knowing how long they would be able to retain support, before it passed to more radical successors. If the currently exiled parties continue banned during the years of negotiation that may lie ahead, it will always be possible for opponents to say that the new leaders are artificial, or men of straw. If they are 'unbanned' the risk must be accepted that those leaders will be swept away.

It seems reasonable to suppose that the parties will remain banned and that black leaders will indeed emerge, ready to do business with government and with some popular backing. Prominent among them, one might expect, will be Chief Buthelezi who, whilst negotiating for KwaZulu, will continue to seek to persuade the world that Inkatha is not a predominantly Zulu party, but one with claims to be considered truly national. Progress towards confederation will no doubt be made and in the short term will solve many problems, notably those of citizenship (with homeland citizenship, but a broader South African nationality) and of international recognition. But if confederation turns out to be little more than a fig-leaf covering the maintenance of white power, only a brave man would forecast that it will prove more than a temporary state of affairs.

* The report of the Buthelezi Commission was published in book form in 1982 and its conclusions are briefly considered in Chapter 18, Postscript.

CHAPTER 15
The Verligte Movement

A number of illustrations have been given of *verligte* thinking and it is now time to tie the threads together, by attempting a more sustained profile of what *verligtes* and *verkramptes* believe and feel. It may help to attempt a sketch of *verkramptheid* first.

The *verkrampte* may or may not be the victim of racial prejudice, but he believes in the absolute necessity of racial discrimination, the purpose of which is to preserve the identity and culture of the whites, by which he means primarily the Afrikaners; (indeed to be *verlig* or *verkramp* is a characteristic of the Afrikaner, and the nationalist at that, whose attribution would only perversely be extended to the English speaker). He may admit that such preservation implies domination by whites, or he may believe that, at least in theory, separation and equality are compatible. In practice, however, he will probably agree that whites need to retain unequal power, in order to administer the separation, and when necessary enforce it.

The *verkrampte* may or may not concern himself with finding any justification for separation and domination. He may rely on a gut feeling that racial divisions are natural and right, so that to observe them is to follow the law of nature, or he may back up his convictions with arguments drawn from theology, anthropology and psychology. In either case he will believe that any small relaxation of *apartheid* is the thin end of the wedge; thus, Group Areas for separate residence; the classification of all individuals as black, white, coloured or Indian; separate schools, hospitals and burial grounds; the prohibition of cross-racial sexual relations or marriage are all equally essential. To remove a single brick is to endanger the whole edifice.

The *verkrampte* is unlikely nowadays to think that he can do without black labour and may even accept that if the economy is to be sustained, the conditions of black labour must be improved, and blacks allowed access to jobs hitherto reserved for whites. But he will see such measures as dangerous and be determined to ensure that economic concessions do not spill over into the social or political spheres. He will be reluctant to accept that the urban black population is there to stay and will oppose any attempt by blacks to retain South African citizenship instead of that of one of the homelands. To retain the shadow of the homelands policy he will tie himself in complex ideological knots.

Poor and uneducated whites naturally have more to fear from black advancement than have the well-to-do and it is understandable if they adopt a last-ditch attitude at the first signs of danger to white privilege, but *verkramptheid* is by no means confined to the poor. There are many Afrikaners in secure positions who take an equally hard line. Thus, an individual's degree of *verkramptheid* is not to be deduced from his class position, though it would not be surprising if the working class tended to be *verkramp* and the bourgeoisie to be *verlig*. However, since individuals of either persuasion or tendency may occupy identical class positions, the distinction between the tendencies is valueless to those who wish to analyse all social phenomena in terms of class; indeed for the Marxist the differences between *verligtes* and *verkramptes* are at best superstructural or inessential, at worst illusory. Similarly, it is difficult to persuade an African that the distinction betokens a real difference, because he will see beyond the convoluted agonizings of some of his rulers to the continuing fact of white power.

Nevertheless, the *verligte* believes that he differs from the *verkramptes* in ways which are meaningful and can be translated into action. He will not, it is true, abandon nationalism, if by that is meant a whole-hearted attachment to the identity and culture of the Afrikaner nation, but he is also likely to believe that the only way to preserve that nation is to dismantle at least some of the apparatus which has been erected for its preservation. He will be convinced that the white man, particularly the Afrikaner, has as good a right to live in South Africa as has any African, coloured or Indian, but at the same time he will see that if power is not shared it will ultimately be taken, and that the civil war which will precede its taking may make it impossible for many whites to stay. Such a persuasion does not necessarily mean that the *verligte* relishes the prospect of sharing power. He may simply have made a cold intellectual calculation, or his intellectual position may also be rooted in morality.

The *verligte*, though still a nationalist, need not be a member of the National Party. On the one hand, he may decide that only by staying in the party and working from within can its stranglehold and that of the Broederbond be broken and he may fear the moral and emotional exile which faces the apostate. A few, however, accept the penalties and go into political opposition, whilst remaining attached to the cultural symbols of Afrikanerdom, notably church and language.

Though the *verligte* is convinced that power must be shared, he may be quite unclear about how this is to be done, while preserving a place in the sun for Afrikanerdom. One difference, perhaps the only essential one, between him and the *verkrampte* is that he is convinced change must come if he is to have a chance of survival, whereas the *verkrampte* is sure that his only chance of survival is to keep things as they are, whatever the cost.

Verligte thinking may be examined under the headings of constitutional, political and socio-economic change. The *verligte* commitment is to work out a future which will satisfy all racial groupings, but there is no unanimity about how this is to be embodied in a new constitutional dispensation. Most *verligtes* would retain the notion of representation through groups as one of the units of constitution building, rather than a unitary state in which individuals would play their political parts directly. The convergence of *verligte* thinking is on some form of federal or confederal arrangement which would put the South African Humpty Dumpty together again by incorporating the 'independent' homelands, with a preference for a confederation, which can be an association entered into by independent states, so that the fiction of homeland sovereignty does not have to be sacrificed. Once the confederation had been created it would be a single state, so that other states would be able to recognize it without involving themselves again in the question of whether or not to recognize the independence of Transkei and other homelands. There is, however, a major obstacle in the way of reconstituting South Africa, which is that some third world states might refuse to recognise the new state. This would be of little practical importance, since most third world states have no overt connections with the Republic in any case, but is nevertheless an outcome which South Africa would wish to avoid.

A further difficulty is that federation is the policy of the Progressive Federal Party and 'race federation' was the solution propounded by the old United Party. In private moments *verligte* nationalists do indeed advocate policies which sound very like those of the PFP, but it is vital for them to avoid saying anything of the kind in public, since to do so leads at least to loss of credibility in Afrikanerdom and at worst may be interpreted by other nationalists as a kind of treachery.

The building bricks of the federation or confederation must be shaped by geography or by race, and this perhaps is where we can find a difference between the PFP and the *verligtes*, though it is more apparent than real. The PFP's federation would be based on geographical units which, although not defined in terms of race, would as a matter of fact each contain a preponderance of a particular racial group. The *verligte* nationalist, whose purpose is exactly the same as the PFP's, namely to preserve 'national' culture without any national group dominating any other, can go further and make no bones about the constituent units being racially defined. Here, however, we come to another difficulty facing the *verligte*: if race is to be the determining factor, then the iniquitous system of race classification must be retained. Yet many *verligtes* would wish to commit themselves to the retention only of customary discrimination and the repeal of all discriminatory laws, of which population classification is one of the most outrageous.

One solution is the PFP's: if the con/federation is based on purely geographical units and if those units follow the residential lines embodied in the Group Areas Act and respect the boundaries of the reserves as laid down in legislation over the years, then as a matter of fact the individual units will be racially pure. That, however, is only at the beginning: if movements of population are to be guarded against something very similar to the Group Areas Act and influx control must be retained. Otherwise, though black units would be unlikely to suffer an influx of whites, black migration could severely dilute areas which initially were entirely, or primarily, white, and white and coloured areas in the Western Cape would become hopelessly muddled.

The last might not be a source of dismay to most *verligtes* because if national identity is based on culture rather than race, most coloured people are simply Afrikaners of mixed race, and some are culturally similar to English speaking whites. There is thus a case, not merely for an alliance between the two racial segments, but a merger, so that so far as whites and coloureds are concerned, the whole apparatus of racial separation could be abandoned. The same is often said of the Indian population, but for the opposite reason; that is, the Indian cultures are so dissimilar from the white, and are so valued by Indians, that there is little likelihood of any large scale mixing and therefore no danger in treating Indians on the same footing as coloureds. The result would be an alliance, but not a merger. Thus, in a con/federation people from the initially white, coloured and Indian areas might be allowed to mingle without regulation, with the result that over time the units would lose their racial purity, though to varying extents. The problem would still remain of distinguishing the African from the non-African population and controlling movement between the two.

This discussion also elucidates the kind of political dispensation envisaged by *verligtes*. Clearly, it must go hand in hand with constitutional arrangements, since if the three non-African groups are to be allowed to merge (it being understood that the attachment of whites and coloureds to their own culture on the one hand, and of Indians to theirs on the other, are likely to preclude large scale social interaction) there can be no objection to their voting on a common parliamentary roll, while if they are merely to be allies, separate rolls remain a necessity. In either case, the *verligte* is committed to one man one vote, though not necessarily on a common roll and almost certainly not in a unitary state. The problem arises, in either case, of what arrangements are to be made for Africans.

The problem is less pressing in the homelands, 'independent' or not, because even if the homelands become economically unimportant and are seen simply as underdeveloped areas whose boundaries become sub-merged in larger regional units, they could still be retained as units for voting purposes. Thus, Africans who actually live in a homeland could vote there; the difficulty is about Africans who live permanently or semi-permanently, with or without permission, in the white area. *Verligtes* accept that 'something must be done about the urban African' and that the conception of all Africans, whether urban or rural, having citizenship and voting rights in one or another homeland, is out of date and irrelevant. Once the urban African population is seen as permanent, then some form of representation in the urban areas becomes essential; the uncertainty is about the degree of control which must be exerted to ensure that Africans do not overflow into white areas and white institutions.

Difficulties also arise over the Africans who live on white-owned farms. If the con/federal units are to be geographical, the sparse white population of many farming areas would be electorally swamped by black workers. If they are to be racial it becomes impossible to repeal discriminatory legislation.

We may turn now to the socio-cultural and economic fields. So far as the economy is concerned, Afrikaner *verligtes* say much the same as English speaking businessmen. African workers should enjoy the same pay and access to training and promotion as whites; they should have freedom of association, though not all *verligtes* would insist that there should be no separate branches for separate races within a union; most *verligtes* would remove the restrictions on trading imposed by Group Areas, even if the Act remained in force to control residence. *Verligtes* recognize that the economy cannot expand unless the pool of skilled blacks is increased and most *verligtes* have outgrown the traditional Afrikaner distrust of capitalist enterprise and identify themselves with the more modern determination of Afrikaners to participate fully in the economy. (However, by 1975 they did so, according to Professor Sadie's 'guesstimates,' only to the extent of 27.5 per cent of GDP, or 44.7 per cent if state enterprises are counted as belonging entirely to the Afrikaner sector: see Sadie 1978: Table 3.)

It is in the socio-cultural field that difficulties arise about how much differentiation between groups and therefore the retention of white (perhaps linked with coloured) national identity, can be left to natural avoidance and how much it must be reinforced by legislation. It is reasonable to suppose that Indians will wish, and can afford, to maintain their own institutions, while at the same time entering a political alliance with the whites, and we have seen that there exist grounds for an alliance, or even a merger, between whites and coloureds. The difficulty, however, concerns the extent to which Africans should share white schools, hospitals, churches, residential neighbourhoods and so on.

Most *verligtes* would repeal the Mixed Marriages Act (which prohibits racially mixed marriages) and the prohibition in the Immorality Act of cross-racial sexual relations, though advocates of repeal have not always thought out whether or not population classification is to be retained for the progeny of any such unions who, as things stand, would be classified as coloured.

Even more difficulty is presented by education and the other aspects of day-to-day life. Africans may well wish to share white schools and hospitals, to attend their churches, live in their suburbs and be buried in their graveyards. To the extent that such a wish is motivated by the superior quality of white facilities, it can in theory be answered by bringing African facilities up to the same standard as white, though in practice to do so would take a very long time and place an impossible burden on the, still largely white, taxpayer. But the quality of facilities may not be the only motivating factor, for the Africans who have so long been exposed to aspects of white culture may have become so affected by them that they wish, not merely to adopt them in separation, but to share them with whites. Such a feeling should, in a sense, bring joy to the nationalist if his attachment to national identity is based upon culture rather than colour, since his culture's appeal to others demonstrates its strength, and there is no reason in logic why people of other colours who share the same culture should not, like the coloured people themselves, be incorporated into the same nation. This, however, is where logic is liable to break down, and the *verligte* has to face the extent to which colour determines or conditions his feeling of national identity, for, if it does to any significant extent, and if customary avoidance between cultural groups does not sufficiently protect his institutions, he will have no choice but to maintain the existing apparatus of legislative separation. All this presents no problem for the *verkrampte*, who will have been convinced from the beginning of the centrality of colour and the need to maintain separation by law, and perhaps by force, but it puts the *verligte* in a dilemma.

Within the *verligte* movement there are many strands of opinion and much confusion. Only the most thorough-going *verligte* will advocate the repeal of all the laws of classification and separation, relying on the innate strength of his own culture (including, perhaps, the consciousness of race) to preserve its own identity. Any lesser commitment, however, inevitably involves the retention of some laws, whose stated purpose may well be to protect all the cultural units in the con/federation, but which will inevitably be perceived as an exercise of white power to preserve white privilege. The question arises, therefore, of how meaningful it is to speak of power-sharing, if the extent and nature of that sharing are to be determined by whites.

It may, of course, be answered that they would not be determined by whites, but in a common parliament drawn from some or all of the current racial groups. But to carry conviction members of that parliament would have to be elected on a common roll, since there can be no reason for separate rolls except the protection of separate group interests, and it cannot be known that other groups than the white would choose to protect their separate interests (if any) through the mechanism of separate rolls. The answer to that question could be found out through a referendum on the kind of constitution desired by the people, but it would first be necessary to decide whether the referendum itself should be held on a common or separate rolls! (At present the nearest South Africa can come to a common roll referendum is through the device of public opinion polls.) It would also be necessary for the inter-racial con/federal parliament to be made up of members in proportion to the population of the constituent units, leading inevitably to whites, coloureds and Indians being outweighed by blacks. *Verligte* whites would say that such an arrangement would not be power sharing, but submission to black power, yet any other arrangement would look like a device to retain white power.

Thus, the central dilemma is that the conditions under which power is shared must either be regulated or not. If they are not, whites will fear that they will be swamped and left with no share of power; if they are regulated, it must be done by some agency, like a parliament; membership and voting rights in that agency must be based on some criterion; if the criterion is population then (whether or not the constitutional units are racially defined) whites must be swamped, unless the blacks choose to vote non-racially. The question facing the *verligte*, therefore, is whether in attempting to share power he is prepared to run the risk of losing it, or whether he will instead himself make the regulations under which power is shared and so open himself to the accusation that the attempt is no more than a last ditch attempt to preserve white domination.

It is, however, important to recognize that, although the *verligtes* may be facing impossible problems, they are facing them genuinely and honestly. Businessmen, constitution-makers, members of parliament, academics, students and many others are, as we have seen, absorbed in a ferment of ideas, both about what reforms are needful and how they are to be brought about. The *verligte* does not advocate giving up power, but sharing it, whilst safeguarding his own future. It may be that the goal is contradictory and should be abandoned in favour either of a *verkrampte* determination to maintain white power, or of a sacrificial willingness, which only the most lion-hearted *verligtes* would contemplate, to give up group power, recognize that eventually individuals rather than groups must be the primary units in the South African political process, and hope that group identity will be protected by tradition and habit, rather than legislation. But no *verligte* who hoped to continue to play a part in the current political process would dare espouse such a programme in public. The *verligte* movement may be implausible, unconvincing and ineffective, but it provides the only route to peaceful reform open to South Africa at present. Whether it can go beyond inessential reform to achieve a constitutional dispensation acceptable to a majority of the population is doubtful, because of the difficulties, both conceptual and practical, discussed in this chapter.

CHAPTER 16

South Africa in Africa

The discussion of confederation as a means to the reconstruction of South Africa leads naturally to consideration of the Republic's ambitions to strengthen its relations with its black African neighbours, through the establishment of a 'constellation of states'. The idea of such a constellation was floated in 1974 by the then Prime Minister, Mr B. J. Vorster and has since been developed by his successor, Mr P. W. Botha. Originally it seems to have been intended to cover the whole of southern Africa, to as far north as Zaïre and Tanzania, but now most of the impetus has been lost and it is likely that not much more is meant by the constellation than the reunification of white South Africa with the 'independent' homelands.

The notion of a constellation was expounded by Mr Botha on 22 November 1979 at the first of his famous meetings with the leaders of South African business (the second was on 12 November 1981) held at the Carlton Centre in Johannesburg; the following paragraphs are based on the account of that meeting—(R.S.A. n.d.)—published by the South African Information Service. The South African Prime Minister took pains then to emphasise that the term 'constellation' was appropriate, because in a constellation the stars remained in fixed positions in relation to each other. The image of a solar system, on the contrary, would suggest planets revolving round a sun in a satellite relationship, which Mr Botha specifically excluded.

The purpose was not to set up new institutions, except perhaps a Southern African Development Bank, but to build upon and expand existing economic links, whilst respecting the sovereignty of each member state and refraining from interference in the internal affairs of others. There was thus no suggestion that the black states, through their membership in a constellation, would be able to influence the Republic's domestic policies; indeed, the possibility was excluded. Nor did such links require the establishment of diplomatic relations (which in black Africa are maintained only by Malawi) though the continuance and extension of 'transnational' connexions at official level would be required, as no doubt would occasional informal contacts at political level.

Mr Botha pointed to the need to develop the peripheral areas in southern Africa and so to counteract the magnetism of the core. He went on:

> We, and the other countries of southern Africa, are thus confronted by the challenge and the opportunity to consolidate, in an evolutionary way, the

undeniable economic interdependence between us to each other's mutual advantage and towards a logical economic grouping (RSA, n.d.:16).

There was, however, a strict limit to what government could do. It would create a framework, within which it was the task of business, not government, to create the desired expansion of economic relations. The alliance between government and capital, symbolized by the Carlton Centre conference, imposed different responsibilities on each partner.

The business men at the conference had been asked to make suggestions and many of them welcomed the constellation as a goal of policy, emphasising the crucial part that the development of agriculture ought to play in its achievement. Mr Harry Oppenheimer also pointed out that business men investing in foreign countries would need some protection against subsequent nationalization of their assets and thought that the success of a constellation would depend upon improvement of South Africa's relations with the west.

This acute observation leads to the question of what the purpose of the constellation should be taken to be, apart from closer economic association. Its emergence could, first, be seen as a success for those who believe that South Africa should finally admit that its 'friends' in Europe are frail ones from whom little can be expected, so that the Republic should turn away from Europe, look for friends in Africa and move towards a neutral posture on East/West relations. Such a renewed movement towards Africa would accord with one strong strand in the advice reaching Ministers, though neutrality between East and West sounds implausible, given South Africa's obsession with the dangers of communism.

Secondly, the constellation might be seen not as a movement away from Europe, but as a means to the Republic's working its passage back into the West's good graces. This might be achieved in two ways, which would appeal to different, though perhaps to an extent overlapping, western constituencies: that is to say, South Africa might both regain western approval by demonstrating that it could maintain peaceful relations with neighbouring black states, and consolidate that approval by showing that such relations did not invalidate its status as a bulwark against communism.

Thirdly, the constellation can be interpreted as a move to build up a ring of friendly black states, which could be expected not to give hospitality to exiled South African guerrillas. Finally, it may be interpreted as evidence of a cynical intention to ensure that the neighbouring states remain dependent upon South Africa. With this intention can be linked such threatening gestures as the Republic's reported maintenance in the Northern Transvaal of about five thousand former auxiliaries, one-time supporters of Bishop Muzorewa, whose presence there is seen by the Zimbabwean Government as a continuing menace. Similarly, South Africa's support (see *Africa Confidential*: July 21 1982) of the Mozambique National Resistance, which actively opposes the Mozambique Government in Manica-Sofala, may be seen as a dual threat in that the Movement both ties down a large part of the

Mozambique army, which might otherwise be deployed near the border with South Africa, and sabotages the railway line from Beira to Harare and so reinforces Mozambique's dependence on the South African transport system. Other gestures are less warlike; for example, South Africa tends to inhibit the movement of Botswana's beef when Botswana's representative speaks against South Africa at the United Nations.

The black states' dependence on South Africa and the Republic's economic dominance over the region are well known and need be only briefly noted. Namibia has long been administered practically as a fifth province of the Republic, although of course when independence is achieved some loosening of the formal ties may be expected. Mozambique sends many thousands of migrant labourers to the Republic, for whom there is no alternative work at home, and relies on South Africans to run its railways and harbours and on South African trade for a large part of the revenue of the port of Maputo; these are relationships which demonstrate that both sides are well able to maintain pragmatically desirable links with an alien political and economic system.

90 per cent of the goods entering and leaving Zimbabwe by rail are carried on the South African rail system; 30–40 per cent of its imports in 1979 originated in (as opposed to passing through) South Africa and Zimbabwe was the source of probably as much as 60 per cent of South Africa's imports from black Africa (Thomas 1980b: 7), a percentage which might have been expected to fall, had South Africa actually carried out its sudden abrogation of the tariff agreement with Zimbabwe in 1981.

Lesotho is entirely surrounded by South Africa and relies overwhelmingly on the Republic for wage employment, though this dependence does not prevent Lesotho taking an independent and robustly anti South African line in the United Nations and elsewhere. Swaziland lies uneasily between South Africa and Mozambique and has an uncertain future after the death of King Sobhuza. Botswana walks a difficult tight-rope between its dependent status as a neighbour of South Africa and active membership of the group of Front Line States, for which it has become something of a go-between with Europe and America. For Zambia, South Africa is the second source of imports, second only to Britain. In Malawi, South Africa has overtaken Britain as the chief supplier of goods and services, with about 38 per cent of its imports coming from South Africa in 1979 (*Ibid*: 6). Finally, Botswana, Lesotho and Swaziland are linked to South Africa in a customs union, and the two last remain members of the rand currency area.

South Africa's trade with black Africa thrives. In the first half of 1980 exports to black Africa, excluding Botswana, Lesotho, Swaziland and the homelands, were 8.4 per cent of the Republic's total exports and, at R539 million, were 65 per cent up on the corresponding period for 1979 (R326 million). For the whole of 1979 exports to black Africa were 39 per cent up, at R748 million from R538 million. Imports from black Africa during 1979 were estimated at R250 million (*Ibid*: 5).

Some further figures may be cited to illustrate South Africa's predominance in the region. In 1976 the Republic's Gross Domestic Product was R29 billion; those of Zimbabwe and Zambia taken together came to R4.5 billion (Cleary, n.d.: 33). The Gross National Product of South Africa in the same year was U.S. $33.7 billion; Zimbabwe came next with $3.5 billion. In 1977 South Africa's income per capita (a misleading measure since it conceals inequality of distribution) was $1340; next came Swaziland with $540; lowest was Malawi with $140 (Barber 1980: 77).

Much of the increase in trade with black Africa consists of goods required for the rehabilitation of Zimbabwe's economy, which can often be obtained more quickly and cheaply from South Africa than from overseas. It is, therefore, hardly surprising that trade representation and some consular functions have been maintained between the two countries, despite the break in diplomatic relations in 1980. But, equally naturally, there is political pressure in Zimbabwe to diversify trade links, as well as sources of aid and expatriate advisers, just as there will be in Namibia when that country achieves independence. Furthermore, Zimbabwe's association with Europe under the Lomé Convention will exert a pull and as conditions improve in Angola and Mozambique a higher proportion of Zimbabwe's trade will be carried on those routes. In 1973, when the Mozambique railways were at their most efficient and Zimbabwe's economy was, of course, less buoyant than at present, Mozambique took 60 per cent of Zimbabwe's exports, compared with 10 per cent in 1981. Early in 1981 the line to Maputo was approaching an average carrying capacity of one train per day, a great improvement on the previous one train per two days. However, the line to Beira is plagued by guerrillas of the MNR and the port of Beira, though able to take ships of a maximum capacity of 29,000 tons, can load only to 23,000 tons.

Despite these factors, it is clear that South Africa will continue to carry a significant proportion of the trade of Zimbabwe and other neighbouring states and in general to retain its economic dominance of the region. To that extent the constellation of states already exists. However, to consolidate it requires not only the extension of economic links (which opponents might call the confirmation of dominance) but also the establishment of political relations of peaceful co-existence. In this respect the policy is a continuation of the earlier 'outward policy' whose goals were dialogue and détente. The difference between the present and those earlier days is that (as the Institute of African Studies at the University of Maputo acutely points out) whereas under the now discredited Minister of Information, Connie Mulder, the purpose was to influence particular decision makers, South Africa's present objective is the far wider one of altering the objective conditions in which decisions are made (Centro de Estudos Africanos, n.d.:4).

Though the facts of current economic life are plain enough, the constellation idea is unpopular with South Africa's neighbours, where opponents, such as the Maputo Institute, see it as liable to perpetuate the unequal international division of labour, to maintain the process of underdevelopment of South Africa's periphery by draining away resources and to prevent the growth of local markets (*Ibid*: 6). Furthermore, to admit that South Africa is the region's natural pole and leave the region's development to market forces, is merely to perpetuate South Africa's dominance. There is thus a perhaps somewhat surprising coincidence of view between Mr Botha, in his remarks at the Carlton conference, and opponents of the constellation (see e.g. Seidman & Makgetla 1980) that if the periphery is to develop, its development must be planned.

There have been sharp reactions to the constellation in neighbouring states, not least because the three 'independent' homelands have joined it. As the late Sir Seretse Khama said in Arusha on 3 July 1979 'we would be bundled together with bantustans and UDI regimes such as Namibia and Zimbabwe'. All the neighbouring states would no doubt be happy to co-operate with a South Africa from which apartheid had been expunged, though with the hope (unrealistic though it may be) that by then South Africa would not dominate the region. Meanwhile, though trade relations may well mature, rather in the manner of trade between eastern and western Europe, closer overt political links seem most unlikely to develop.

The African states have not merely attacked South Africa's expansionist vision orally. Partly in response to the constellation, nine states (Tanzania, Malawi, Zambia, Zimbabwe, Angola, Mozambique, Botswana, Lesotho, Swaziland) have founded the Southern African Development Coordination Conference (SADCC). The process of its foundation started at a meeting in Gaborone in May 1979 of the Foreign Ministers of the (then five) 'front line states' after intensive lobbying by Mr Archie Mogwe, Botswana's Foreign Minister. It is thought that SADCC was the brainchild of Sir Seretse Khama, the President of Botswana, who wished to maintain the valuable liaison established between the five over the Rhodesian question and, by promoting constructive joint action, to prevent their political energies from seeping away into sterile confrontation with South Africa. He may also have wished to draw Angola and Mozambique closer to the West, and, by creating a diversion from undiluted confrontation with South Africa, to avoid pressure to give greater support to the ANC.

The initial meeting led to the first SADCC meeting at Arusha in July 1979 (known as SADCC 1) at which Khama made the remark quoted above. There followed a summit meeting at Lusaka on 1 April 1980, (for the documents presented at Arusha and Lusaka see Nsekala (Ed) 1981) when the group was enlarged to include representatives of Malawi, Lesotho, Swaziland and Zimbabwe, (and which was also attended by, among others, a representative of the Economic Commission for Africa and Mr Sam Nujoma, the leader of SWAPO); there followed a meeting of 21 Ministers of the nine in Salisbury on 11 September 1980 (the first conference of African governments to be held in independent Zimbabwe) to finalize projects for SADCC 2 and in November 1980 in Maputo, SADCC 2 itself. (Zaïre is said to wish to join SADCC, but to have been re-buffed, because its present government is unacceptable to most of the nine).

Thus SADCC is a young, but already potentially important, organization. Its two aspirations are to free black Africa from South African dominance (so that in this respect it may be seen as a 'counter constellation') and, more generally, to promote the economic independence of the nine, six of which are land locked, through the coordination of economic development. These aspirations only became feasible (though their achievement is still remote) when Zimbabwe reached independence, for Zimbabwe is the natural fulcrum of the region. Indeed, some fear that it will come to dominate it, as in the days of the Central African Federation (1953–63) made up of the then colonial territories of Northern and Southern Rhodesia and Nyasaland.

To ask whether the SADCC's dominant objective is economic development or detachment from South Africa is perhaps to ask the wrong question, because the two are entwined, and different spokesmen have given answers of varying emphases, but the impetus behind SADCC, as it was in the case of the Federation, is certainly political; it must at present be an open question whether the political will for greater economic independence of South Africa would survive the transition to majority rule and the abolition of apartheid there. Meanwhile such decisions as the one to hold SADCC 3 in Malawi in November 1981, must be perceived in the Republic as unkind cuts. A reading of the Maputo communiqué may also suggest to South African observers that it was drafted by the same hand as was responsible for the rather anti South African communiqué of the Arusha meeting, in contrast to the milder form adopted, on Malawi's insistence, at Lusaka.

SADCC 2 was a major gathering of representatives of 30 foreign governments (though the Soviet Union and China refused to attend) and 18 international organisations. It was important, not only as a forum in which projects could be presented and promises of aid given, but politically and symbolically. Because it was an African initiative it was seen as an opportunity to escape from the frustrations of the north-south dialogue and by some as a watershed in aid giving. It also provided an opportunity for the world to show that it took the nine seriously as a potential economic unit and for governments and donor agencies to demonstrate their approval of the multi-racial systems of the black states and, by implication, disapproval of South Africa's racism, (see interview with Monsieur Claude Cheysson, then Commissioner for Development, Commission of the European Communities, in *Financial Mail*, Johannesburg: 12 December 1980).

The SADCC countries have identified transport and communications as the first priorities and have set up the Southern African Transport and Communications Commission, with its secretariat in Maputo, while other countries have been asked to study other areas of co-operation; for example, Zimbabwe has responsibility for food security. Meanwhile, the major document presented to SADCC 2 was an outline of projects in transport and communications, prepared by Danish consultants (for the documents see Kgarebe (Ed) 1981). The projects include: rehabilitation of the railway line from Nacala to the Mozambique border and of the Botswana railway; upgrading roads in Lesotho; road-building in Tanzania; deepening and increasing the capacity of the ports of Beira and Maputo; and building new terminal facilities at Harare airport. These projects account for $1,007 million of the total $1,946 million estimated expenditure (*South*: January 1981). In addition to transport, much emphasis is laid upon the need to improve telecommunications; it is, for example, said to be easier at present to telephone Lisbon than Harare from Maputo. Much, too, of the work to be done in the field of surface transport is of a bread and butter nature; for instance there is a need to systematize standards of road construction and regulations concerning the weights which may be carried on the roads.

In the event SADCC 2 yielded pledges of $650 million (all conditional upon detailed project approval) and several expressions of interest by international agencies which do not make pledges. The largest single pledge, $384 million spread over 1981/86, came from the African Development Bank, though this seems to have come from funds already earmarked for the region. The European Community, similarly, pledged funds ($100 million) already earmarked under Lomé. The United States gave $50 million, which was considered a disappointing figure, the Netherlands $32 million, Sweden $22 million and Italy $15 million; West Germany gave a token $2 million and Britain, France and Japan nothing at all (Zimbabwe Project, *News Bulletin* January 1981). In some quarters the total was seen as evidence that the rich countries are more interested in safeguarding their investments in South Africa and not antagonizing the South African Government than in assisting the wider development of southern Africa. But the total is not inconsiderable, and may equally be taken to indicate that some investors may be hedging their bets and that some countries, particularly the smaller ones, may be thinking of the great new markets and sources of raw materials which the region may eventually offer.

At SADCC 2 President Samora Machel of Mozambique referred to:

> . . . The acute state of underdevelopment bequeathed by colonial domina-
> tion. . . . The economies of the southern African countries were conceived and
> organised as functions of South Africa.

President Quett Masire of Botswana, on the other hand, did not see the effort to reduce dependence on South Africa as a signal for confrontation with the Republic, but rather as an expression of Pan-Africanism. Dr Bernard Chidzero, Zimbabwe's Minister of Economic Planning and Development, indicated how large were the aspirations of some participants when he said: 'We have set ourselves the challenge and the task to change the course of history in southern Africa.' (*South*: January 1981).

Of course not all the SADCC countries are involved to the same extent. For example Angola is preoccupied with its own internal problems, notably the civil war with UNITA, and in any case has poor transport links with the rest of the region. Zambia may be disappointed that no major new projects have been mooted of direct benefit to it and would particularly welcome the establishment of a railway link with the Indian Ocean. Nevertheless, all the nine stand to gain in the long term from the successful progress of SADCC projects.

One of the most hopeful signs is that, though the sums of money involved are large, the objectives are in a sense modest. The leaders of the nine are well aware of past failures to promote joint economic activities in Africa, so that in SADCC the accent is on co-ordination. There is no commitment to develop a common market or preferential trade area (p.t.a.) for the nine (though plans do exist eventually to establish a much wider p.t.a. of eighteen African states) and any SADCC member is allowed to enter into special relationships, such as Lomé, with non-members. Nor are the leaders anxious to set up new organizations with expensive bureaucracies, partly because they are only too conscious that nationalist jealousies could cause problems over the siting of institutions (though the decision to keep the permanent secretariat in Botswana, which had provided the interim secretariat, seems to have been reached with little difficulty).

Not all experts, however, agree with the high priority given to transport projects. It is true that, if the main thrust of development is to be industrial, then railways and heavy duty roads are essential, but if agriculture and rural light industry are the first priorities, then much less need be spent on physical communications. Professor Michael Lipton has pointed out (in a letter to *The Times* of 5 November 1980) that massive communications networks provide neither food nor employment, which are the two prime needs in poor countries with rapidly growing populations. Instead they drain off cash and skills and in southern Africa the first beneficiaries of new and improved transport links will be South African exporters. Other experts, on the other hand, see the future in terms of heavy industry, such as steel works, oil refineries and so on, which do require a sophisticated infrastructure.

Ann Seidman and Neva Makgetla for example, are proponents of a primarily industrial development strategy where the priorities would be: industries directed to the improvement of agricultural productivity; bicycle and vehicle production; production of consumer necessities and finally the development of pole of growth industries in each member state. The problems of industrialization are in their view primarily institutional. The region's underdevelopment has been created by colonial adventurers and transnational corporations (TNCs), but in the future financial institutions, import-export and wholesale trade must be entirely state controlled, though the TNCs would not be completely expropriated until local personnel had been trained to run them. By the year 2000 (for this is the time scale) the authors envisage an accumulated regional investable surplus of $150 billion (of which $12 billion would be generated in the twentieth year) and an annual market of $48 billion. Meanwhile a great new mineral province could be developed in the region, though it must be added by way of comment that the massive investment needed would not be available locally for some years and meanwhile is unlikely to be committed by mining houses (even if they have it at their command) without guarantees against expropriation which would be so comprehensive and binding that governments would feel unable to give them.

Seidman and Makgetla continue that a regional industrial strategy above all demands planning, which in turn requires inter-state financial institutions to garner and invest the surplus. Planning, unselfishness between states, state control, a movement towards a common currency, long term interstate contracts and co-ordination of taxation and income policies, should make it possible for each state to build on the assets it already has to the benefit of all. For example iron and steel production would be based in Zimbabwe, fertilizer in Tanzania, oil in Angola, meat packing in Botswana. All this, Seidman and Makgetla conclude, would also be in the interest of outside capitalists, who would be attracted by the rapidly growing regional market whilst weakening South Africa and promoting liberation:

> Together with a liberated further industrialized South Africa, characterized by a more equitable distribution of income, their (the SADCC states') market could grow to almost six times that of South Africa's current market.
> (Seidman and Makgetla, 1980: 353).

It is too soon to tell whether the leaders of southern Africa will decide on a primarily agricultural or a primarily industrial strategy. Much will depend upon the availability of capital and skills, which in turn depends on the confidence engendered in foreign capitalists, since aid alone would be insufficient to meet the region's potentially vast capital needs and it must be some years before the financial institutions necessary for the planning and disbursement of the investable surplus are in operation.

Meanwhile the SADCC countries will have to weigh up the relative strength of their dual, though not incompatible objectives, regional independence as a good in itself and independence from a South Africa ruled by whites. If the latter objective is predominant they will need to consider the possibility that by the time SADCC has achieved any significant degree of independence South Africa may have in any case passed through the transition from apartheid to majority rule. It might, of course, still be considered desirable, in that future state of affairs, to pursue independence from South Africa, but that is a different decision, and one which lies beyond the time-span of most politicians.

CHAPTER 17

The Way Forward

The purpose of this book has been to assess the prospects for change in South Africa, looking particularly at changes generated within the white political system. That system is dominated by nationalist Afrikaners; hence the emphasis throughout has been on trends of opinion within the Afrikaner élite and on the prospects of the *verligte* movement gaining the ascendancy.

I began by considering various approaches to South Africa's problems: the homelands, or 'Bantustans' policy; liberalism; and the revolutionary option, which might more properly be called the violent option. I concluded that none of these by itself provides the way forward. The homelands policy's essential purpose has been to excise the old reserves from South Africa, induce them to accept independent statehood and define all Africans as citizens of one or another homeland. The policy is widely discredited because it fails to solve any problems, except on paper, and has been frustrated by the refusal of some homelands, notably KwaZulu, to accept independence. It is true that there continue to be some 'successes', most recently the independence of the Ciskei in December 1980, but even in the official mind the emphasis has moved away from the pure Verwoerdian conception of separate development to a more sophisticated vision of South Africa as a series of economic regions, which, though not abolishing homeland boundaries, will reduce their importance.

Liberalism has in recent years been more of a state of mind than a policy and, although liberals have kept a respect for human rights and other traditional liberal values alive in some white minds, and continue to do so in the press, the Anglican Church and in Parliament, they have achieved little that is tangible and have negligible influence. They will no doubt play some part in the negotiations leading up to a settlement, but are likely to have most to contribute in the subsequent period of reconstruction.

As for violence, that is to say black violence, rather than the structural violence implicit in the total system of apartheid, it appears that the South African army can withstand any threat posed by guerrilla operations for the foreseeable future, whether these be generated internally, or carried out by externally trained personnel who infiltrate back into the Republic. On the other hand, though guerrilla warfare is still in its very early stages, the South African authorities clearly expect its tempo and scale to increase, and there is little reason to suppose that they will be able to stamp it out altogether. It seems more probable that sporadic outbreaks, perhaps

192

leading in some areas to sustained fighting, will continue in the background. Violence by itself will not persuade the Republic to negotiate, still less force a surrender, but, as in Zimbabwe, it seems likely to be an essential component of the long preamble to negotiations, and to continue until a settlement is reached.

Meanwhile it is true that changes are taking place in South Africa, though not to anything like the extent claimed by the Republic's apologists. The changes are largely in the thinking of the Afrikaner and business élites, but some have been translated into fact. They include improvements in wages and conditions of service, to some extent stimulated by the European Community's Code of Conduct, and by other codes, and some extension of trade union rights, though with many safeguards, both to protect minorities (that is, the whites) and to restrain unions from 'political' action. Furthermore, the changes inspired by Dr Riekert's recommendations have the effect of stabilizing the urban African population (though at the price of exporting unemployment to the homelands even more systematically than before) so that it is no longer possible for any but the most dyed-in-the-wool reactionary to argue that all blacks in white South Africa should properly be regarded as impermanent migrants.

At the political level, there is much debate about South Africa's constitutional future and there seems to be a convergence of opinion that some form of federation or confederation will be the outcome, perhaps including those homelands which have accepted independence, so that the old South Africa would be reconstituted in a different form. Such an arrangement would have the advantage, from the white point of view, that South Africa would be able to present itself to the world as a single state, whilst internally there would be very great devolution of power to the con/federation's constituent parts. Even if race nowhere appeared on paper as a defining characteristic of social groups and racial discrimination disappeared from all con/federally controlled institutions, it seems highly probable that under the new dispensation the way would be left open for groups to maintain racial discrimination at the local level if they so wished. Thus, at that level, customary self-segregation might continue to be reinforced by law; election to local, or state, parliaments could be on separate racial rolls, and in predominantly white areas the right to vote might even be reserved to whites, as at present.

In other words, a con/federal future need not greatly reduce the privileges currently enjoyed by whites, and if the electorate is to accept any such future, this aspect of it will have to be strongly emphasized. If, however, black, Indian and coloured leaders are to be persuaded to negotiate on this basis, there must be some arguments to persuade them that they can do so without losing all credibility with their supporters. Such arguments are not altogether easy to find.

Perhaps the best that can be said is that negotiation must start somewhere, and if black leaders are convinced that the whites' opening offer is the best that can be obtained, they may make the courageous decision to take part. But they will only do so if they are also convinced that the opening offer will be improved, for no black leader (except those of the 'independent' homelands) will dare take back to his people a constitutional blueprint which maintains white supremacy, in all but name, in those parts of the country which are attractive to whites. They will have, in other words, to show some willingness to extend the sectors in which racial discrimination is abolished, perhaps by establishing 'joint venture areas' or 'grey areas' under the direct control of a non-racial con/federal government.

A constitutional conference may lie years ahead, if, indeed, it ever takes place at all, and may itself be of some years' duration, though some optimistic commentators have suggested that the process of institutionalized negotiation has already begun, with the establishment of the President's Council. It is, perhaps, too soon to judge this body's potential, though the lack of African representation, which prompted the PFP's refusal to take part, must raise doubts and its limited record so far does not suggest that it will rapidly evolve into a powerful and dynamic body. Even if it does so evolve, it is most unlikely to do so at a pace acceptable to the black population, or even to *verligte* nationalists.

An additional political initiative is needed if negotiation is to begin in a reasonable time, but whether one will be taken depends upon the fluctuating strength and self-confidence of the *verligte* movement, especially of the *verligte* members of Cabinet, most of all of the Prime Minister himself. The strength shown by the HNP in the 1981 elections has obviously been a restraining influence; on the other hand it is hard to see what changes in current conditions would improve the chances of electoral popularity for a distinct move towards a constitutional conference.

It may be objected that more time is needed, not for preparing the electorate, but for preparatory thinking and writing. It seems doubtful, however, whether much more of value will be produced in a political vacuum. Constitutional proposals abound; what is needed now is for some proposals to be given the authority of governmental support and subjected to detailed scrutiny and negotiation. As at all constitutional conferences, all sorts of detailed changes would no doubt be made, perhaps even major changes of principle, but without the stimulus of live negotiation it is unlikely that much further progress will be made.

Once the long range decision to hold a conference has been made, there are the immediate problems of deciding which bodies are to be invited, and then of securing their attendance. There would be no particular difficulty about the white representation, which would include government and opposition, perhaps also the private sector and the state corporations. On the black side, homeland leaders, and almost certainly Inkatha, would not wish to be excluded, though some difficulty might be experienced, both in deciding which of the more radical, though still legal bodies, like AZAPO, should be included, and then in persuading their leaders to attend. The real problem, however, is presented by the banned ANC (of which Inkatha regards itself as the legal embodiment within South Africa) the PAC and perhaps the Black Consciousness Movement.

Without these organizations a conference would lack credibility with a proportion, unquantifiable, but probably large, of the black population, though this is not to say that their image within South Africa accords with the exiled reality. Even outside South Africa their absence, particularly that of the ANC, would be badly received, though the western industrial powers might be expected to withhold adverse public judgment at first. On the other hand, even if *verligte* leaders could persuade themselves of the necessity of the banned parties being represented, they would have extraordinary difficulty in persuading public opinion, and the agreement of other potential participants, like the homeland leaders, and perhaps even Inkatha, might not be readily forthcoming.

Despite the difficulties it seems unlikely that any even relatively peaceful deliverance from South Africa's problems will be achieved, except through negotiation, though even that process will, no doubt, take place against a background of grumbling guerrilla activity, perhaps growing into civil war.

THE INTERNATIONAL DIMENSION

The future of South Africa is not of interest only to South Africans, though they will have to decide it, but is of consuming interest to the world in general. Frequently the problem of South Africa is pushed to one side by more brightly burning political issues, like the Middle East, but once the process of moving towards decisions begins, it is likely to absorb so much international energy as to make the disruption caused by the Rhodesian problem look a mere nothing. The question, therefore, arises of what the outside world's attitude, and particularly that of the West, should be.

It is clear that the West has a general interest in change in South Africa, because without it there may be revolution, which, quite apart from the opportunities it might offer to the Soviet Union, would jeopardize the interests in safeguarding mineral supplies, trade relations and investment which the western powers share, though in different degrees. For the same reasons, not to mention moral and humanitarian considerations, the western interest lies in peaceful, rather than violent, change and, once the judgment is made that things cannot indefinitely continue as they are, the question becomes that of how peaceful change may best be encouraged.

The opportunities for the exertion of influence, without incurring charges of undue interference, are not great. Such charges are unacceptable to western governments because their relations with South Africa are at least nominally friendly, though often embarrassing, and in some sectors, notably business, relationships are cordial, as well as close. These limits notwithstanding, there are certain steps which can be taken.

First, the existing policy can be pursued of encouraging *verligte* elements within the Afrikaner élite and maintaining informal relationships with some of the legal black organizations in South Africa. There must, however, be doubts about the strength of the *verligte* movement and the

195

current influence of most black bodies, though perhaps not of Inkatha's. That being so, it is incumbent upon western governments to give thought to what more they can do to promote peaceful change, while continuing to protect interests at present believed essential.

The way forward lies more in the establishment of a new trend in policy and the creation of a new atmosphere, than in any single dramatic act. It goes without saying that the West should examine all alternative sources of minerals, take seriously the long term trading opportunities offered by the SADCC states and (though this might be less generally agreed upon) not encourage new investment in South Africa. Such policies, although their effects would not be immediate, would go part of the way to establishing a new relationship with the Republic, which, though still perfectly correct, would demonstrate to white South Africans that western friendship cannot be relied upon indefinitely.

The West could go further and, whilst not departing from its generally held view that the future of South Africa must be decided by South Africans, give some indication of the programme of change expected and a possible timetable. There are obvious difficulties about such a course: it might be counter-productive, by angering *verkrampte* whites into increased reaction; the programme of change put forward might be insufficiently radical, and the timetable too leisurely, to satisfy many members of the United Nations; if the targets were achieved it might prove impossible to deliver a reward. Nevertheless, if the West is to move into a more energetic attitude towards the Republic, which can perhaps not be done until its current preoccupation with Namibia is removed, then this seems the most fruitful direction in which to move.

The relationship, moreover, should not be solely with white South Africans and the black organizations tolerated by them. The time has surely come for western governments to move into some sort of relationship, however informal and even symbolic at first, with the ANC and other exiled bodies. Even the extension to their leaders of some of the courtesies given to Mr Sam Nujoma of SWAPO would serve notice on South Africa that western leaders have not closed their eyes to the future. Of course, the difficulties are great: not all western governments would agree to any such change of direction; it might well anger the South African Government; sections of western public opinion might be outraged. These, however, are arguments for conducting the manoeuvre with delicacy, rather than for not considering it at all.

CONCLUSION

This brief discussion of western policy is a digression from the main theme of change within South Africa, but it serves to remind us that the Republic is a world problem, little though white South Africans may relish the thought.

The questions outsiders ask themselves are whether the changes which have lately occurred in South Africa are significant, and whether they represent the beginning of an irreversible process, or should rather be seen as isolated events.

I conclude that significant, if limited, changes have been achieved and that, if the thinking of *verligte* members of the élite can be translated into action, much more can be done. However, the process which in 1980 looked full of promise can now be seen to have suffered severely from the elections of 1981 and the split in the National Party, though in some fields, notably industrial relations and black employment, it will no doubt continue. Left to itself progress will be slow; sometimes so slow as to be virtually undetectable, though to some extent it can be encouraged by outside pressure, by the threat of violence and by the growth of legal and organized action by such bodies as black trade unions.

The prospects of sufficient change being achieved to satisfy the majority of South Africa's population are slim, but they still exist. However, they can only be taken seriously if South Africa's leaders judge that the alternative is too bleak to be contemplated. In that case, they may gather the courage to take a new political initiative, leading eventually to negotiation and the prospect of a settlement.

CHAPTER 18

Postscript

In 1982 some of the themes in South African politics gathered new emphasis, though it cannot be said that any new directions were embarked upon. The National Party split in March and Dr Treurnicht founded the Conservative Party of South Africa (here referred to as KP, for Konserwatiewe Party, to avoid confusion with the Communist Party); in May the President's Council produced its constitutional report and in July the Prime Minister presented the government's thinking about the report to a Federal Congress of the Party, held in advance of the various Provincial Congresses. On the economic front the government's thinking on industrial devolution was embodied in a White Paper (RSA 1982). Meanwhile the Buthelezi Commission reported in March, and in June the Government's long-rumoured intention to cede part of South Africa to Swaziland became public. The land to be ceded included a section of KwaZulu, which naturally produced a strong adverse reaction from Chief Buthelezi. In neighbouring Zimbabwe a large part of the Air Force was sabotaged on the ground in July, which many commentators almost automatically ascribed to South Africa, as part of the policy of destabilization. Others, however, thought such an operation would not be beyond the expertise gained during the long guerrilla war by Mr Nkomo's opposition.

The trouble in the NP was sparked off by an editorial written by Dr Jan Grobler, the party's chief information officer and MP for Brits, in the January edition of a party publication, *Nat 80's*, which said that coloureds, Indians and whites lived in one country and should logically have one government. This provoked much speculation that a multiracial government might be intended and on Sunday 21 February *Rapport* claimed that Dr Treurnicht was upset about the issue. The Prime Minister thereupon issued a statement, in which he said that a country could only have one central government, though there might be several instruments of government, and that this principle had been embodied in the 1977 proposals. These had provided for an executive State President and a joint Council of Cabinets under the State President's chairmanship. Thus, Mr Botha was concerned to show that if Dr Treurnicht dissented, he was dissenting from principles established five years earlier and of which he must be presumed to have approved, since otherwise he would not have accepted Cabinet office. Dr Treurnicht's real fears, however, were of what the President's Council might propose in its forthcoming report.

There was much debate about whether the new approach entailed 'power-sharing' between the races, a form of words which provoked instinctive distaste among Nationalists, because it was associated with the PFP. Mr Botha's statement went on:

> Too many bogeymen are conjured up around the term 'power-sharing'. We and the PFP do not think in the same terms about 'power-sharing'. That party is working towards a unitary state, we are not.

> For us the concept of consultation and joint decision-making is indeed a healthy form of power-sharing without destroying self-determination. However we prefer the term joint responsibility. (*The Citizen* [NP advertisement]: 25 March 1982).

Some of Mr Botha's opponents wondered whether 'healthy power-sharing' was like 'healthy suicide'! *Beeld* pointed out on 23 February that he had never used the term approvingly before and it is difficult not to suspect that he did so deliberately, knowing Dr Treurnicht's sensitivity to anything that smacked of PFP policy. Be that as it may, the Prime Minister clearly expected trouble at the Cabinet meeting on 22 February, which was crucial, but secret and not much reported; one account says that he raced through the agenda in order to allow a clear hour for Dr Treurnicht to state his case, but that the latter avoided doing so.

The scene then shifted to the NP's Parliamentary caucus meeting on 24 February where, as *Beeld* put it the following day, 'the gauntlet was thrown down and everyone had to state his position'. As the *Rand Daily Mail* suggested on 25 February, Dr Treurnicht may have been trapped into voting on a motion he could not support; by his own account (*Citizen*: 25 February) he had asked to be allowed a difference of opinion on power sharing and it seems certain that he was pushed, partly by the Prime Minister, partly by his own supporters, into a confrontation he wished to avoid. The question remains open of whether the Prime Minister engineered the confrontation solely of his own volition, or whether he too was pushed.

In any event Mr S. P. Botha, as leader of the Assembly, moved a motion in the caucus of 'confident and unqualified support for the Prime Minister for his leadership and interpretation of National Party policies'. Although there was no mention of 'power-sharing' Dr Treurnicht felt obliged to vote against, and was accompanied by one Minister, Dr Hartzenberg, and twenty backbenchers. Six of them, however, returned to the NP fold in the week's grace allowed by the Prime Minister. Of the remaining sixteen, twelve belonged to the most *verkrampte* group (group 4) of MPs distinguished in our research in 1980 (see Chapter 13); three were in group 3, and one had entered Parliament since the research was conducted. (Of the six who returned, three belonged to group 4 and one was a new member). All but one of the sixteen represented Transvaal constituencies.

Some of the twenty-two rebels now asked for an emergency meeting of the 'Head Committee' of the NP in the Transvaal to be held within 14 days, as the rules provided, and it was called for the following Saturday, 27 February. In the interval former President Vorster announced his support for Dr Treurnicht. The 230 member committee consisted of MPs and Members of the Provincial Council, an elected representative of each Transvaal constituency and 16 co-opted members. At the meeting a motion identical to the one passed in the Parliamentary caucus was carried by 172—36, (only 18 of the 36 were MPs) an overwhelming vote of confidence for the Prime Minister. The latter had flown to Pretoria that morning, officially to celebrate his daughter's birthday, and was invited to the meeting at the suggestion of Mr F. W. de Klerk (he in any case had the right to attend, though not to vote). It is fairly generally thought that his presence made a big difference to the vote. (A survey published by *Beeld* on 26 February found that 89 members of the Head Committee favoured Mr Botha, 34 were for Dr Treurnicht, 57 not sure or unwilling to commit themselves and 50 unavailable for comment).

Another motion, carried by 140–33, provided that any MPs failing to fall into line by the following Tuesday, 2 March, would automatically forfeit any office in the Transvaal NP; meanwhile they would be suspended from office.

Thereafter, events moved swiftly. Dr Treurnicht and Dr Hartzenberg resigned from Cabinet on 2 March and Dr Treurnicht was expelled from the party on 8 March (though his party divisional committee backed him 131–26, despite the efforts of Mr F. W. de Klerk and General Magnus Malan). Most of the remaining rebels were expelled a week later (though many were resoundingly endorsed by their divisional committees), two resigned and one was expelled after a reprieve. The press consensus on 2 March was that Dr Treurnicht would not found a new party; instead there was much speculation that he would join Jaap Marais' HNP, though it was pointed out that Mr Marais had never forgiven Dr Treurnicht for failing to go with him when the HNP was founded in 1969. *Beeld* (3 March) also pointed to the class difference between the HNP and Dr Treurnicht's supporters: the latter tended to come from comfortably off areas, the former had a rather 'blue collar' image. Professor Laurence Schlemmer thought that a Treurnicht party in alliance with the HNP might gain approximately 24 per cent of the vote; the nationalists would gain English speakers from the NRP and rise to 37 per cent, leaving 24 per cent with the PFP and 14 per cent undecided or floating (*Sunday Times*: 28 February 1982). Another experienced observer thought the KP could win 5 Transvaal seats in an immediate election, and have a chance in another 15 (Personal communication).

In fact Dr Treurnicht and his 15 supporters founded the Conservative Party, with which Dr Connie Mulder and his National Conservative Party threw in their lot, at a rally of about 10,000 people at Pretoria on 20 March. Dr Treurnicht made a point of delivering part of his speech in English to emphasize that the new party should be seen as a conservative, rather than a purely Afrikaner movement. (*The Guardian*: 22 March 1982). A few days earlier Dr Treurnicht had been tumultuously received at the University of Pretoria by a crowd of 2,000 students (*Argus*: 11 March 1982; other estimates ranged to 3,000 or more) and 10 of the university's 14 hostels had formed KP branches by early April (*Cape Times*: 3 April 1982). The party announced that it would hold its first Congress in August and by May a poll, reported in *Oggendblad* (4 May 1982) gave it 20 per cent of the electorate, mostly from the HNP, with some from the NP and the formerly undecided. *Beeld* reported on the same day that the HNP retained only 3 per cent. A poll in *Rapport* (reported in *The Guardian*: 4 May 1982) gave the KP 38 per cent of Afrikaners in the Transvaal against 44 per cent for the NP; in the country at large, among English and Afrikaans speaking voters, they had 18 and 43 per cent respectively.

The KP was thus able to go forward confidently to its first congress. The *Transvaler* commented (6 August 1982) that the approach and atmosphere there and at the NP's Federal Congress (see below) had been so different that one wondered what had kept the people in the same party for so long. The NP's new dispensation was cautious to a degree, but attendance at the KP congress made one see that it also contained an important element of daring, because it was light years away from the things the KP still clung to.

The KP's draft constitution had been leaked in advance (*Transvaler*: 20 July 1982) and was extremely reactionary, the core being absolute apartheid and geographical separation, with homelands (or 'heartlands') being established for coloureds and Indians. Blacks with established rights of residence in white South Africa would be deprived of them, although black homelands would not be extended beyond the limits laid down in 1936. According to *Beeld* (3 August 1982) Dr Treurnicht's opening address contained four main criticisms of government policy: he objected to the proposed powers of the President to decide which matters are of common concern to one race, and which to more than one; to a mixed cabinet, which meant power-sharing; to one parliament with three chambers, which amounted to a unitary system and to 'old United Party policy'; and to the proposed powers of the President's Council, without responsibility to Afrikanerdom.

Dr Treurnicht was roundly attacked in *Beeld* for all this and the KP's programme was condemned in other Afrikaans papers as backward-looking and unreasonable, but that is unlikely to diminish the KP's following. More probably it will continue to tap the deep fear of any change, 'the thin end of the wedge', that exists among many whites.

In May the President's Council presented its long awaited report. Although far less detailed than had been hoped, it recommended equal political rights for Indians, coloureds and whites (but not blacks though there have been reports of hints by Dr Worrall, chairman of the Council's Constitutional Committee, that negotiations should be started, at least with urban blacks), an Executive President indirectly elected by an electoral college of the three non-black groups, and an appointed Cabinet. The purpose would be to create a body above ethnic interests and strong enough to initiate and push through reform measures: to speed up the process the first President should be elected for a seven year term by the present white House of Assembly.

In a simultaneous report on local government the Council recommended the maximum devolution of power to local authorities, which would probably, but not necessarily, be uni-racial. Above them would be metropolitan authorities in the main urban areas, which would consist of members of all the local authorities in their areas, and so be multi-racial. 'Hard', or non-controversial functions, like water and electricity supplies, would be left to metropolitan authorities, while local authorities would deal with 'soft', or sensitive functions, such as schools and residential rights (*The Guardian:* 13 May 1982). The proposals have naturally been rejected by blacks and right wing whites and there have been widespread misgivings about the great powers to be allowed the President. Chief Buthelezi, with the PFP's leader, Dr Van Zyl Slabbert, beside him on the platform at a packed meeting in Durban, denounced the President's Council as a 'forum for racism and racial hatred' (*Ibid*: 27 May 1982).

The government was slow to make public its position in response to the proposals, but it did succeed in obtaining a mandate for reform at a meeting of the NP's parliamentary and provincial caucuses early in June (*The Times*: 7 June 1982). However the party vetoed the President's Council's recommendation that MPs appointed to Cabinet should give up their seats. (*The Guardian*: 8 June 1982). According to the *Transvaler* (7 June 1982) the caucuses had also accepted that the State President should (contrary to the Council's recommendation) function as Prime Minister as well; that there should be a mixed Cabinet drawn proportionately from the three population groups; that the legislature should consist of one tri-cameral Parliament; and the President's Council should continue in being. The paper also reported that government circles did not regard the new guidelines as deviating from the 1977 proposals sufficiently to necessitate a referendum.

The Government's proposals were at length made publicly known at a Federal Congress of the party (the first for nearly twenty years) at Bloemfontein on July 30 and 31 and were unanimously accepted. In the words of Allister Sparks (*Observer*: 1 August 1982, under the apt headline 'Botha loses his nerve and turns clock back'), this 'symbolically anti-climactic event . . . turned out to be a step back five years . . . to the 1977 model, with a few trimmings . . .'. There would be three separate parliamentary chambers, sitting together only on ceremonial occasions. Legislation affecting one community would be passed by the relevant chamber, if it affected two or three, each must pass it separately (there might also be joint Standing Committees) and when the chambers were in conflict the President's Council would decide between them. The Council would have 20, 10 and 5 members, elected by the white, coloured and Indian chambers

202

respectively and a further 25 to be nominated by the new Executive President. The President, to be elected by a college of 50 white, 25 coloured and 13 Indian MPs, would pick his Cabinet from inside and outside Parliament, and might include coloureds and Indians, as well as whites.

These proposals do indubitably support Mr Botha's contention at the time of the National Party's split that his thinking had not departed from the spirit of 1977, and that there was therefore no need for Dr Treurnicht to leave the party. No doubt the Prime Minister, in formulating the proposals, had an eye on the KP's evident support among the electorate and therefore did not take any of the slightly more radical options which the President's Council left open to him. Nevertheless, the breach with Dr Treurnicht seems irreversible and the coloured and Indian leaders were in great doubt about whether to participate in the new dispensation. The *Transvaler* (2 August 1982) congratulated the government on its bold and resolute approach, but the London *Times*' leading article of the same day said of the proposals, under the headline 'Mr Botha's mouse': 'They spell, not change, but defiance of change—which is the more disappointing because Mr Botha had seemed until recently, to be speaking the language of change'. That is a verdict with which I see no reason to quarrel.

While these dramatic, if inconclusive, happenings were going on in white South Africa, the report of the Buthelezi Commission was made public; this is an important document, which was ignored by the NP, disclaimed by the NRP with what the *Financial Mail* (2 April 1982: 47) called 'unseemly haste', and widely noticed overseas.

Central to the report was an exhaustive attitude survey of respondents from all population groups, both within and outside Natal/KwaZulu, directed by Professor Lawrence Schlemmer, who was also Secretary to the Commission. The survey found that blacks were intensely interested in politics and attached great value to the vote. Negative perceptions of black political conditions had risen from the 65–70 per cent in Hanf's 1977 study to 80 per cent in 1980. The largest rise in the 'angry' category had occurred in the middle class, where it had increased from 45 to 68 per cent.

Eight out of ten black respondents were very impressed by Mr Robert Mugabe, the new Prime Minister of Zimbabwe, Inkatha members marginally more than others, and rural Africans not significantly less. Militancy in the rural areas had increased; 21 per cent in Natal/KwaZulu and 31 per cent on the Rand accepted that 'nothing will work, only bloodshed'; virtually all blacks expected violence if their life conditions did not change within the next ten years; revolution had become a familiar idea; four out of ten, and in some groups many more, would secretly aid the ANC, which seemed to have gained ground from Black Consciousness.

There had been fluctuations in the popularity of black leaders on the Rand, where Chief Buthelezi was second behind the ANC, having been top in 1977, and temporarily outstripped by Dr Motlana, of the Committee of 10, in the interim. The popular recognition of the exiled ANC leadership had climbed rapidly. Even in KwaZulu/Natal, where Inkatha was the most popular political organization, the ANC had made big advances, so that, as Professor Schlemmer commented, on these results it was no longer possible to see the ANC as an 'underground' organization.

78 per cent of all Zulu speakers attached a very high priority to 'one man one vote in a unitary state' but a marginally higher majority also supported elected homeland leaders joining whites on a consociational basis. A majority (a large one in the Transvaal) were against homeland independence and partition was the least attractive option of all. Given the acceptance of consociationalism (essentially, negotiation in an executive body between respected black and white leaders, who would be able to carry their legislature with them) and a majority in favour, if only as second best, of a regional solution for Natal/KwaZulu alone, the Commission believed that there were 'magnificent opportunities . . . to explore creative compromises'.

On the other hand, they could distinguish four types of black discontent: some displayed apolitical dissatisfaction with their material circumstances; others suffered relative deprivation, i.e. were dissatisfied with the comparison between their own and other groups' conditions, but moderate in terms of their acceptance of political alternatives—this was the largest group; there were also urban lower class and middle class radicals; the fourth group were militants, who were not, however, necessarily radical ideologically. There was widespread expectation of violence in the third and fourth groups and some in the second, so that the Commission was led to the conclusion that '. . . our results show an emergent situation which could become very serious indeed'.

Nevertheless, the flexibility of black South Africans, and the readiness for change shown by many whites, caused the Commission to recommend government under consociational agreement between representatives of groups, which need not be racially defined. They went on:

> It is not necessarily a long term governmental system. It is likely to provide a period of government during which co-operative decision making will minimise the high level suspicion that exists in a deeply segmented society and may, in improved circumstances, mean that the need for consociational government could disappear and a new form of government can be devised by agreement. (Buthelezi Commission 1982, I: 112)

In the first instance the executive would consist equally of representatives of the (white) Natal Provincial Executive (since Natal is controlled by the NRP that party's initial reaction to the Report is highly unfortunate) and of the (black) KwaZulu Government, with some representation of Indians and coloureds. Later the groups would be found (the Commission optimistically believed):

> . . . to have changed toward common political and economic interests and by agreement the groups represented on the executive could be varied under an amended consociational agreement. (*Ibid*: 114)

The legislature would be elected by proportional representation, with some minimum group representation, from areas which would, initially, be to a large extent racially defined, but would move towards being areas of common political and economic interests. The new Natal/KwaZulu would not be independent, but the Commissioners do not go into the details of the future relationship with the central South African Government.

It may of course be said that any scheme such as this is so inherently over-optimistic as to be unworthy of consideration, especially as the South African Government missed the opportunity (for which it was reproached in the Afrikaans press) of entering into serious discussion of it. Nevertheless, the Commission was, as Chief Buthelezi himself said, the first major black initiative in the constitutional debate, and for that reason may be remembered after many exclusively white agonizings have been forgotten. Furthermore, the fact that the Commissioners could envisage their solution as not necessarily being permanent must increase the chances of its being considered a worth while interim goal.

Finally, in this consideration of recent developments in South African politics, we come to the government's decision (the intention had long been the subject of rumour, but was announced only on 14 June) to excise from the Republic some black areas adjoining Swaziland and hand them over to Swaziland. The areas concerned are the greater part of the Swazi homeland of Kangwane, and the whole of a part of KwaZulu, known as Ingwavuma, possession of which would give Swaziland access to the sea through Kosi Bay. The plan has been strenuously denounced by Mr E. J. Mabuza, Chief Minister of Kangwane, and by Chief Buthelezi. (*The Guardian*: 15 June 1982). Nor was the *Transvaler* of the same day in favour of it, largely because of the bloodshed it might cause. There was also unfavourable comment in the Afrikaans press on the secrecy with which the negotiations had been conducted, and the failure to consult the people whose land was to be transferred. *Oggendblad* (17 June 1982) pointed out that King Sobhuza was an old man, who might well be succeeded by a Marxist son, who could be expected to maintain close relations with Mozambique so that South Africa would have gained nothing. On the other hand *Oggendblad*'s editor wrote only the next day that the transfer was to be applauded, because it was in the true spirit of Separate Development!

There followed the dissolution by the central government of Kangwane's Legislative Assembly. The Natal Provincial Council and the KwaZulu Government planned referenda, and both were confident that the cession of land would be decisively rejected. As Chief Buthelezi said: 'Pretoria's abolition of its own creation means it has abandoned all pretence of carrying out even its own fraudulent policy'. Dr Willem de Klerk, in his column in *Rapport* on 20 June, supported Chief Buthelezi and urged upon the South African Government the need to maintain good relations with him: 'I know I speak for a large group of important Afrikaners when I respectfully ask the Chief Minister to be strong enough to fight his rage and bitterness with Christian patience!

According to *Vaderland* (28 June 1982) Ingwavuma has always been overwhelmingly Swazi and its transfer to KwaZulu in 1976 was an administrative mistake; the same might be said of the Southern Sotho homeland, QuaQua, established almost on the Lesotho border. But *Vaderland* had got wind of a whole 'package deal' with Swaziland; this included a military agreement, covering action against the ANC and development of Kosi Bay into a harbour which could be used for the defence of the southern Indian Ocean and would also take take traffic away from Maputo; Swazi agreement in principle to join an eventual confederation of southern Africa; and considerable expansion of economic ties. With all this went a South African Cabinet decision to force a confrontation with Chief Buthelezi, and work instead with King Goodwill Zwelethini.

The government may, indeed, have forced more of a confrontation than it expected, since Chief Buthelezi has embarked on a battle in the Supreme Court against the transfer and announced that there is more common ground between him and the ANC than ever before. The transfer has also bred strange alliances; Libya has backed Swaziland, apparently in return for Swazi support at the OAU, and the front-line states, the ANC and the OAU have said they will not oppose the deal. The latter decision must have been extremely difficult; on the one hand, to condone the transfer entailed both accepting interference with established boundaries and not opposing an action which the South African Government presents as a logical extension of its policy of separate development. On the other hand, to oppose the transfer was to thwart a fellow member state of the OAU, in favour of a homeland leader who has been vilified by the ANC because he has used the institutions of apartheid.

The motives of the South African Government are no doubt complicated, not to say Machiavellian. One major intention may be to deprive not only the inhabitants of Ingwavuma and Kangwane of their South African citizenship, but also the entire Swazi population of the Republic, perhaps as many as a million people; Mr Mabuza's purpose, on the other hand, is for his people to retain South African citizenship and fight for improvements from within. Some other South African intentions were probably: to prevent any radical successor to King Sobhuza from giving aid to the ANC; to embarrass Chief Buthelezi, the ANC and the OAU; to detach Swaziland from Mozambique's influence; to interpose a Swazi buffer between northern KwaZulu and southern Mozambique, and to confer respectability on the homelands policy by negotiating about it with a sovereign state, which might eventually be persuaded to join the 'constellation'. It is too soon to tell whether the deal will be judged a success by South Africa's rulers, though it seems probable that several of the purposes behind it will be achieved.

In conclusion, we may say that recent months have seen the working out of old themes in South African politics; the events have generated considerable amounts of heat but whether they point towards changes which will significantly benefit the black population is more doubtful. The split in the NP, the full results of which, as they spread through Afrikaner organizations, have yet to be seen, is likely to render slower than ever the process of change; indeed its effects are already to be seen in the caution of the constitutional proposals put forward by the government. The proposals are of no direct relevance to Africans, though for Indians and coloureds they present the very difficult problem of whether or not to accept them.

The Buthelezi Commission's report would, if it were acted upon, give the black population some hope. It is surprising that the South African Government has so decisively ignored it, since the Commission's line of argument is, after all, consistent with the government's own con/federal intentions, with the new form of the old policy of decentralized industrialization and with such manifestations of *verligte* thinking as the Lombard plan. Finally, the cession to Swaziland of parts of South Africa can be seen as the radical continuation of the old policy of uniting members of the same ethnic group; it is unlikely to benefit the inhabitants of the areas ceded, and for the other Swazis in the Republic may carry the penalty of loss of South African citizenship.

In short, and to return to the title of this book, changes have been taking place in South Africa in recent years; they are cautious, grudging, hampered by the strength of right wing white opinion and, above all, slow, but they do provide evidence of a new climate of thought among sections of the élite. In other words, there are new directions. The danger is not so much that those who take them will get lost in blind alleys, as that their energy will be dissipated for very little return. If the end of apartheid is to be negotiated in tolerably peaceful conditions, it is the pace of change which must drastically increase.

Bibliography

Adam, H. and Giliomee, H., 1979. *The Rise and Crisis of Afrikaner Power*. Cape Town: David Philip.

Ademiluyi, A., 1978. *Strikes in Natal, January and February 1973*. Unpublished M.A. Dissertation, University of York (U.K.), (Centre for Southern African Studies).

African Communist, 1977. 'The Way Forward from Soweto: Political Report adopted by the Plenary session of the Central Committee of the South African Communist Party in April 1977.' *The African Communist* **70**: 21–50.

African Communist, 1980. 'Role of Trade Unions in the South African Revolution', by 'A Reader'. *The African Communist* **82**: 81–89.

Akeroyd, A. V. *et al* (Eds.), 1981. *European Business and South Africa: An Appraisal of the E.C. Code of Conduct*. Mainz: Grünewald; and Munich: Kaizer.

Ballinger, M., 1960. 'A Programme for Progress towards a Democratic South Africa', in H. Spottiswoode (Comp.) *South Africa, the Road Ahead*. Cape Town: Timmins, 13–27.

Banton, M., 1967. *Race Relations*. London: Social Science Paperbacks in association with Tavistock Publications.

Baran, P. A., 1970. 'On the Political Economy of Backwardness', in R. I. Rhodes (Ed.) *Imperialism and Underdevelopment*. New York and London: Monthly Review Press, 285–301.

Barber, J., 1980. 'Zimbabwe's Southern African Setting', in W. H. Morris-Jones (Ed.) *From Rhodesia to Zimbabwe: Behind and Beyond Lancaster House*. London: Cass, 69–84.

Bell, R. T., 1973. *Industrial Decentralisation in South Africa*. Cape Town: Oxford University Press.

Bloch, J., 1977. *The Legislative Framework of Collective Bargaining in South Africa*. Unpublished LL.M. Dissertation, University of London. London School of Economics.

Blumer, H., 1965. 'Industrialisation and Race Relations', in G. Hunter (Ed.) *Industrialisation and Race Relations: A Symposium*. London: Oxford University Press for Institute of Race Relations, 220–253.

Bonner, P., 1979. 'Focus on FOSATU', *South African Labour Bulletin* **5** (1), (May): 5–24.

Botha, P. R., 1978. *South Africa: Plan for the Future*. Johannesburg: Perskor.

Bozzoli, B., 1978. 'Capital and the State in South Africa'. *Review of African Political Economy*, No. 7 (Jan. – April): 40–50.

Brett, E. A., 1972. *Colonialism and Underdevelopment in East Africa*. London: Heinemann.

Bunting, B., 1975. *Moses Kotane: South African Revolutionary*. London: Inkululeko.

Bureau of Economic Policy and Analysis, University of Pretoria, 1980a. 'Political Stability'. *Focus on Key Economic Issues* 26 (July). J. A. Lombard *et al* (Comps.). Johannesburg: Mercabank.

——1980b. 'Alternatives to the Consolidation of KwaZulu'. *Special Focus* 2. J. A. Lombard (Ed.). Pretoria: Bureau of Economic Policy and Analysis.

Buthelezi Commission, (n.d., but 1982). *The Requirements for Stability and Development in KwaZulu and Natal*. Two volumes. Durban: H & H Publications.

Carter, G. *et al* 1967. *South Africa's Transkei: The Politics of Domestic Colonialism*. Chicago: North Western University Press.

Caygill, M., 1980. *Black Trade Unions in South Africa*. Unpublished M.A. Dissertation, University of York (U.K.), (Centre for Southern African Studies).

Centro de Estudos Africanos, 1980. *South Africa: Is Botha's Total Strategy a Programme of Reform?* Maputo: Universidade Eduardo Mondlane, Centro de Estudos Africanos. Mimeo.

——n.d. *The Constellation of Southern African States: A New Strategic Offensive by South Africa in the Region*. Mimeo

Cheadle, H., 1979. 'A Guide to the Industrial Conciliation Amendment Act'. *South African Labour Bulletin* 5(2) (August): 102–126.

——1980. 'Letter to SALB'. *South African Labour Bulletin* 5 (6 & 7) (March): 7–9.

Ciskei Commission, 1980. *Report*. Pretoria: Conference Associates. [The Quail Report].

Claasens, A., 1979. 'The Riekert Commission and Unemployment: the KwaZulu Case'. *South African Labour Bulletin* 5(4) (November): 49–64.

Clarke, S., 1978. 'Capital, Fractions of Capital and the State: Neo-Marxist Analysis of the South African State'. *Capital and Class* 5: 32–77.

Cleary, S. n.d. 'The "New Initiative": the Formation of a neo-Colonial Empire'. *Two Views on South Africa's Foreign Policy and the Constellation of States*. Johannesburg: South African Institute of Race Relations, Occasional Papers of the Research Department, no. 2.

Cooper, C., 1979. 'The Mine Workers' Strike'. *South African Labour Bulletin* 5(2) (August): 102–126.

Cooper, C., 1980. *Strikes in South Africa, 1979*. Johannesburg: South African Institute of Race Relations.

Cooper, C. and Ensor, L., 1980. 'The 1979 TUCSA Conference: Moving in for the Kill'. *South African Labour Bulletin* 5(6 & 7) (March): 116–121.

Cowley, C., 1975. 'South West Africa: its Problems and Prospects'. *Optima* No. **3**: 171–196.

Curle, R., 1978. *South Africa's Border Industries: Geographical Perspectives on their Location and Viability*. Unpublished M.A. Dissertation, University of York (U.K.), (Centre for Southern African Studies).

Davies, R., 1979. 'Capital Restructuring and the Modification of the Racial Division of Labour in South Africa'. *Journal of Southern African Studies* **5**(2) (April): 181–198.

Davis, D., 1976. 'African Unions at the Crossroads'. *The African Communist* **64**: 93–104.

De Klerk, W. A., 1976. *The Puritans in Africa*. Harmondsworth: Penguin Books.

Douwes Decker, L. C. G., 1980. 'Industrial Peace and Industrial Justice—are these Attainable in the 1980 Decade?' Paper presented at the fiftieth annual council meeting of the South African Institute of Race Relations. Cape Town.

Duncan, P., 1965. 'Is Apartheid an Insoluble Problem?' *Race* **6**(4) (April): 263–266.

Ellis, C. F. R., 1980. 'Black Unemployment in South Africa—A Problem'. *South African Outlook* (April): 61–62.

Esterhuyse, W. P., 1979. *Afkeid van Apartheid: Opstelle oor Rassie-diskriminasie*. Cape Town: Tafelberg.

Feit, E., 1970. 'Urban Revolt in South Africa: A Case Study'. *Journal of Modern African Studies* **8**(1): 55–72.

Feit, E. and Stokes, R. G., 1976. 'Racial Prejudice and Economic Pragmatism: A South African Case Study', *Journal of Modern African Studies* **14**(3): 487–506.

First, R., 1977. 'After Soweto: A Response'. *Review of African Political Economy* No. **11** (Jan. – April): 93–100.

FOSATU (Federation of South African Trade Unions), 1979. *Documents on E.E.C. Code of Conduct*. (August). Typescript. (Documents presented at an ICFTU Conference, Brussels, February 1980).

——1980. 'Memorandum. The Parallel Union Thesis'. *South African Labour Bulletin* **5**(6 & 7) (March): 78–98.

Frank, A. G., 1969. *Capitalism and Underdevelopment in Latin America*. New York: Monthly Review Press.

Furnivall, J. S., 1948. *Colonial Policy and Practice: A Comparative Study of Burma and Netherlands India*. Cambridge: Cambridge University Press.

Gagiano, J., *et al.* 1982 (March). *Opvattings van Studente aan die Universiteit van Stellenbosch*. Universiteit van Stellenbosch: Departement Staatsleer en Publieke Administrasie.

Greenberg, S. 1980. *Race and State in Capitalist Development*. New Haven: Yale University Press.

Guelke, A., n.d. 'Apartheid and the Labour Market' in C. R. Hill and P. Warwick (Eds.) *Southern African Research in Progress*. University of York (U.K.), Centre for Southern African Studies, *Collected Papers*; **1**: 96–117.

Hanf, T. *et al* 1981. *South Africa: The Prospects of Peaceful Change—An Empirical Inquiry into the Possibility of Democratic Conflict Negotiation.* London: Rex Collings; Cape Town: David Philip; and Bloomington: Indiana University Press.

Hendler, P., 1980. 'The Organisation of Parallel Unions'. *South African Labour Bulletin* 5(6 & 7) (March): 99–115.

Henson, D., 1978. 'Trade Unionism and the Struggle for Liberation in South Africa'. *Capital and Class* 6: 1–41.

Hill, C. R., 1964. *Bantustans: the Fragmentation of South Africa.* London: Oxford University Press for Institute of Race Relations.

——(Ed.), 1969. *Rights and Wrongs: Some Essays on Human Rights.* Harmondsworth: Penguin Books.

——1976. 'British Reactions to Transkeian Independence'. Paper presented to South African Institute of International Affairs Conference, Umtata, November.

——1977a. 'Business and Politics in South Africa: Preliminary Observations'. University of York (U.K.), Centre for Southern African Studies. Unpublished paper.

——1977b. 'South Africa 1976'. Unpublished report to Southern African Studies Trust.

——1982. 'Regional Co-operation in Southern Africa'. Paper presented to International Social Science Conference, University of Malawi, July.

Hirson, B., 1981. 'Language in Control and Resistance in South Africa'. *African Affairs* 80(319) (April): 219–237.

Horwitz, R., 1967. *The Political Economy of South Africa.* London: Weidenfeld and Nicholson.

Houghton, D. Hobart, 1970. *Enlightened Self Interest and the Liberal Spirit* (Alfred and Winifred Hoernlé Memorial Lecture). Johannesburg: South African Institute of Race Relations.

Hudson, W. E. (Ed.), 1969. *The Is-Ought Question.* London: Macmillan.

Hugo, P., 1977. 'Academic Dissent and Apartheid in South Africa'. *Journal of Black Studies* 7(3) (March): 243–262.

Hurley, D. E., 1966. *Human Dignity and Race Relations* (Presidential Address). Johannesburg: South African Institute of Race Relations.

Johns, S., 1965. *Marxism-Leninism in a Multi-Racial Environment: The Origins and Early History of the Communist Party of South Africa 1914–1933.* Unpublished Ph.D. Thesis, Harvard University.

Kantor, B. S. and Kenny, H. F., 1976. 'The Poverty of Neo-Marxism: the Case of South Africa'. *Journal of Southern African Studies* 3(1) (October): 20–40.

Kantor, B. S., 1980. 'Is there an Unemployment Problem in South Africa?' *Businessman's Law* (February).

Kgarebe, A. (Ed.), 1981. *SADCC 2—Maputo.* London: SADCC Liaison Committee.

Kotzé, D., 1976. *African Politics in South Africa: Parties and Issues.* London: C. Hurst.

Leftwich, A. (Ed.), 1974. *South Africa: Economic Growth and Political*

Change—with Comparative Studies of Chile, Sri Lanka and Malaysia. London: Allison and Busby.

Legassick, M., 1976. 'Race, Industrialisation and Social Change in South Africa: the Case of R. F. A. Hoernlé'. *African Affairs* **75**(299) (April): 224–239.

Legassick, M. and Innes, D., 1977. 'Capital Restructuring and Apartheid: A Critique of Constructive Engagement'. *African Affairs* **76**(305) (October): 437–482.

Levy, N., 1978. 'Problems of Acquisition of Labour for the South African Goldmining Industry: The Asian Labour Alternative and the Defence of the Wage Structure', in C. R. Hill and A. V. Akeroyd (Eds.) *Southern African Research in Progress.* University of York (U.K.), Centre for Southern African Studies, *Collected Papers* **3**: 58–72.

Leys, C., 1975. *Underdevelopment in Kenya: the Political Economy of Neo-Colonialism.* London: Heinemann Educational Books.

Lipton, M., 1976. 'British Investment in South Africa: Is Constructive Engagement Possible?' *South African Labour Bulletin* **3**(3) (October): 10–48.

Locke, J., 1690. *The Second Treatise of Government.*

Lombard, J., *et al*, 1980a and 1980b. *See* Bureau of Economic Policy and Analysis.

Luckhardt, K. and Wall, B., 1980. *Organise or Starve. The History of the South African Congress of Trade Unions.* London: Lawrence and Wishart.

Macpherson, C. B., 1962. *The Political Theory of Possessive Individualism: Hobbes to Locke.* London: Oxford University Press.

Mafeje, A., 1978. 'Soweto and its Aftermath'. *Review of African Political Economy* No. **11** (Jan. – April): 17–30.

Mason, P., 1962. *Common Sense about Race.* London: Oxford University Press.

Matanzima, K. D., 1976. *Independence My Way.* Pretoria: Foreign Affairs Association.

Mayer, P., 1962. 'Labour Migrancy and the Social Network' in J. F. Holleman *et al* (Eds.) *Problems of Transition.* Pietermaritzburg: Natal University Press, 21–51.

McCabe, H., 1980. 'The Class Struggle and Christian Love', in R. Ambler and D. Haslam (Eds.) *Agenda for Prophets: Towards a Political Theology for Britain.* London: Bowerdean Press, 153–169.

McGregor, L., 1980. 'The Fatti's and Moni's Dispute'. *South African Labour Bulletin* **5**(6 & 7) (March): 122–131.

Midlane, M., n.d. 'Aspects of the South African Liberal Tradition', in C. R. Hill and P. Warwick (Eds.) *Southern African Research in Progress.* University of York (U.K.), Centre for Southern African Studies, *Collected Papers* **1**, 71–95.

Minogue, K., 1963. *The Liberal Mind.* London: Methuen.

Moodie, T., 1975. *The Rise of Afrikanerdom: Power, Apartheid and the Afrikaner Civil Religion.* Berkeley: University of California Press.

Naudé, G., 1969. 'Banning in South Africa: a Technique of Repression' in C. R. Hill (Ed.) *Rights and Wrongs: Some Essays on Human Rights*. Harmondsworth: Penguin Books.

Nicol, M., 1980. 'Legislation, Registration, Emasculation'. *South African Labour Bulletin* 5(6 & 7) (March): 44–56.

No Sizwe, 1979. *One Azania, One Nation—The National Question in South Africa*. London: Zed Press.

Nsekela, A. J. (Ed.) 1981. *Southern Africa: towards Economic Liberation. Papers presented at the Arusha and Lusaka Meetings of the Southern Africa Development Co-ordination Conference*. London: Rex Collings.

O'Dowd, M., 1974. 'South Africa in the light of the stages of Economic Growth', in A. Leftwich (Ed.) *South Africa: Economic Growth and Political Change—with Comparative Studies of Chile, Sri Lanka and Malaysia*. London: Allison and Busby, 29–43.

O'Meara, D., 1977. 'The Afrikaner Broederbond 1927–1948: Class Vanguard of Afrikaner Nationalism'. *Journal of Southern African Studies* 3(2) (April): 156–186.

Oxaal, I., *et al* (Eds.), 1975. *Beyond the Sociology of Development: Economy and Society in Latin America and Africa*. London: Routledge and Kegan Paul.

Palmer, R. and Parsons, N. (Eds.), 1977. *The Roots of Rural Poverty in Central and Southern Africa*. Berkeley: California University Press; and London: Heinemann.

Republic of South Africa, 1964. *Report of the Commission of Inquiry into the Affairs of South-West Africa* [Odendaal Report] R.P. 12/1964. Pretoria: Government Printer.

——1976. *Commission of Enquiry into Matters Relating to the Coloured Population Group* [Theron Report] R. P. 38/1976. Pretoria: Government Printer.

——1979a. *Report of the Commission of Enquiry into Legislation affecting the Utilisation of Manpower (Excluding the Legislation Administered by the Departments of Labour and Mines)* [Riekert Report] R.P. 32/1979. Pretoria: Government Printer.

——1979b. Department of Labour and of Mines, *Report of the Commission of Inquiry into Labour Legislation, Part I*. [Wiehahn Report] R.P. 47/1979. Pretoria: Government Printer.

——1979c. *White Paper on Part I of the Report of the Commission of Inquiry into Labour Legislation*. W.P.S./1979. Pretoria: Government Printer.

——1980a. *Report of the Commission of Inquiry into Labour Legislation, Part II*. R.P. 38/1980. Pretoria: Government Printer.

——1980b. *White Paper on Part II of the Report of the Commission of Enquiry into Labour Legislation*. W.P.N./1980. Pretoria: Government Printer.

——1980c. *Interim Report of the Commission of Enquiry on the Constitution* [Schlebusch Report]. R.P. 68/1980. Pretoria: Government Printer.

——1982. *Promotion of Industrial Development as an Element of Co-ordinated Regional Development Strategy for Southern Africa*. White Paper and Information Document.

213

——n.d. Department of Information: *Towards a Constellation of States in Southern Africa*. Pretoria: Government Printer.

Robertson, J., 1971. *Liberalism in South Africa*. London: Oxford University Press.

Rostow, W. W., 1960. *The Stages of Economic Growth: A Non-Communist Manifesto*. Cambridge: Cambridge University Press.

Sachs, E. S., 1965. *The Anatomy of Apartheid.* London: Collet's.

Sadie, J. L., 1978. 'The Afrikaner in the Southern African Economy'. Unpublished paper.

SALDRU, 1979. 'The Wiehahn Commission: A Summary'. *South African Labour Bulletin* **5**(2) (August): 13–52.

Seidman, A. and Makgetla, N., 1980. *Outposts of Monopoly Capitalism: Southern Africa in the Changing Global Economy*. Westport: Lawrence Hill; London: Zed Press.

Slabbert, F. Van Zyl and Welsh, D., 1979. *South Africa's Options: Strategies for Sharing Power*. London: Rex Collings; and Cape Town: David Philip.

Slovo, J., 1977. 'South Africa: No Middle Road', in R. Segal (Ed.) *Southern Africa: The New Politics of Revolution*. Harmondsworth: Penguin Books, 106–210.

Smith, R., 1981. 'Labour and Management in South Africa. Problems of Adaption to Change', in A. V. Akeroyd *et al* (Eds.) *European Business and South Africa: An Appraisal of the E.C. Code of Conduct*, Mainz: Grünewald; and Munich: Kaizer, 60–79.

Sondashi, H., 1980. *The Politics of the Voice: An Examination and Comparison of British Pressure Groups (Capricorn Africa Society, The Africa Bureau and The Movement for Colonial Freedom) which sought to Influence Colonial Policies and Events, The Case of Central Africa, 1949–1962*. Unpublished M.Phil. Thesis, University of York (U.K.) (Centre for Southern African Studies).

South African Federated Chamber of Industries, 1979. *Annual Report*.

——1980. *Guidelines for Industrial Relations in the 1980s*.

South African Institute of Race Relations, 1980 (and annually, 1981, 1982). *Survey of Race Relations in South Africa, 1979 (1980, 1981)*. Johannesburg: S.A.I.R.R.

South African Labour Bulletin, 1979. 'Critique of the Wiehahn Commission and the 1979 Amendments of the Industrial Conciliation Act', by The Editors. *South African Labour Bulletin* **5**(2) (August): 53–79.

Southall, R. J., 1977. 'The Beneficiaries of Transkeian Independence'. *Journal of Modern African Studies* **15**(1) (March): 1–23.

SPRO-CAS, 1973. *South Africa's Political Alternatives* (Spro-Cas Publications Number 10). Johannesburg: Ravan Press.

Suckling, J. R., 1977. 'Factors Affecting the Promotion and Payment of Black Labour in South Africa'. University of York (U.K.), (Centre for Southern African Studies). Unpublished paper.

Temkin, B., 1976. *Gatsha Buthelezi: Zulu Statesman*. Cape Town: Purnell.

Thomas, D., 1981. 'Some Comments on Aspects of South African Law and

Institutions Relevant to the E.C. Code', in A. V. Akeroyd *et al* (Eds.) *European Business and South Africa: An Appraisal of the E.C. Code of Conduct.* Mainz: Grünewald; and Munich: Kaizer, 87–94.

Thomas, W. H., 1980a. *Economic Development in Namibia: Towards Acceptable Development Strategies for Independent Namibia.* Mainz: Grünewald; and Munich: Kaizer.

——1980b. 'South Africa and her Neighbours: Prospects for Co-operation'. Paper presented to the International Conference on South Africa, Hamburg, on September 23, 1980.

Thönessen, W., 1980. 'Statement of Trade Union Activity', in A. V. Akeroyd *et al* (Eds.) *European Business and South Africa: An Appraisal of the E.C. Code of Conduct.* Mainz: Grünewald; and Munich: Kaizer, 80–86.

Turok, B., 1974. *Strategic Problems in South Africa's Liberation Struggle: A Critical Analysis.* Richmond, Canada: Liberation Support Movement Information Center.

Union of South Africa, 1948. *Report of the Native Laws Commission 1946–1948.* [Fagan Report] U.G. 28/1948. Pretoria: Government Printer.

——1955. *Report of the Commission for the Socio-Economic Development of the Bantu Areas within the Union of South Africa.* [Tomlinson Report] U.G. 61/1955. Pretoria: Government Printer.

Urban Foundation, 1980. *Annual Report.* Johannesburg.

Van der Merwe, H. W, *et al* 1974. *White South African Elites: a Study of Incumbents of Top Positions in the Republic of South Africa.* Cape Town: Juta.

Vosloo, W. B., 1979. 'Consociational Democracy as a Means to Accomplish Peaceful Political Change in South Africa: An Evaluation of the Constitutional Change Proposed by the National Party in 1977'. *Politikon* **6**(1) (June): 13–28.

Wassenaar, A. D., 1977. *Assault on Private Enterprise: The Freeway for Communism.* Cape Town: Tafelberg.

Welsh, D., 1974. 'The Political Economy of Afrikaner Nationalism', in A. Leftwich (Ed.) *South Africa: Economic Growth and Political Change—with Comparative Studies of Chile, Sri Lanka and Malaysia.* London: Allison and Busby, 249–285.

Western Province General Workers Union (W.P.G.W.U.), 1980. 'Registration, Recognition and Organisation: The Case of the Cape Town Stevedores'. *South African Labour Bulletin* **5**(6 & 7) (March): 57–75.

Whisson, M., *et al*, n.d. (but 1979). *The Sullivan Principles at Ford.* Johannesburg: South African Institute of Race Relations.

Wilkins, I. and Strydom, H., 1978. *The Super-Afrikaners.* Johannesburg: Jonathan Ball.

Woods, D., 1978. *Biko.* New York and London: Paddington Press.

Workers Movement, n.d. (but latter half of 1979). *The Workers Movement, SACTU and the A.N.C.: A Struggle for Marxist Policies.*

Worrall, D., 1978. 'The South African Government's 1977 Constitutional

Proposals', in J. Benyon (Ed.) *Constitutional Change in South Africa*. Pietermaritzburg University of Natal Press, 127–135.

Wright, H. M., 1977. *The Burden of the Present: Liberal-Radical Controversy over South African History*. Cape Town: David Philip; and London: Rex Collings.

Yudelman, D., 1975. 'Industrialisation, Race Relations and Change in South Africa'. *African Affairs* **74**(294) (January): 82–96.

Index

218

election results, 153
evidence to Schlebusch Commission, 162–4
Ndjoba, Pastor, 14
Niewoudt, Artie, 82
Niewoudt, Professor Charles, 11
No Sizwe, 37, 39
Nujoma, Sam, 187, 196

Odendaal Report, 1964, 14
O'Dowd, Michael, 4, 25–7
Oppenheimer, Harry, 4, 59, 184
Orange Free State, University of, 135, 138
Organisation for African Unity (OAU), 52, 206
Ovamboland, 14, 15

Pan-Africanist Congress (PAC), 2, 19, 35, 38, 46, 92, 195
parliament, 144–53
nominated members, 147, 157
Paulus, Ari, 95
parallel unions, 117–8
Petersen, Bob, 40–2
Phatudi, Dr Cedric, 18
Physical Planning and Utilization of Resources Act, 1957, 66
pluralism, 4, 158–9
Polstu, 137–42
population of SA, 50–1
Port Elizabeth Black Civic Organisation (PEBCO), 109, 113–4
Port Elizabeth, University of (UPE), 85
Potchefstroom, University of, 138, 139–40
power sharing, 49, 181–2
Pretoria, Univeristy of, 125, 140, 201
Progressive Federal Party (PFP), 33, 124, 126, 137, 150, 156, 157, 177
election results, 150, 153
exposition of policy, 156, 159–61
parliamentary representation, 150–1, 153
Schlebusch Commission, 157
University of Stellenbosch, 124, 126, 142
President's Council, 123, 129, 139, 145, 147, 156–7, 167–8, 194
constitutional report 1982, 198, 201–2; government response, 202–3, 207
report on local government, 202
Prime Minister, see P. W. Botha

Prohibition of Mixed Marriages Act, 1949, 55, 58, 123, 139, 161, 167, 180

Quail Report, see Ciskei Commission
Qua Qua, 206

Rand Afrikaans University (RAU), 125, 139
Raubenheimer, A. J., (SA Minister of Water Affairs and Forestry), 146
Rhodesia, (see Zimbabwe)
Richards Bay, 51, 76
Riekert Commission and Report, 6, 11, 27, 49, 64, 78, 96, 97–107
Ruiterwag, 127, 142

Sadie, Professor J. L., 129
Saldanha, 51
Sasolburg, 39, 170
Schlebusch, Dr Alwyn, (Vice-President of SA), 139, 146
Schlebusch Commission, 50, 97, 157, 161–5, 166
Schlemmer, Professor Laurence, 200, 203–4
Schoeman, H., (SA Minister of Agriculture), 146
Sebe, Chief, 16–19
Sharpeville, 55
Shaw, Gerald, 145
Silverton, 108
Slabbert, Dr F. van Zyl, MP (SA), 124, 133, 145, 202
exposition of PFP policy, 156, 159–61
University of Stellenbosch, 126, 136
Slovo, Joe, 38
Smit, H. H., (SA Minister of Posts and Telecommunications; retired July 1982), 146
Snelling, Sir Arthur, 15
Sobhuza II, King, 185, 205–6
South Africa, University of (UNISA), 85, 97, 125–6
Institute of Labour Relations, 120
South African Boilermakers' Society, 113
South African Broadcasting Corporation, 127
South African Bureau of Racial Affairs (SABRA), 71, 127, 130
South African Communist Party (SACP), see CPSA
South African Congress of Trade Unions (SACTU), 35, 40–2, 45, 88, 92–3, 114
South African Council of Churches, 156

222